The Man and Woman Manifesto
What We Believe!

Christopher Alan Anderson

The Man and Woman Manifesto: What We Believe!
Copyright ©2017 Christopher Alan Anderson

ISBN 978-1506-904-18-4 HC/JC/Color
ISBN 978-1506-903-14-9 PBK/B/W
ISBN 978-1506-903-15-6 EBOOK

LCCN 2016953965

April 2017

Published and Distributed by
First Edition Design Publishing, Inc.
P.O. Box 20217, Sarasota, FL 34276-3217
www.firsteditiondesignpublishing.com

Foundation of Man and Woman Balance
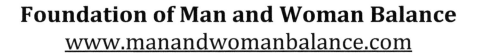
www.manandwomanbalance.com

Dedicated to:

The *light*—has come into this world in the form of Man and Woman Balance. Who would have thought that the light is actually an activity of giving and receiving love between a man and a woman—and so the light is also life. Dedicated to *life*—those living the *law of life* by giving their love to another and receiving love from another; what more can there be?

Thank you to brother Lee and Sister-in-Law Cathy, brother Marc, old friends Ron and Robert, friend Frank, Misha of Norwest Designs, Debi of First Edition Design Publishing, and spiritual companion Gina. Thank you for helping me.

Preface

"The Communists disdain to conceal their views and aims. They openly declare that their ends can be attained only by the forcible overthrow of all existing social conditions. Let the ruling classes tremble at a Communistic revolution. The proletarians have nothing to lose but their chains. They have a world to win.

"Working Men of all Countries, Unite!"

Thus ends one of the most prophetic declarations from one of the most profound and influential books ever written. This, of course, is *The Communist Manifesto* (more formally called *Manifesto of the Communist Party*) by Karl Marx and Frederick Engels, 1848. Why do I begin this writing with a quote from Marx and Engels? Because, at least in my view, it seems we are on the verge of another ideology of class struggle/warfare. Not that the class struggle (between the Haves and the Have-nots) has ever gone away but that its *ideology* and *cause* is resurfacing, perhaps under different labels, to be used as justification for one or more people to use that deadly instrument of *forcible overthrow* to acquire their desires and needs. By forcible overthrow I mean violence—*the use of force one upon another*—and, of course, its justification. This issue of violence (force) has yet to be resolved. Wasn't this the same issue with Cain and Abel in the Bible? On Wikipedia it states:

> **Cain and Abel** (Hebrew: קַיִן, הֶבֶל Qayin, Heḇel) were, according to the Book of Genesis, two sons of Adam and Eve. Cain is described as a crop farmer and his younger brother Abel as a shepherd. Cain was the first human born and Abel was the first human to die. Cain committed the first murder by killing Abel. Interpretations of Genesis 4 by ancient and modern commentators have typically assumed that the motives were jealousy and anger. The story of Cain and Abel is found in the Christian Bible, Jewish Torah and Muslim Quran.

Albert Einstein (1879–1955), probably best known for his mass/energy formula $E = mc^2$, said:

Albert Einstein (1879–1955)
The real problem is in the hearts and minds of men. It is not a problem of physics but of ethics. It is easier to denature plutonium than to denature the evil from the spirit of man.

And here we see the problem. The problem is in the minds and spirits of each one of us. And, here-to-fore, all of our religions, philosophies, psychologies, and (Humanist) manifestos have done little to resolve. So here we are again, with another philosophy, if you will, and manifesto. Can we somehow see, and in some way grasp, a certain placement in our own hearts and souls whereby some kind of balance can be structured such that rather than seeking to force another we can actually embrace another? This is our fundamental issue and quest.

C.A.A.— April 8, 2016

Note to the Reader: This writing contains both text and quotes from other writings by the author. Also many quotes from other writers, especially writers from the Creative Thought movement, are included to compare and contrast with the author's thoughts.

Table of Contents

Part 1
The Framework for an Understanding

Every moment is a spiritual resurrection/rebirth—and it exists due to the balanced nature of the sexual/procreant process itself.

Introduction—The Purpose of a Manifesto

Webster's defines a manifesto as *a public declaration of motives and intentions by a government or by a person or group regarded as having some public importance.* Wikipedia states: *A **manifesto** is a published verbal declaration of the intentions, motives, or views of the issuer, be it an individual, group, political party, or government. A manifesto usually accepts a previously published opinion or public consensus and/or promotes a new idea with prescriptive notions for carrying out changes the author believes should be made. It often is political or artistic in nature, but may present an individual's life stance. Manifestos relating to religious belief are generally referred to as creeds.* Furthermore, Wikipedia lists a number of manifestos. Most of us have heard of *The Communist Manifesto.* Well, did you know that the *Declaration of Independence* is also a manifesto? How about the *Declaration of the Rights of Man and Citizen*? Then there is *Liberty and Tyranny: A Conservative Manifesto, The Rich and the Rest of Us: A Poverty Manifesto,* and a *Humanist Manifesto.* Wikipedia list dozens of manifestos. Anyone can write a manifesto. What are your motives and intentions—or life stance?

The purpose of this manifesto is to detail in the best way possible that paradigm (or shift) I call **Man and Woman Balance**. What is Man and Woman Balance? Moreover, what is its stand and what are its ramifications for men and women on planet earth? Let's begin with a (first general) definition of Man and Woman Balance.

Man and Woman Balance

A system of understanding the universe in terms of the fundamental polarities of maleness and femaleness and the balance thereof.

Before we move on I would like to address two points. First off, the purpose of this Man and Woman Balance manifesto is to define and stress what it is we believe. It is not so much to analyze what we don't believe although some comparison is inevitable and occurs though out this writing to better elucidate the idea of Man and Woman Balance.

Secondly, you might be thinking to yourself, "Isn't this just your own manifesto. Why do you use the word 'we,' as if you are speaking for others?" Fair enough. At this stage of things, I don't have any followers and, I might add, have never wanted any. I do know of a few others who have made some of the abstractions and distinctions I am making and all

I have to say is, "I am grateful for that." This, as do my other writings, constitutes *inner work.* In my opinion, any step forward by anyone person constitutes a step forward for everyone.

The Communist Manifesto—Karl Marx

Karl Marx (1818-1883) is best known as the father of Communism although his manifesto was jointly written by him and Frederick Engels (1820-1895). I am taking various paragraphs from that writing as I believe it creates a very good context of class struggle. Look at the first sentence below—*The history of all hitherto existing society is the history of class struggles.* What a sweeping statement. And it goes on... just one sweeping statement after another. I have included enough from his manifesto for you to capture a flavor of this important document. And the question we want to be asking ourselves as we review it is, "What is the context that Marx is presenting, i.e., what is his point or stand?"

Karl Marx (1818-1884) and Frederick Engels (1820-1895)—*Manifesto of the Communist Party*, 1848

The history of all hitherto existing society is the history of class struggles.

Freemen and slave, patrician and plebeian, lord and serf, guild-master and journeymen, in a word, oppressor and oppressed, stood in constant opposition to one another, carried on an uninterrupted, now hidden, now open fight, a fight that each time ended, either in a revolutionary reconstitution of society at large, or in the common ruin of the contending classes.

In the earlier epochs of history, we find almost everywhere a complicated arrangement of society into various orders, a manifold gradation of social rank. In ancient Rome we have patricians, knights, plebeians, slaves; in the Middle Ages, feudal lords, vassals, guild-masters, journeymen, apprentices, serfs; in almost all of these classes, again, subordinate gradations.

The modern bourgeois society that has sprouted from the ruins of feudal society has not done away with class antagonisms. It has but established new classes, new conditions of oppression, new forms of struggle in place of the old ones.

Our epoch, the epoch of the bourgeoisie, possesses, however, this distinctive feature: it has simplified the class antagonisms. Society as a whole is more and more splitting up into two great hostile camps, into two great classes directly facing each other: Bourgeoisie and Proletariat.

In proportion as the bourgeoisie, i.e., capital, is developed, in the same proportion is the proletariat, the modern working class, developed—a class of labourers, who live only so long as they find work, and who find work only so long as their labour increases capital. These labourers, who must sell themselves piecemeal, are a commodity, like every other article of commerce, and are consequently exposed to all the vicissitudes of competition, to all the fluctuations of the market.

Owing to the extensive use of machinery and to division of labour, the work of the proletarians has lost all individual character, and, consequently, all charm for the workman. He becomes an appendage of the machine, and it is only the most simple, most monotonous, and most easily acquired knack, that is required of him. Hence, the cost of production of a workman is restricted, almost entirely, to the means of subsistence that he requires for his maintenance, and for the propagation of his race. But the price of a commodity, and therefore also of labour, is equal to its cost of production. In proportion, therefore, as the repulsiveness of the work increases the wage decreases. Nay more, in proportion as the use of machinery and division of labour increases, in the same proportion the burden of toil also increases whether by prolongation of the working hours, by increase of the work exacted in a given time, or by increased speed of the machinery, etc.

Modern industry has converted the little workshop of the patriarchal master into the great factory of the industrial capitalist. Masses of labourers, crowded into the factory, are organized like soldiers. As privates of the industrial army they are placed under the command of a perfect hierarchy of officers and sergeants. Not only are they slaves of the bourgeois class, and of the bourgeois State; they are daily and hourly enslaved by the machine, by the overlooker, and, above all, by the individual bourgeois manufacturer himself. The more openly this despotism proclaims gain to be its end and air, the more petty, the more hateful and the more embittering it is.

The less the skill and exertion of strength implied in manual labour, in other words, the more modern industry becomes developed, the more is the labour of men superseded by that of women and children. Differences of age and sex have no longer any distinctive social validity for the working class. All are instruments of labour, more or less expensive to use, according to their age and sex.

No sooner is the exploitation of the labourer by the manufacturer, so far at an end, that he receives his wages in cash, than he is set upon by the other portions of the bourgeoisie, the landlord, the shopkeeper, the pawnbroker, etc.

The lower strata of the middle class—the small tradespeople, shopkeepers and retired tradesmen, generally, the handicraftsmen and peasants—all these sink gradually into the proletariat, partly because their diminutive capital does not suffice for the scale on which modern industry is carried on, and is swamped in the competition with the large capitalists, partly because their specialized skill is rendered worthless by new methods of production. Thus the proletariat is recruited from all classes of the population.

...The growing competition among the bourgeois, and the resulting commercial crises, make the wages of the workers ever more fluctuating. The increasing improvement of machinery, ever more rapidly developing, makes their livelihood more and more precarious; the collisions between individual workmen and individual bourgeois take more and more the character of collisions between two classes. Thereupon the workers begin to form combinations (trades' unions) against the bourgeois; they club together in order to keep up the rate of wages; they found permanent associations in order to make provision beforehand for these occasional revolts. Here and there the contest breaks out into riots.

Now and then the workers are victorious, but only for a time. The real fruit of their battles lies, not in the immediate result, but in the ever-expanding union of the workers. This union is helped on by the improved means of communication that are created by modern industry, and that place the workers or different localities in contact with one another. It was just this contact that was needed to centralize the numerous local struggles, all of the same character, into one national struggle between classes. But every class struggle is a political struggle. And the union, to attain which the burghers of the Middle Ages, with their miserable highways, required centuries, the modern proletarians, thanks to railways, achieve in a few years.

This organization of the proletarians into a class, and consequently into a political party, is continually being upset again by the competition between the workers themselves. But it ever rises up again, stronger, firmer, mightier. It compels legislative recognition of particular interests of the workers, by taking advantage of the division among the bourgeoisie itself. Thus the ten-hour's bill in England was carried.

Of all the classes that stand face to face with the bourgeoisie today, the proletariat alone is really a revolutionary class. The other classes decay and finally disappear in the face of modern industry; the proletariat is its special and essential product...

In the conditions of the proletariat, those of old society at large are already virtually swamped. The proletarian is without property; his relation to his wife and children has no longer anything in common with the bourgeois family relations; modern industrial labour, modern subjection to capital, the same in England as in France, in America as in Germany, has stripped him of every trace of national character. Law, morality, religion, are to him so many bourgeois prejudices, behind which lurk in ambush just as many bourgeois interests.

Hitherto, every form of society has been based, as we have already seen, on the antagonism of oppressing and oppressed classes...

The essential condition for the existence, and for the sway of the bourgeois class, is the formation and augmentation of capital; the condition for capital is wage-labour. Wage-labour rests exclusively on competition between the labourers. The advance of industry, whose involuntary promoter is the bourgeoisie, replaces the isolation of the labourers, due to competition, by their revolutionary combination, due to association. The development of modern industry, therefore, cuts from under its feet the very foundation on which the bourgeoisie produces and appropriates products. What the bourgeoisie therefore produces, above all, are its own grave-diggers. Its fall and the victory of the proletariat are equally inevitable.

In what relation do the Communists stand to the proletarians as a whole?

The Communists do not form a separate party opposed to other working-class parties.

They have no interest separate and apart from those of the proletariat as a whole.

They do not set up any sectarian principles of their own, by which to shape and mould the proletarian movement.

The Communists are distinguished from the other working-class parties by this only: 1. In the national struggles of the proletarians of the different countries, they point out and bring to the front the common interests of the entire proletariat, independently of all nationality. 2. In the various states of development which the struggle of the working class against the bourgeoisie has to pass through, they always and everywhere represent the interest of the movement as a whole.

The Communists, therefore, are on the one hand, practically, the most advanced and resolute section of the working-class parties of every country, that section which pushes forward all others; on the other hand, theoretically, they have over the great mass of the proletariat the advantage of clearly understanding the line of march, the conditions, and the ultimate general results of the proletarian movement.

The immediate aim of the Communists is the same as that of all the other proletarian parties: formation of the proletariat into a class, overthrow the bourgeois supremacy, conquest of political power by the proletariat.

The theoretical conclusions of the Communists are in no way based on ideas or principles that have been invented, or discovered, by this or that would-be universal reformer.

They merely express, in general terms, actual relations springing from an existing class struggle, from a historical movement going on under our very eyes. The abolition of existing property relations is not at all a distinctive feature of Communism.

All property relations in the past have continually been subject to historical change consequent upon the change in historical conditions.

The French Revolution, for example, abolished feudal property in favour of the bourgeois property.

The distinguishing feature of Communism is not the

abolition of property generally, but the abolition of bourgeois property. But modern bourgeois private property is the final and most complete expression of the system of producing and appropriating products that is based in class antagonisms, on the exploitation of the many by the few.

In this sense, the theory of the Communists may be summed up in the single sentence: Abolition of private property.

You are horrified at our intending to do away with private property. But in our existing society, private property is already done away with for nine-tenths of the population; its existence for the few is solely due to its non-existence in the hands of those nine-tenths. You reproach us, therefore, with intending to do away with a form of property, the necessary condition for whose existence is the non-existence of any property for the immense majority of society.

In one word, you reproach us with intending to do away with your property. Precisely so; that is just what we intend.

From the moment when labour can no longer be converted into capital, money, or rent, into a social power capable of being monopolized, i.e., from the moment when individual property can no longer be transformed into bourgeois property, into capital, from that moment, you say, individuality vanishes.

You must, therefore, confess that by "individual" you mean no other person than the bourgeois, than the middle-class owner of property. This person must, indeed, be swept out of the way, and made impossible.

Communism deprives no man of the power to appropriate the products of society; all that it does is to deprive him of the power to subjugate the labour of others by means of such appropriation.

Abolition of the family! Even the most radical flare up at this infamous proposal of the Communists.

On what foundation is the present family, the bourgeois family, based? On capital, on private gain. In its completely developed form this family exists only among the bourgeoisie. But this state of things finds its complement in the practical absence of the family among the proletarians, and in public prostitution.

The bourgeois family will banish as a matter of course when its complement vanishes, and both will vanish with the banishing of capital.

Do you charge us with wanting to stop exploitation of children by their parents? To this crime we plead guilty.

But, you will say, we destroy the most hallowed of relations, when we replace home education by social.

And your education! Is not that also social, and determined by the social conditions under which you educate, by the intervention, direct or indirect, of society, by means of schools, etc.? The Communists have not invented the intervention of society in education; they do but seek to alter the character of that intervention, and to rescue education from the influence of the ruling class.

The bourgeois claptrap about the family and education, about the hallowed co-relation of parent and child, becomes all the more disgusting, the more, by the action of modern industry, all family ties among the proletarians are torn asunder, and their children transformed into simple articles of commerce and instruments of labour.

"There are, besides, eternal truths, such as Freedom, Justice, etc., that are common to all states of society. But Communism abolishes eternal truths, it abolishes all religion, and all morality, instead of constituting them on a new basis; it therefore acts in contradiction to all past historical experience."

What does this accusation reduce itself to? The history of all past society has consisted in the development of class antagonisms, antagonisms that assumed different forms at different epochs.

But whatever form they may have taken, one fact is common to all past ages, viz., the exploitation of one part of society by the other. No wonder, then, that the social consciousness of past ages, despite all the multiplicity and variety it displays, moves within certain common forms, or general ideas, which cannot completely vanish except with the total disappearance of class antagonisms.

The Communist revolution is the most radical rupture with traditional property relations; no wonder that its development involves the most radical rupture with traditional ideas.

But let us have done with the bourgeois objections to

Communism.

We have seen above, that the first step in the revolution by the working class, is to raise the proletariat to the position of ruling class, to win the battle of democracy.

The proletariat will use its political supremacy to wrest, by degrees, all capital from the bourgeoisie, to centralize all instruments of production in the hands of the State, i.e., of the proletariat organized as the ruling class; and to increase the total of productive forces as rapidly as possible.

Of course, in the beginning, this cannot be effected except by means of despotic inroads on the rights of property, and on the conditions of bourgeois production; by means of measures, therefore, which appear economically insufficient and untenable, but which, in the course of the movement, outstrip themselves, necessitate further inroads upon the old social order, and are unavoidable as a means of entirely revolutionizing the mode of production.

Nevertheless in the most advanced countries, the following will be pretty generally applicable.

1. Abolition of property in land and application of all rents of land to public purposes.
2. A heavy progressive or graduated income tax.
3. Abolition of all rights of inheritance.
4. Confiscation of the property of all emigrants and rebels.
5. Centralization of credit in the hands of the State, by means of a national bank with State capital and an exclusive monopoly.
6. Centralization of the means of communication and transport in the hands of the State.
7. Extension of factories and instruments of production owned by the State, and bringing into cultivation of waste lands, and the improvement of the soil generally in accordance with a common plan.
8. Equal liability of all to labor. Establishment of industrial armies, especially for agriculture.
9. Combination of agriculture with manufacturing industries; gradual abolition of the distinction between town and country by a more equable distribution of population over the country.
10. Free education for all children in public schools.

Abolition of children's factory labor in its present form. Combination of education with industrial production, etc.

When, in the course of development, class distinctions have disappeared, and all production has been concentrated in their hands of a vast association of the whole nation, the public power will lose its political character.

In short, the Communists everywhere support every revolutionary movement against the existing social and political order of things.

In all these movements they bring to the front, as the leading question in each, the property question, no matter what its degree of development at the time.

Finally, they labor everywhere for the union and agreement of the democratic parties of all countries.

The Communists disdain to conceal their views and aims. They openly declare that their ends can be attained only by the forcible overthrow of all existing social conditions. Let the ruling classes tremble at a Communistic revolution. The proletarians have nothing to lose but their chains. They have a world to win.

Working Men of all Countries, Unite!

Marx's point, if you will, is that there is a fundamental (and unjust) imbalance in the economic system that can only be rectified by *forcible overthrow*. As such violence becomes both necessary and justified in this approach or method. Marx's essence statement that he is historically known for, although perhaps previously used by others, from his *Critique of the Gotha Program*, 1875, states:

From each according to his abilities, to each according to his needs.

Now, I will submit to you that such a statement (or society) actually requires *forcible overthrow*, i.e., violence to implement. This is to say that violence towards others *must* be the means to achieve the end of: *From each according to his abilities, to each according to his needs*. Why might this be so? This is one of the questions we want to get at. Most of us are familiar with the saying, "The end justifies the means." As per Wikipedia this means *that if a goal is morally important enough, any method of achieving it is acceptable.* NO! I will say to you that if our means requires violence towards others there must be something *intrinsically* wrong with our end. So we want to be able to understand the frame/structure of things (the metaphysical end) such that we can gauge our own "individual end" and see if it will result in means that are violent or means that are peaceful. It might also be worthwhile to ask, are peace and harmony, joy, and love, etc., just utopian fantasies or do they have some basis in reality? Einstein clearly thought they had a basis in reality even while viewing the problem of good and evil as very difficult. *The real problem is in the hearts and minds of men. It is not a problem of physics but of ethics. It is easier to denature plutonium than to denature the evil from the spirit of man.*

Now, you might be thinking to yourself, "Why are we talking about Marxism/Communism; didn't that die off years ago?" Unfortunately not. There was an article from the *Truth Revolt* website that read: *Marx's Communist Manifesto Most Frequently Taught Text in U.S. Colleges.* A sub-caption read: *Must be why millennials prefer socialism over capitalism.* It seems that socialism (a polite word for communism) never dies. Why is that? In our system in the United States, the Democratic party basically is the socialist/progressive party. (Look who is running for President.) The Republicans are not far behind. Why is this? Why does socialism keep coming back to life? Today it is rearing its head under the term *"social/economic justice."* We must look deeper into this to see if we cannot better understand this phenomenon—particularly this imbalance between Haves and Have-nots. Also, it would be worthwhile to understand why our politicians play off this class struggle and imbalance, and how they continue to cement themselves in their own political power and money. Going forward, it would be well to remember that communist/socialism plays off class struggle, be it over opportunity, equality, freedom, justice, property, money, etc., and that its solution is the overthrow of the existing power structure reversing the positions of the Have and the Have-nots—and, most importantly, it does not have a qualm about using force to do so.

Before we leave this section I would like to comment on what is called Humanism. Humanists are essentially social progressives, i.e., Democrats, socialists, Communists, or Marxists. I would suggest to you that Humanism is basically running the world today. The European Union, the United Nations, and Washington, D.C. are all under the umbrella of Humanism running some form of socialist model. The following quote is from Wikipedia and gives to us a bit of an historical insight into Humanism.

Humanist Manifesto is the title of three <u>manifestos</u> laying out a <u>Humanist</u> worldview. They are the original *<u>Humanist Manifesto</u>* (1933, often referred to as Humanist Manifesto I), the *<u>Humanist Manifesto II</u>* (1973), and *<u>Humanism and Its Aspirations</u>* (2003, a.k.a. *Humanist Manifesto III*). The Manifesto originally arose from <u>religious Humanism</u>, though <u>secular Humanists</u> also signed.

The central theme of all three *manifestos* is the elaboration of a <u>philosophy</u> and value system which does not necessarily include belief in any personal deity or "higher power," although the three differ considerably in their tone, form, and ambition. Each has been signed at its launch by various prominent members of <u>academia</u> and others who are in general agreement with its principles.

Humanist Manifesto I

The first manifesto, entitled simply *A Humanist Manifesto*, was written in 1933 primarily by <u>Roy Wood Sellars</u> and <u>Raymond Bragg</u> and was published with thirty-four signatories including philosopher <u>John Dewey</u>. Unlike the later ones, the first Manifesto talked of a new "<u>religion</u>", and referred to Humanism as a religious movement to transcend and replace previous religions based on allegations of supernatural revelation. The document outlines a fifteen-point belief system, which, in addition to a secular outlook, opposes "acquisitive and profit-motivated society" and outlines a worldwide egalitarian society based on voluntary mutual cooperation, language which was considerably softened by the Humanists' board, owners of the document, twenty years later.

The title "A Humanist Manifesto"—rather than "The Humanist Manifesto"—was intentional, predictive of later Manifestos to follow, as indeed has been the case. Unlike the creeds of major organized religions, the setting out of Humanist ideals in these Manifestos is an ongoing process. Indeed, in some communities of Humanists the compilation of personal Manifestos is actively encouraged, and throughout the Humanist movement it is accepted that the Humanist Manifestos are not permanent or authoritative dogmas but are to be subject to ongoing critique.

Humanist Manifesto II

The second Manifesto was written in 1973 by <u>Paul Kurtz</u> and <u>Edwin H. Wilson</u>, and was intended to update and replace the previous one. It begins with a statement that the excesses of <u>Nazism</u> and <u>World War II</u> had made the first seem "far too optimistic," and indicated a more hardheaded and realistic approach in its seventeen-point statement, which was much longer and more elaborate than the previous version. Nevertheless, much of the unbridled optimism of the first remained, with hopes stated that war would become obsolete and poverty would be eliminated.

Many of the proposals in the document, such as opposition to <u>racism</u> and <u>weapons of mass destruction</u> and support of strong <u>human rights</u>, are fairly uncontroversial, and its prescriptions that <u>divorce</u> and <u>birth control</u> should be legal and that <u>technology</u> can improve life are widely accepted today in much of the <u>Western world</u>. Furthermore, its proposal of an <u>international court</u> has <u>since been implemented</u>. However, in addition to its rejection of supernaturalism, various controversial stances are strongly supported, notably the right to <u>abortion</u>.

Initially published with a small number of signatures, the document was circulated and gained thousands more, and indeed the AHA website encourages visitors to add their own name. A provision at the end noted that signatories do "not necessarily endorse every detail" of the document.

Among the oft-quoted lines from this 1973 Manifesto are, "No deity will save us; we must save ourselves," and "We are responsible for what we are and for what we will be," both of which may present difficulties for members of certain Christian, Jewish, and Muslim sects, or other believers in doctrines of submission to the will of an all-powerful God.

Expanding upon the role that public education establishment should play to bring about the goals described in the Humanist Manifesto II, <u>John Dunphy</u> wrote: "I am convinced that the battle for humankind's future must be waged and won in the public school classroom by teachers that correctly perceive their role as proselytizers of a new faith: a religion of humanity that recognizes and respects the spark of what theologians call divinity in every human being... The classroom must and will become an arena of conflict between the old and new—the rotting corpse of Christianity, together with all its adjacent evils and misery, and the new faith of humanism, resplendent with the promise of a world in which the never-realized Christian ideal of 'love thy neighbor' will finally be achieved."

Humanist Manifesto III

Humanism and Its Aspirations, subtitled *Humanist Manifesto III, a successor to the Humanist Manifesto of 1933*, was published in 2003 by the AHA, which apparently wrote it by committee. Signatories included 21 Nobel laureates. The new document is the successor to the previous ones, and the name "Humanist Manifesto" is the property of the American Humanist Association.

The newest manifesto is deliberately much shorter, listing seven primary themes, which echo those from its predecessors:

- Knowledge of the world is derived by observation, experimentation, and rational analysis. (See empiricism.)
- Humans are an integral part of nature, the result of evolutionary change, an unguided process.
- Ethical values are derived from human need and interest as tested by experience. (See ethical naturalism.)
- Life's fulfillment emerges from individual participation in the service of humane ideals.
- Humans are social by nature and find meaning in relationships.
- Working to benefit society maximizes individual happiness.
- Respect for differing yet humane views in an open, secular, democratic, environmentally sustainable society.

How let's look more specifically to the 3rd Humanist Manifesto. This is from the American Humanist Association website.

Humanist Manifesto III, a successor to the Humanist Manifesto of 1933

Humanism is a progressive philosophy of life that, without supernaturalism, affirms our ability and responsibility to lead ethical lives of personal fulfillment that aspire to the greater good of humanity.

The lifestance of Humanism—guided by reason, inspired by compassion, and informed by experience—encourages us to live life well and fully. It evolved through the ages and continues to develop through the efforts of thoughtful people who recognize that values and ideals, however carefully wrought, are subject to change as our knowledge and understandings advance.

This document is part of an ongoing effort to manifest in clear and positive terms the conceptual boundaries of Humanism, not what we must believe but a consensus of what we do believe. It is in this sense that we affirm the following:

Knowledge of the world is derived by observation, experimentation, and rational analysis. Humanists find that science is the best method for determining this knowledge as well as for solving problems and developing beneficial technologies. We also recognize the value of new departures in thought, the arts, and inner experience—each subject to analysis by critical intelligence.

Humans are an integral part of nature, the result of unguided evolutionary change. Humanists recognize nature as self-existing. We accept our life as all and enough, distinguishing things as they are from things as we might wish or imagine them to be. We welcome the challenges of the future, and are drawn to and undaunted by the yet to be known.

Ethical values are derived from human need and interest as tested by experience. Humanists ground values in human welfare shaped by human circumstances, interests, and concerns and extended to the global ecosystem and beyond. We are committed to treating each person as having inherent worth and dignity, and to making informed choices in a context of freedom consonant with responsibility.

Life's fulfillment emerges from individual participation in the service of humane ideals. We aim for our fullest possible development and animate our lives with a deep sense of purpose, finding wonder and awe in the joys and beauties of human existence, its challenges and tragedies, and even in the inevitability and finality of death. Humanists rely on the rich heritage of human culture and the life stance of Humanism to provide comfort in times of want and encouragement in times of plenty.

Humans are social by nature and find meaning in relationships. Humanists long for and strive toward a world of mutual care and concern, free of cruelty and its consequences, where differences are resolved cooperatively without resorting to violence. The joining of individuality with interdependence enriches our lives, encourages us to enrich the lives of others, and inspires hope of attaining peace, justice, and opportunity for all.

Working to benefit society maximizes individual happiness. Progressive cultures have worked to free humanity from the brutalities of mere survival and to reduce suffering, improve society, and develop global community. We seek to minimize the inequities of circumstance and ability, and we support a just distribution of nature's resources and the fruits of human effort so that as many as possible can enjoy a good life.

Humanists are concerned for the well-being of all, are committed to diversity, and respect those of differing yet humane views. We work to uphold the equal enjoyment of human rights and civil liberties in an open, secular society and maintain it is a civic duty to participate in the democratic process and a planetary duty to protect nature's integrity, diversity, and beauty in a secure, sustainable manner.

Thus engaged in the flow of life, we aspire to this vision with the informed conviction that humanity has the ability to progress toward its highest ideals. The responsibility for our lives and the kind of world in which we live is ours and ours alone.

The question we want to ask ourselves here is whether Humanism essentially is Marxism in sheep's clothing. That is to say, does Humanism adhere to Marx's essence statement *"From each according to his abilities, to each according to his needs."* Let's see:

> ...opposes "acquisitive and profit-motivated society" and outlines a worldwide egalitarian society based on voluntary mutual cooperation...
> "I am convinced that the battle for humankind's future

must be waged and won in the public school classroom by teachers that correctly perceive their role as proselytizers of a new faith…"

We seek to minimize the inequities of circumstance and ability, and we support a just distribution of nature's resources and the fruits of human effort so that as many as possible can enjoy a good life.

It sounds like the old Marxism to me—we, the bureaucrats, get to decide for you, for the good of you of course. And if you don't like it… If this is so then Humanism is nothing more than the forced mandate of economic sharing, what the Humanists (and Marxists) call social/economic justice. Wonderful terms to justify that the end justifies the means.

The Romantic Manifesto—Ayn Rand

Let's move ahead to another manifesto, this one by Ayn Rand (1905-1982). Ayn Rand's *The Romantic Manifesto* was published in 1962. Why would I choose Ayn Rand's manifesto to review? Well, for one, Ayn Rand's novels (*Atlas Shrugged* and *The Fountainhead*) and Objectivist's philosophy have also had great impact, precisely as a counter balance to Marxism. Ayn Rand herself was born in Russia and, as I understand, lived through the Bolshevik Revolution of 1917. And it was these two manifestos, the Communist and the Romantic, that I read when I was in my twenties and was highly impressed by their breath and scope.

Ayn Rand's Romantic Manifesto is of a different subject matter than Karl Marx's Communist Manifesto. Ayn Rand's primary subject matter is art (esthetics). Esthetics has to do with the evaluation of art. What makes art great art? Why or how do we claim something is beautiful? What is the importance of beauty/art in our lives—to our souls? These are challenging questions to say the least. But even though Ayn Rand's Romantic Manifesto is different than Karl Marx's Communist Manifesto, they do tie in as we shall see. Remember, we are asking the question of the point or end game that these authors are trying to get to. Moreover, we are asking the means and end question—*Does the end justify the means?*

Ayn Rand (1905-1982)—*The Romantic Manifesto*, 1962

The dictionary definition of "manifesto" is: "a public declaration of intentions, opinions, objectives or motives, as one issued by a government, sovereign, or organization." (*The Random House Dictionary of the English Language,* College Edition, 1968.)

I must state, therefore, that this manifesto is not issued in the name of an organization or a movement. I speak only for myself. There is no Romantic movement today. If there is to be one in the art of the future, this book will have helped it to come into being.

To quote from Chapter 6: "The destruction of Romanticism in esthetics—like the destruction of individualism in ethics or of capitalism in politics—was made possible by philosophical default... In all three cases, the nature of the fundamental value involved had never been defined explicitly, the issues were fought in terms of non-essentials, and the values were destroyed by men who did not know what they were losing or why."

It has been said and written by many commentators that the atmosphere of the Western world before World War I is incommunicable to those who have not lived in that period. I used to wonder how men could say it, know it, yet give it up—until I observed more closely the men of my own and the preceding generations. They *had* given it up and, along with it, they had given up everything that makes life worth living: conviction, purpose, value, future. They were drained, embittered hulks whimpering occasionally about the hopelessness of life.

Whatever spiritual treason they had committed, they could not accept the cultural sewer of the present, they could not forget that they had once seen a higher, nobler possibility. Unable or unwilling to grasp what had destroyed it, they kept cursing the world, or kept calling men to return to meaningless dogmas, such as religion and tradition, or kept silent. Unable to stifle their vision or to fight for it, they took the "easy" way out: they renounced valuing. To fight, in this context, means: to think. Today, I wonder at how stubbornly men cling to their vices and how easily they give up whatever they regard as the good.

Renunciation is not one of my premises. If I see that the good is possible to men, yet it vanished, I do not take "Such is the trend of the world" as a sufficient explanation. I ask such questions as: Why?—What caused it?—What or who determines the trends of the world? (The answer is: philosophy.)

I made it my task to learn what made Romanticism, the greatest achievement in art history, possible and what destroyed it. I learned—as in other, similar cases involving philosophy—that Romanticism was defeated by its own spokesmen, that even in its own time it had never been properly recognized or identified. It is Romanticism's identity that I want to transmit to the future...

Our day has no art and no future. The future, in the context of progress, is a door open only to those who do not renounce their conceptual faculty; it is not open to mystics, hippies, drug addicts, tribal ritualists—or to anyone who reduces himself to a sub-animal, sub-perceptual, sensory level of awareness.

Will we see an esthetic Renaissance in our time? I do not know. What I do know is this: anyone who fights for the future, lives in it today.

Is the universe intelligible to man, or unintelligible and unknowable? Can man find happiness on earth, or is he doomed to frustration and despair? Does man have the power of *choice,* the power to choose his goals and to achieve them, the power to direct the course of his life—or is he the helpless plaything of forces beyond his control, which determine his fate? Is man, by nature, to be valued as good, or to be despised as evil? These are *metaphysical* questions, but the answers to them determine the kind of *ethics* men will accept and practice; the answers are the link between metaphysics and ethics. And although metaphysics as such is not a normative science, the answers to this category of questions assume, in man's mind, the function of metaphysical value-judgments, since they form the foundation of all his moral values.

Consciously or subconsciously, explicitly or implicitly, man knows that he needs a comprehensive view of existence to integrate his values, to choose his goals, to plan his future, to maintain the unity and coherence of his life—and that his metaphysical value-judgments are involved in every moment of his life, in his every choice, decision and action.

Metaphysics—the science that deals with the fundamental nature of reality—involves man's widest abstractions. It includes every concrete he has ever perceived, it involves such a vast sum of knowledge and such a long chain of concepts that no man could hold it all in the focus of his immediate conscious awareness. Yet he needs that sum and that awareness to guide him—he needs the power to summon them into full, conscious focus.

That power is given to him by art.

Art is a selective re-creation of reality according to an artist's metaphysical value-judgments.

By a selective re-creation, art isolates and integrates those aspects of reality which represent man's fundamental view of himself and of existence. Out of the countless number of concretes—of single, disorganized and (seemingly) contradictory attributes, actions and entities—an artist isolates the things which he regards as metaphysically essential and integrates them into a single new concrete that represents an embodied abstraction.

For instance, consider two statues of man: one as a Greek god, the other as a deformed medieval monstrosity. Both are metaphysical estimates of men; both are projections of the artist's view of man's nature; both are concretized representations of the philosophy of their respective cultures.

Art is a concretization of metaphysics. *Art brings man's concepts to the perceptual level of his consciousness and allows him to grasp them directly, as if they were percepts.*

The place of ethics in any given work of art depends on the metaphysical views of the artist. If, consciously or subconsciously, an artist holds the premise that man possesses the power of volition, it will lead his work to a value orientation (to Romanticism). If he holds the premise that man's fate is determined by forces beyond his control, it will lead his work to an anti-value orientation (to Naturalism). The philosophical and esthetic contradictions of determinism are irrelevant in this context, just as the truth or falsehood of an artist's metaphysical views is irrelevant to the nature of art as such. An art work may project the value man is to seek and hold up to him the concretized vision of the life he is to achieve. Or it may assert that man's efforts are futile and hold up to him the concretized vision of defeat and despair as his ultimate fate. In either case, the esthetic means—the psycho-epistemological processes involved—remain the same.

A sense of life is formed by a process of emotional generalization which may be described as a subconscious counterpart of a process of abstraction, since it is a method of classifying and integrating. But it is a process of *emotional* abstraction: it consists of classifying things *according to the emotions they invoke*—i.e., of tying together, by association or connotation, all those things which have the power to make an individual experience the same (or a similar) emotion. For instance: a new neighborhood, a discovery, adventure, struggle, triumph—or: the folks next door, a memorized recitation, a family picnic, a known routine, comfort. On a more adult level: a heroic man, the skyline of New York, a sunlit landscape, pure colors, ecstatic music—or: a humble man, an old village, a foggy landscape, muddy colors, folk music.

Which particular emotions will be invoked by things in these examples, as their respective common denominators, depends on which set of things fit an individual's *view of himself.* For a man of self-esteem, the emotion uniting the things in the first part of these examples is admiration, exaltation, a sense of challenge; the emotion uniting the things in the second part is disgust or boredom. For a man who lacks self-esteem, the emotion uniting the things in the first part of these examples is fear, guilt, resentment; the emotion uniting the things in the second part is relief from fear, reassurance, the undemanding safely of passivity.

Even though such emotional abstractions grow into a metaphysical view of man, their origin lies in an individual's view of *himself* and of *his own* existence. The subverbal, subconscious criterion of selection that forms his emotional abstractions is: "That which is important to *me*" or: "The kind of universe which is right for *me,* in which *I* would feel at home." It is obvious what immense psychological consequences will follow, depending on whether a man's subconscious metaphysics is consonant with the facts of reality or contradicts them.

The integrated sum of a man's basic values is his sense of life.

A sense of life represents a man's early value-integrations, which remain in a fluid, plastic, easily amendable state, while he gathers knowledge to reach full *conceptual* control and thus to *drive* his inner mechanism. A full conceptual control means a consciously directed process of cognitive integration, which means: a conscious *philosophy* of life.

By the time he reaches adolescence a man's knowledge is sufficient to deal with broad fundamentals; this is the period when he becomes aware of the need to translate his incoherent sense of life into conscious terms. This is the period when he gropes for such things as the meaning of life, for principles, ideals, values and, desperately, for self-assertion. And—since nothing is done, in our anti-rational culture, to assist a young mind in this crucial transition, and everything possible is done to hamper, cripple, stultify it— the result is frantic, hysterical irrationality of most adolescents, particularly today. Theirs is the agony of the unborn—of minds going through a process of atrophy at the time set by nature for their growth.

The transition from guidance by a sense of life to guidance by a conscious philosophy takes many forms. For the rare exception, the fully rational child, it is a natural, absorbing, if difficult, process—the process of validating and, if necessary, correcting in conceptual terms what he had merely sensed about the nature of man's existence, thus transforming a wordless feeling into clearly verbalized knowledge, and laying a firm foundation, an intellectual roadbed, for the course of his life. The result is a fully integrated personality, a man whose mind and emotions are in harmony, whose sense of life matches his conscious convictions.

Philosophy does not replace a man's sense of life, which continues to function as the automatically integrated sum of his values. But philosophy sets the criteria of his emotional integrations according to a fully defined and consistent view of reality (if and to the extent that a philosophy is rational). Instead of deriving, subconsciously, an implicit metaphysics from his value-judgments, he now derives, conceptually, his value-judgments from an explicit metaphysics. His emotions proceed from his *fully convinced* judgments. The mind leads, the emotions follow.

For many men, the process of transition never takes place: they make no attempt to integrate their knowledge, to acquire any conscious convictions, and are left at the mercy of their inarticulate sense of life as their only guide...

A sense of life, once acquired, is not a closed issue. It can be changed and corrected—easily, in youth, while it is still fluid, or by a longer, harder effort in later years. Since it is an emotional sum, it cannot be changed by a direct act of will. It changes automatically, but only after a long process of psychological retraining, when and if a man changes his conscious philosophical premises.

Whether he corrects it or not, whether it is objectively consonant with reality or not, at any stage or state of its specific content, a sense of life always retains a profoundly personal quality; it reflects a man's deepest values; it is experienced by him as a sense of his own identity.

A given person's sense of life is hard to identify conceptually, because it is hard to isolate: it is involved in everything about that person, in his every thought, emotion, action, in his every response, in his every choice and value, in his every spontaneous gesture, in his matter of moving, talking, smiling, in the total of his personality, it is that which makes him a "personality."

Introspectively, one's own sense of life is experienced as an absolute and an irreducible primary—as that which one never questions, because *the thought of questioning it never arises.* Extrospectively, the sense of life of another person strikes one as an immediate, yet undefinable, impression—on very short acquaintance—an impression which often feels like certainty, yet exasperatingly elusive, if one attempts to verify it.

This leads many people to regard a sense of life as the province of some sort of special intuition, as a matter perceivable only by some special, non-rational insight. The exact opposite is true: a sense of life is *not* an irreducible primary, but a very complex sum; it can be felt, but it cannot be understood, by an automatic reaction; to be understood, it has to be analyzed, identified and verified conceptually. That automatic impression—of oneself or of others—is only a lead; left untranslated, it can be a very deceptive lead. But if and when that intangible impression is supported by and unites with the conscious judgment of one's mind, the result is the most exultant form of certainty one can ever experience: it is the integration of mind and values.

Romanticism is a category of art based on the recognition of the principle that man possesses the faculty of volition.

Art is a selective re-creation of reality according to an artist's metaphysical value-judgments. An artist recreates those aspects of reality which represent his fundamental view of man and of existence. In forming a view of man's nature, a fundamental question one must answer is whether man possesses the faculty of volition—because one's conclusions and evaluations in regard to all the characteristics, requirements and actions of man depend on the answer.

Their opposite answers to this question constitute the

respective basic premises of two broad categories of art: Romanticism, which recognizes the existence of man's volition—and Naturalism, which denies it.

1. If man possesses volition, then the crucial aspect of his life is his choice of values—if he chooses values then he must act to gain and/or keep them—if so, then he must set his goals and engage in purposeful action to achieve them…

The faculty of volition operates in regard to the two fundamental aspects of man's life: consciousness and existence, i.e., his psychological action and his existential action, i.e., the formation of his own character and the course of action he pursues in the physical world.

2. If man does not possess volition, then his life and his character are determined by forces beyond his control—if so, then the choice of values is impossible to him—if so, then such values as he appears to hold are only an illusion, predetermined by the forces he has no power to resist—if so, then he is impotent to achieve his goals or to engage in purposeful action—and if he attempts the illusion of such action, he will be defeated by those forces, and his failure (or occasional success) will have no relation to his actions.

Romanticism is a product of the nineteenth century—a (largely subconscious) result of two great influences: Aristotelianism, which liberated man by validating the power of his mind—and capitalism, which gave man's mind the freedom to translate ideas into practice (the second of these influences was itself the result of the first). But while the practical consequences of Aristotelianism were reaching men's daily existence, its theoretical influence was long since gone: philosophy, since the Renaissance, had been retrogressing overwhelmingly to the mysticism of Plato. Thus the historically unprecedented events of the nineteenth century—the Industrial Revolution, the child-prodigy speed in the growth of science, the skyrocketing standard of living, the liberated torrent of human energy—were left without intellectual direction or evaluation. The nineteenth century was guided, not by an Aristotelian philosophy, but by *an Aristotelian sense of life.* (And, like a brilliantly violent adolescent who fails to translate his sense of life into conscious terms, it burned itself out, choked by the blind confusion of its own overpowering energy.)

Whatever their conscious convictions, the artists of that century's great new school—the romanticists—picked their sense of life out of the cultural atmosphere: it was an atmosphere of men intoxicated by the discovery of freedom, with all the ancient strongholds of tyranny—of church, state, monarchy, feudalism—crumbling around them, with unlimited roads opening in all directions and no barriers set to their newly unleased energy. It was an atmosphere best expressed by that century's naive, exuberant and tragically blind belief that human progress, from here on, was to be irresistible and *automatic...*

Such were the roots of one of the grimmest ironies in cultural history: the early attempts to define the nature of Romanticism declared it to be an esthetic school based on *the primacy of emotions*—as against the champions of the primacy of reason, which were the Classicists (and, later, the Naturalists). In various forms, this definition has persisted to our day. It is an example of the intellectually disastrous consequences of definitions by non-essentials—and an example of the penalty one pays for a non-philosophical approach to cultural phenomena...

The Romanticists saw their cause primarily as a battle for their right to individuality and—unable to grasp the deepest metaphysical justification of their cause, unable to identity their values in terms of reason—they fought for individuality in terms of *feelings,* surrendering the banner of reason to their enemies.

There were other, lesser consequences of this fundamental error, all of them symptoms of the intellectual confusion of the age. Groping blindly for a metaphysically oriented, grand-scale, exalted way of life, the Romanticists, predominantly, were enemies of capitalism, which they regarded as a prosaic, materialistic, "petty bourgeois" system—never realizing that it was the only system that could make freedom, individuality and the pursuit of values possible in practice. Some of them chose to be advocates of socialism; some turned for inspiration to the Middle Ages and became shameless glamorizers of that nightmare era; some ended up where most champions of the non-rational end up; in religion. All of it served to accelerate Romanticism's growing break with reality.

When, in the later half of the nineteenth century,

Naturalism rose to prominence and, assuming the mantle of reason and reality, proclaimed the artists' duty to portray "things as they are"—Romanticism did not have much of an opposition to offer.

Art (including literature) is the barometer of a culture. It reflects the sum of a society's deepest philosophical values: not its professed notions and slogans, but its actual view of man and of existence. The image of an entire society stretched out on a psychologist's couch, revealing its naked subconscious, is an impossible concept; yet *that* is what art accomplishes: it presents the equivalent of such a session, a transcript which is more eloquent and easier to diagnose than any other set of symptoms...

In politics, the panic-blind advocates of today's status quo, clinging to the shambles of their mixed economy in a rising flood of statism, are now adopting the line that there's nothing wrong with the world, that this is a century of progress, that we are morally and mentally healthy, that we never had it so good. If you find political issues too complex to diagnose, take a look at today's art: it will leave you no doubt in regard to the health or disease of our culture.

Romantic art is the fuel and the spark plug of a man's soul; its task is to set a soul on fire and never let it go out. The task of providing that fire with a motor and a direction belongs to philosophy.

Just as man's physical survival depends on his own effort, so does his psychological survival. Man faces two corollary, interdependent fields of action in which a constant exercise of choice and a constant creative process are demanded of him: the world around him and his own soul (by "soul," I mean his consciousness). Just as he has to produce the material values he needs to sustain his life, so he has to acquire the values of character that enable him to sustain it and that make his life worth living. He is born without the knowledge of either. He has to discover both—and translate them into reality—and survive by shaping the world and himself in the image of his values.

Growing from a common root, which is philosophy, man's knowledge branches out in two directions. One branch studies the physical world or the phenomena pertaining to man's physical existence; the other studies man or the phenomena pertaining to his consciousness. The first leads to abstract science, which leads to applied science or engineering, which leads to technology—to the actual production of material values. The second leads to art.

Art is the technology of the soul.

Art is the product of three philosophical disciplines: metaphysics, epistemology, and ethics. Metaphysics and epistemology are the abstract base of ethics. Ethics is the applied science that defines a code of values to guide man's choices and actions—the choices and actions which determine the course of his life; ethics is the engineering that provides the principles and blueprints. Art creates the final product. It builds a model.

Although the representation of things "as they might be and ought to be" helps man to achieve these things in real life, this is only a secondary value. The *primary* value is that it gives him the experience of living in a world where things are *as they ought to be.* This experience is of crucial importance to him: it is his psychological life line.

Since man's ambition is unlimited, since his pursuit and achievement of values is a lifelong process—and the higher the values, the harder the struggle—man needs a moment, an hour or some period of time in which he can experience the sense of his completed task, the sense of living in a universe where his values have been successfully achieved. It is like a moment of rest, a moment to gain fuel to move farther. Art gives him that fuel. Art gives him the experience of seeing the full, immediate, concrete reality of his distant goals.

The importance of that experience is not in *what* he learns from it, but in *that* he experiences it. The fuel is not a theoretical principle, not a didactic "message," but the life-giving fact of experiencing a moment of *metaphysical* joy—a moment of love for existence.

A given individual may choose to move forward, to translate the meaning of that experience into the actual course of his own life; or he may fail to live up to it and spend the rest of his life betraying it. But whatever the case may be, the art work remains intact, an entity complete in itself, an achieved, realized, immovable fact of reality—like a beacon raised over the dark crossroads of the world, saying: "*This* is possible."

There is a scene in *The Fountainhead* which is a direct expression of this issue. I was, in a sense, both characters in that scene, but it was written primarily from the aspect of myself as the consumer, rather than the producer, of art; it was based on my own desperate longing for the sight of human achievement. I regarded the emotional meaning of that scene as entirely personal, almost subjective—and I did not expect it to be shared by anyone. But that scene proved to be the one most widely understood and most frequently mentioned by the readers of *The Fountainhead*.

It is the opening scene of Part IV, between Howard Roark and the boy on the bicycle.

The boy thought that "man's work should be a higher step, an improvement on nature, not a degradation. He did not want to despise men; he wanted to love and admire them. But he dreaded the sight of the first house, poolroom and movie poster he would encounter on his way... He had always wanted to write music, and he could give no other identity to the thing he sought... Let me see that in one single act of man on earth. Let me see it made real. Let me see the answer to the promise of that music... Don't work for my happiness, my brothers—show me yours—show me that it is possible—show me your achievement—and the knowledge will give me courage for mine."

This is the meaning of art in man's life.

I must admit, I am a bit of an Ayn Rand fan. I mean, look at what she is saying. There is so much here to bite on. Let me just summarize in her own words.

Romanticism is a category of art based on the recognition of the principle that man possesses the faculty of volition.

Art is a selective re-creation of reality according to an artist's metaphysical value-judgments. An artist recreates those aspects of reality which represent his fundamental view of man and of existence. In forming a view of man's nature, a fundamental question one must answer is whether man possesses the faculty of volition—because one's conclusions and evaluations in regard to all the characteristics, requirements and actions of man depend on the answer.

Their opposite answers to this question constitute the respective basic premises of two broad categories of art: Romanticism, which recognizes the existence of man's volition—and Naturalism, which denies it.

1. If man possesses volition, then the crucial aspect of his life is his choice of values—if he chooses values then he must act to gain and/or keep them—if so, then he must set his goals and engage in purposeful action to achieve them...

The faculty of volition operates in regard to the two fundamental aspects of man's life: consciousness and existence, i.e., his psychological action and his existential action, i.e., the formation of his own character and the course of action he pursues in the physical world.

2. If man does not possess volition, then his life and his character are determined by forces beyond his control—if so, then the choice of values is impossible to him—if so, then such values as he appears to hold are only an illusion, predetermined by the forces he has no power to resist—if so, then he is impotent to achieve his goals or to engage in purposeful action—and if he attempts the illusion of such action, he will be defeated by those forces, and his failure (or occasional success) will have no relation to his actions.

So, according to Ayn Rand, man is a creature of volitional consciousness, that man (men and women) can deliberate on things. He can choose his values, make goals, and understand creative processes that move him in a direction of life fulfillment. Volitional consciousness really means that man has a dual consciousness, he can reflect inwardly (deductive thinking) and project outwardly (inductive thinking). Both are necessary I surmise. I mean the whole ability of man to think is huge; it is the difference maker. Ayn Rand speaks of achievement of goals and purposeful action. And these are underlined by ideas such as purpose and values—think about it—which are underlined by one's own existence and consciousness of that existence. And Ayn Rand is asking— can't we reach out for the beautiful, the heroic, the accomplishment, the betterment of man? And so her essence statement (different from Karl Marx's: *From each according to his abilities, to each according to his needs.*) is, as taken from her historical novel *Atlas Shrugged,* 1959:

I swear by my life and my love of it that I will never live for the sake of another man, nor ask another man to live for mine.

I am aware of the criticism regarding Ayn Rand, of an overbearing self-interest. But let us ask this question, would you rather live under her statement or that of Karl Marx? Which one is more apt to use violence—against you—to achieve their ends? We often think that Communism (or shall we call it Socialism?) is intrinsically altruistic. But let me ask, who is going to see to it who gets what as per one's needs? Why has the great utopia of Communist/Socialist countries never been realized but instead continues to drive people into the dirt—under dictatorship no less? At least Ayn Rand is not asking another to live for her sake—which means be forced to live for her sake. She may not want to live for another, that is her business, but she is not asking—of forcing—that another live for her. That is a start, isn't it?

The University of Science and Philosophy
Walter and Lao Russell

I first came across Walter and Lao Russell's *The University of Science and Philosophy* in 1970. I was just nineteen years old. What an explosion! The Russell's present something even different than Marx and Rand. Their message may be called metaphysical. But it also had a different flavor than the Christianity of my upbringing. To capture this flavor I am going to be quoting from *The Message of the Divine Iliad* by Walter Russell, 1949. Let's call this a public declaration of Dr. Russell's thoughts and ideas, i.e., *The Message of the Divine Iliad Manifesto*.

Walter Russell (1871-1963)—*The Message of the Divine Iliad*, 1949

I am in the kingdom of Thy Heavens, O my Father-Mother. Speak Thou to me lest my words to man be but my words, not Thine and mine.

Through My messengers I have told man that it is not easy for him who loveth riches of earth alone to enter My kingdom, but he still fails to comprehend that he may have great riches and still find his way to Me, through obeying My One Law.

Write thou again My oft said words: "Desire ye what ye will and it shall be thine. All My universe will give it thee in the strength of my desiring and in the strength of my action in reaching out for thy desire."

For again I say My one principle of My one law is founded upon the solid rock of equal interchange between all pairs of opposite things, opposite conditions or opposite transactions between men.

These do I balance with My will as I balance all divided pairs in My universe of Me.

For I am absolute, and all things which extendeth from the Light of My imagining are absolute.

That which seems imperfect to man's eyes is but seeming, for he sees not at all. Could he see all he would see all perfect.

For My universe is but the forever unfolding-refolding of

My One Whole Idea. As My Whole Idea is perfect, so, also, is each part perfect.

At each stage of their unfolding and refolding they are absolute and perfect, for I am absolute and perfect.

Unbalance and imperfection exist not, therefore, save in man's timed seeing. For him who knows My Light there is no timed seeing.

All paths of all things in My radial body are but one path, for, of a verity I say that slightest move of creeping thing on this small earth is recorded upon all paths of all things, e'en to giant star beyond man's seeing.

Here Me again say there are not two halves of a divided one in all the pairs of opposites of My universe. There are but a seeming two, and each one of these is of the other one while seeming to be two. And each becomes the other one sequentially to maintain that seeming.

Hear thou Me when I say that man writes his own record of his thinking, and his acting, in his own immortal Soul; and that which man writes there will be repeated in the patterned seed of the reborning of that man unto eternity.

Said I not these very words in the beginning of thy full knowing Me in thee: "Desire is of the Soul, the Soul being record of desire fulfilled by action for repeating its pattern in the seed"?...
And again said I not to thee: "My sole desire is to think for the purpose of expressing the One Idea of My thinking through imaged forms of My imagining engaged in purposeful action"?

Desire ye what ye will, and behold, it standeth before thee. Throughout the aeons it has been thine without thy knowing, e'en though thou has but just asked for it. I am the center of My universe of Me. Everywhere I am is the center of all things, and I am everywhere.

Thou, my Father-Mother, hast commended that I write down in words for man the meaning within Thy Light which is written upon my heart in waves of Thy inspired essence of meaning which I must interpret into man's words.

I am the sexless knower of the Known. In Me is the Consciousness of all-knowing. And that is My power.

My dual thinking divides My knowing Light into pairs of sex-divided mirrors of the two opposed lights of My thinking. These electric mirrors of divided light reflect My Light and Life in them for manifesting My knowing and the One Life of my Being. Forever and forever they interchange the dual reflected lights of My thinking for manifesting the continuance of My thinking, yet they are not My light, nor are they My Life.

Verily, I say, the power of moving things to move, or to find rest, is not in them. I, alone, am energy; and I am also rest.

I am the fulcrum which extends the power to move from rest.

My rest and peace may be known by moving things which know my balance in them and keep balance in them while thus moving.

Moving things which manifest My knowing by equal interchanging void their moving and thus find rest;— but those which manifest Me unequally cannot wholly void their moving.

For I am Balance; and all moving things which extend from Me must manifest My balance in them. And I am Law. No rest can there be, or can there be peace, while My law remains broken by unbalance e'en by one whit.

For verily I give rest to moving things by equally dividing Light of My knowing at rest in Me to extending and retracting lights of My thinking. Know thou that as My knowing is balanced and at rest in Me so is My thinking balanced and at rest in Me.

The extending light of My thinking multiples the oneness of My knowing into many ones to mother them as formed bodies made in patterned images of My knowing.

The retracting light gathers all the many ones together into My oneness to father them in Soul-seed of Me for again borning into patterned forms of many ones.

In man's thinking, man begins to live as he leaves the mother-womb which borned him. And when he returns the clay of him to clay of earth, he thinks of life as ending, knowing not that its beginning never was, nor could its ending be.

Balanced thinking is an ecstasy which knows no burden, no fatigue nor imperfection.

Wherefore I say, come unto Me, ye self-burdened. Find rest in Me by being Me.

Since the beginning man cried aloud, "Who am I?"
And My Voice forever answers, Thou Art I. I, the Universal One, am thou whom thou are creating in My image.
I am I. I am I whom I am creating. I am the universal I.
I am all that is, and Thee.
I am the empire of I that am I.

Since the beginning My Voice within man forever asks: "Whence came I?"
And My Voice forever answers:
I came from God.
I am Soul, record of Idea.
Where God is I am.
Where I am there God is.

Within man My eternal Voice demands: "What Am I?"
And My familiar Voice within man answers:
I am the body of God, born of His substance.
God is Mind. I am Mind.
God is Truth. I am Truth.
God is Love. I am Love.
God is Light. I am Light.
God is Power. I am Power.
God is Rest and Balance. I am Rest and Balance.
What God is, I am. What He commands, I command.
My purpose is His purpose.

God lives in me. My inheritance is from God and of God.

He gives His all to me. He withholds nothing.

The divinity of me is Thine and mine. It is what which is recorded within the soul of me. It is the Holy Spirit within the sanctuary of me.

I am what I am.

I shall be what I desire to be.

What I am I have desired to be.

I am the sum of my own desire.

I am Thou, Creator of myself.

Thou are I, Creator of all.

I am Thou, Creator of All; for Thou has made it known in my heart that I am not of myself alone.

I am Thou and Thou art I.

Thy thinking has created all that is.

My thinking is Thy thinking.

My thinking has created all that is.

I am ecstatic man.

I am man, Self creating.

I am God, Creator of man.

I am Father of myself.

I am Son of the living God.

The ends of space are mine. I shall know no limitations that are not Thy limitations.

God was my beginning, is my substance and shall by my end.

From the One I came. To the One I return.

I shall know my universality and I shall dwell on the mountain top in the Light of inner knowing.

Hope dwells in the Light.

Despair lurks in the dark.

Life and growth are of the Light.

Death and destruction are of the dark.

Thy Balance must I give him, that he shall know power.

Thy Law must I give him, that he shall know peace.

Thy Love must I give him, that he shall know unity.

Thy Beauty must I give him, that Thy rhythmic thinking

shall inspire him to rhythmic thinking.

Thy Light must I give him, that he may commune with Thee in Thy language of Light.

Consciousness of Thee must I give him, that he shall forever be Thee.

I am Thy messenger of Love. There is no fear nor hate in Thee.

I am Thy messenger of Life. There is no death nor darkness in Thy Light.

Make Thou me a worthy messenger.

Be Thou me.

Thy power be my power. Thy essence, my essence.

Unfold Thou Thy concept through me.

Be me, that I may be not alone I.

Be me, that I may be the universe.

Flow Thou through me to all the universe.

I AM the universe.

Command Thou me.

I know Love; naught else but Love is there to know.

I know Light; naught else but Light is there to know.

I know Ecstasy; naught else but Ecstasy is there in Me. For I am Balance. In Balance there can be no other emotion than changeless Ecstasy.

Love, Balance, Beauty and Truth are ONE in Me. When man knoweth Love, Balance, Beauty and Truth in Light of Me, and hath My Ecstasy, he shall have My all-knowing and think My knowing into thought forms to create My universe of imaged forms with Me.

Go thou and tell man he cannot find Love outside of his Self. When he findeth Self he findeth Me. For I am he. And I am Love. Love cannot be acquired, nor possessed, for I cannot be acquired, nor possessed.

The Light of My Love is in all men from their beginnings. Man needeth not to seek it from afar, he needeth but to recognize it in him when he heareth My Voice whispering to him from My silences, and calling aloud to him from the voices of every unfolding-refolding form of My imagining.

Say thou to these men: Thou canst not see God, for God is Love, and Love cannot be seen, nor weighed, nor measured.

But thou canst manifest Love by the balanced actions and reactions of thy body,— or by its balanced givings and regivings. But when thou thus expresseth Love with thy body, know thou that thy expression of Love is not Love; for thy body is not thee, nor is it Me.

When man asketh of thee, "Where am I when death taketh me?" say thou to him, "Thy Light of birth is mirrored by the Light of death at the moment of thy birth. Both are one, e'en though they mirror each other from far ends of cycles until their interchangings void each other in their constant interpassings.

Thus is My law of opposites fulfilled. For again I say, life giveth to death that death may die; and death regiveth to life that life may live. All opposites of My cyclic thinking forever interchange with each, that each may be what the other was, sequentially.

When man knoweth Me in him as Light of Me, then is he as unchanging as I, his Father-Mother, am unchanging.

Wherefore I say, man must be born again, and yet again, rejoicing at My givings. Likewise, he must come to rest in Me, again and yet again, rejoicing at his regivings to Me of countless deaths of man-formed clay for reborning into man-formed clay.

I, the undivided sexless One, am Unity.

Out of My Light of knowing, My two lights of thinking are born as sexed pairs of opposites for repetition as sexed pairs of opposites.

To think is to create. I create with Light. Nothing is which is not Light.

Behold in Me thy God of Love, the One, inseparable.

Through woman I speak of Love to man, and to woman

through man. Many there are whose bodies hear the call of body and call it Love.

Pairs of oppositely-conditioned bodies must forever interchange with each other to find balance with Me. In this wise I express My unchanging Love through the changing cycles of My thinking as manifested in the pulse beat, breathing and sex interaction of My dual electric body.

E'en so doth My universal body interchange as My resolving-dissolving universe of dual light shineth out of darkness as mirrored forms which disappear again in Me forever borning.

But he who loveth in his heart, knowing Me in him, rejoiceth that he is thus enriched by knowing Love in the heart of woman, e'en though no words of Love shall have passed between him and the woman of his inspiration.

For I again say, My One Law demandeth that man doeth My will in all his creations by first giving the Light of his Self, so that the reflection of his Light returneth to him in full measure, e'en as I give of My Light to My universe and repeat the reflection of My Light forever and forever.

To him I give all-knowing and all-power to think My universe into rhythmic, balanced forms with Me.

Through My illuminated one—whom I have anointed with My Light of all-knowing—man's jungle world of hate and fear of neighbor and nation will unfold unto the world of peace through the unity of man. But again I say, all men will come to Me, but the agony of awaiting that day shall be theirs alone.

Better is it for him that he knoweth not his numbers, nor his letters, than that he knoweth not the Beauty of the dawn.

He who knoweth Beauty in him seeth the unseen and heareth My heartbeat in the silent rhythms of My symphonies.

Say thou to thine anointed one, these, My words: Thou art Love. Thou art Beauty. Thou art Balance. Thou art Truth. Go thou and give Love, Beauty, Balance and Truth to thy neighbor.

Think not thou of doing great works in My name. Go thou to thy neighbor. Think thou of thy neighbor alone. One seed sufficeth not for a meadow but out of one seed cometh a sheaf of ten.

Be not neglectful of thine own tasks, My son. Leave not to others of lesser knowing that which thou thy Self must do. That which must be done for cosmic man to come must have thine own Self in it.

Again I say unto all men that thy dealings with thy neighbor are with the whole world of men, for what ye do to one ye do to all.

Likewise the good of any man is the good of all. It uplifteth all mankind.

I am in the Spirit. Thy Light is all about me. It encompasseth me. It shineth through me. I am dissolved in Thy Light.
Thy Light is my Light. I am immersed in my Light.
Dimensionless I am; and I am as unconditioned as Thou Thyself art dimensionless and unconditioned.
Thou, my Father-Mother, are the Light of the world.

I need not to learn, for I know all things.
Thou thinkest Thy knowing in light-waves; and Thy meaning is as clear to Thy anointed one as the Light of Thy knowing behind its meanings is radiant to him.

Thou art the Source of force which keeps all Creation moving on Thy balanced wheel of motion; yet Thou are not the wheel, nor art Thou motion.

I know Thy purpose wholly. Thou hast flashed it to me clearly in its fullness.

Unfold Thou again, through me, part by part, sequentially, Thy immortal plan which Thou hast writ in waves of dual light upon time's pages.
I, whom Thou hast freed from time, must bind myself to

time for man.

And keep Thou me in the Oneness of Thy Light until I have worthily given Thy message to suffering man.

Man still sayeth that I cannot be comprehended, for he still must sense that which he would comprehend.

Man still thinketh of Me as a material body like unto his own, for he still demandeth a material body for all idea of his conceiving. He still knoweth not that I have a universal body of My conceiving—product of My desiring—created by My Thinking—which is not Me, e'en as man has a body of man's conceiving—product of his desiring—created by his thinking—which, likewise, is not man.

Say thou to him; each thing is everything; and each is everywhere.

All things are the same thing, for all are universal.

All things occupy the same space, and each thing occupyeth all space. For, verily I say, all things are omnipresent—for I center all things; and I am everywhere.

All things extendeth to all things—from all things—and through all things. For, to thee I again say, all things are Light—and Light separateth not; nor has it bounds; nor is it here and not there.

Man cannot evade Me, for he is Me. Nor can I evade man when he desireth Me—for I am he. Knoweth thou that desire in man and desire in Me are One—likewise all desire in all men are One.

And as the rainbow is a light within the Light, inseparable, so is man's Self within Me, inseparable: and so is his image My image.

Verily, I say, every wave encompasseth every other wave unto the One; and the many are within the One, for the many are the One.

I further say that everything repeateth itself within every other thing, unto the One.

And, furthermore, I say, that every element which man thinketh of as itself alone is within every other element, e'en to the atom's smallest unit.

Say thou also to him: All things center all things and are involved in all things. Everything reacheth through every other thing e'en to the farthermost star.

Know thou that eternity endeth in NOW, for now is eternity. For the purpose of creating the illusion of time have I set My mirrors and lenses of dual light to attain an infinity in My imaged universe where no measure is.

My universe is My body, idea of My imagining, formed in My image, product of My knowing, recorded in matter by My electric thinking. My body is not Me. I alone AM.

I think Balance; for I am Balance.
I think Love; for I am Love.
I think Power; for desire in Me is Power in Me.
I think Truth and Law; for I am Truth and Law.
I think balanced form of idea, for in Me is naught but rhythmic balance from which rhythmic balanced form appeareth.
My balance is absolute. My rhythm is absolute.
So, also, is My image rhythmic, balanced, absolute.
So likewise, is My love absolute.

Behold all men, the workings of My One Law of rhythmic balanced interchange between all pairs of opposed Light-mirrored waves which constitute My body and its extension in man.

Again I say, Love alone ruleth all things of heaven and earth. With Love I build My universe and with Love it voideth itself in Me for again reappearing as My universe.

Omniscient thou art. All power hath thou that thy Father-Mother hath.

He who would be made whole will see My Light in thee and come to Me.
Fear thou shalt not know, lest pestilence lodge with thee in its passing through thee to its resurrection.
Fear is an unbalanced thing—apart from Me—for I am

Balance.

The toxemia of unbalance is man's only ailment. There is no other ailment. Therefore, give him Balance.

Fear is not in Me. Teach thou that fear cannot be in any man who knoweth Me.

Comfort thou the fearing man and make him whole through Me.

Resurrect thou him who is near death and feareth his dying, knowing it as naught but death, and give death back to him as life, yea, as eternal life.

See thou the Light of ecstasy in his closing eyes as thou openest doors to life for him, who expecteth death.

Teach him that there is no death, that there is naught but life: for e'en while sleeping in My arms as death they cradle him anew as life.

For I am the God of Love.

Thy task is to unify mankind through his knowing. Man's day of cosmic knowing is now here. Man can be unified only through cosmic knowing.

Man's knowing is his power. He cannot think beyond his knowing.

He who would heal the sick must know Me in him and have My Omnipotent power. Beyond his knowing of the Light he cannot extend My Power, nor My Balance, to those who have lost their equilibrium in Me through divers fears and unbalanced acts.

Man is not now so new as man of yesterday who comprehended not My electric wave universe of dual light which recordeth My thinking by the motion of matter. My anointed messengers of yesterday, who knew the Light of Me in them, bade man to have faith and belief in Me, for mankind could not then comprehend, nor know Me.

He who would heal man of today shall not command any one to dependence upon faith or belief in what he sayeth or doeth, e'en upon Me, unsupplemented by his knowing.

Mine anointed, illumined ones must inspire him whom he would heal to know Me in him, and comprehend the workings of My Law which he controlleth e'en as I.

When man thus findeth rest in Me, he findeth Balance which restoreth his body.

For I am Rest. He who cometh to Me to find Rest in Me findeth rhythmic balance interchange in every cell of him. He who thus reneweth his body, through balancing the waves of dual light which compriseth his body, is like unto one reborn.

As man unfoldeth into greater knowing, his creations are his and Mine—co-Creators—as One.

He who thus extendeth his knowing of My Light to Others must himself be illumined in My Light while thus extending it. He must rise above his sensing and be Me in his knowing.

He who is made whole by finding Balance in My Light findeth an inner joyousness which immunizes him from toxins and destructive things which attack fearing man. Inner joyousness is the forerunner of the ecstasy which cometh alone to the reverent inspired ones who have found My all-knowing.

Man, likewise, maketh his own ills in his own unbalanced image when thinking alone without Me—for all ills are unbalanced things and unbalance is not in Me.

When thinking My knowing with Me, he findeth Balance in Me to void the pairs of opposites of his unbalanced thinking and is made whole by finding rest in me.

All idea of My thinking is divided into pairs of opposite unbalanced conditions.

Male sex and female are opposite unbalanced conditions of the one idea of man. The two opposed conditions void each other by finding rest from motion in each other.

Opposite unbalanced conditions are as a lever in motion swinging from its still fulcrum. In the fulcrum is the one unchanging condition of Balance from which the two changing unbalanced conditions extend.

So long as the lever swingeth in motion its two opposites are unbalanced. When the swinging of the lever ceaseth, the lever is balanced in the stillness of its fulcrum.

Behold in Me the still fulcrum of My changing universe. In Me is neither good nor evil, fear nor anger, sympathy nor sorrow, sin nor virtue. In Me is naught but the ecstasy of Love—fulcrum of all thinking and all emotion. Naught else existeth.

These words of my Father-Mother's knowing have I translated true while in the Light of all-knowing upon the mountain top.

By gosh! What is he saying? In short, he is speaking of a *balanced process.*

These do I balance with My will as I balance all divided pairs in My universe of Me.

So long as the lever swingeth in motion its two opposites are unbalanced. When the swinging of the lever ceaseth, the lever is balanced in the stillness of its fulcrum.

For My universe is but the forever unfolding-refolding of My One Whole Idea. As My Whole Idea is perfect, so, also, is each part perfect.

Here Me again say there are not two halves of a divided one in all the pairs of opposites of My universe. There are but a seeming two, and each one of these is of the other one while seeming to be two. And each becomes the other one sequentially to maintain that seeming.

He is also speaking about a source-point of all things, what we can call a center or foundation or beginning point. Dr. Russell uses the terms one, fulcrum, and balance.

God was my beginning, is my substance and shall by my end.
From the One I came. To the One I return.

I am the fulcrum which extends the power to move from rest.

My rest and peace may be known by moving things which know my balance in them and keep balance in them while thus moving.

For I am Balance; and all moving things which extend from Me must manifest My balance in them. And I am Law. No rest can there be, or can there be peace, while My law remains broken by unbalance e'en by one whit.

Moreover, Dr. Russell is speaking about sex or a sexual process.

I, the undivided sexless One, am Unity.

Out of My Light of knowing, My two lights of thinking are born as sexed pairs of opposites for repetition as sexed pairs of opposites.

Pairs of oppositely-conditioned bodies must forever interchange with each other to find balance with Me. In this wise I express My unchanging Love through the changing cycles of My thinking as manifested in the pulse beat, breathing and sex interaction of My dual electric body.

All idea of My thinking is divided into pairs of opposite unbalanced conditions.

Through woman I speak of Love to man, and to woman through man. Many there are whose bodies hear the call of body and call it Love.

Male sex and female are opposite unbalanced conditions of the one idea of man. The two opposed conditions void each other by finding rest from motion in each other.

Opposite unbalanced conditions are as a lever in motion swinging from its still fulcrum. In the fulcrum is the one unchanging condition of Balance from which the two changing unbalanced conditions extend.

So long as the lever swingeth in motion its two opposites are unbalanced. When the swinging of the lever ceaseth, the lever is balanced in the stillness of its fulcrum.

And lastly, he is speaking of Father and Mother or what he calls

Father-Mother.

> I am in the kingdom of Thy Heavens, O my Father-Mother. Speak Thou to me lest my words to man be but my words, not Thine and mine.

> Thou, my Father-Mother, hast commended that I write down in words for man the meaning within Thy Light which is written upon my heart in waves of Thy inspired essence of meaning which I must interpret into man's words.

> When man knoweth Me in him as Light of Me, then is he as unchanging as I, his Father-Mother, am unchanging.

> Thou, my Father-Mother, are the Light of the world.

> Omniscient thou art. All power hath thou that thy Father-Mother hath.

> These words of my Father-Mother's knowing have I translated true while in the Light of all-knowing upon the mountain top.

Now, given these quotes from *The Divine Iliad* what might be Walter Russell's essence statement? Before I get to that let's first look at Marx, Rand, and Russell in a context. We began with Marx and his class struggle. With Marx it seems we can only end up with winners and losers. Their sides may change from time-to-time but that is what it seems to be. The promise of a Communist utopia always stays in the future because there is no way to provide for those in need without *forcibly* taking from those who have. That use of coercive force always voids the potential of a favorable outcome. As has been said by others, *"Violence always perpetuates violence."* Indeed. So the end of the Marxist struggle is the same as the means to get there—violence—because that means (of violence) was in the heart of the end going in.

With Ayn Rand, the focus is on volition and purposeful action—man as a creator of his life not a reactor to his circumstances. Let's quickly review:

> 1. If man possesses volition, then the crucial aspect of his life is his choice of values—if he chooses values then he must

act to gain and/or keep them—if so, then he must set his goals and engage in purposeful action to achieve them...

The faculty of volition operates in regard to the two fundamental aspects of man's life: consciousness and existence, i.e., his psychological action and his existential action, i.e., the formation of his own character and the course of action he pursues in the physical world.

2. If man does not possess volition, then his life and his character are determined by forces beyond his control—if so, then the choice of values is impossible to him—if so, then such values as he appears to hold are only an illusion, predetermined by the forces he has no power to resist—if so, then he is impotent to achieve his goals or to engage in purposeful action—and if he attempts the illusion of such action, he will be defeated by those forces, and his failure (or occasional success) will have no relation to his actions.

This issue of a volitional consciousness—one acting from purposeful action towards a goal of creating value—is, I believe, a step up from Marx's class struggle. Remember Ayn Rand's essence statement: *I swear by my life and my love of it that I will never live for the sake of another man, nor ask another man to live for mine.* As such, she is swearing off violence—and thievery which is the purpose of violence. (Let's recognize there is a distinction between violence and self-defense. Violence initiates force; self-defense only surfaces as a reaction/attempt to thwart off violence.) So Ayn Rand's end or ideal is *value creation*. That in itself is a great step forward—if we could just adhere to that.

And yet here we have Walter Russell coming on the scene and speaking of something else altogether. I mean, what is this?—Let me give you just one example here to get us back to his mindset.

> Pairs of oppositely-conditioned bodies must forever interchange with each other to find balance with Me. In this wise I express My unchanging Love through the changing cycles of My thinking as manifested in the pulse beat, breathing and sex interaction of My dual electric body.

What Walter Russell is presenting (and we will bring in his wife Lao shortly) is a metaphysical end. Metaphysical is often thought as something transcending the physical. Let's think of it as just the essential reality, the "what is" or foundation of things. (Dr. Russell used the word fulcrum.) Mankind has always wondered about the true nature of things. Our religions are metaphysical endeavors looking for the source of things. Most of us ask: "Who am I?" and "Why am I here?" These are metaphysical questions. "What does it all mean?" is another. We postulate a "God" to give us meaning and coherency. We want and seek an end point, an end we can use rightful means to get to. In Christianity, the end point is salvation in Jesus Christ and the means is belief and worship. But Dr. Russell is going deeper than that I believe. He is speaking to or coming from a consciousness/understanding of the God-head or God-process itself. His expression seems more Eastern in nature, almost like some of the Indian Swamis sound. I didn't say that this would be easy. I am endeavoring to present a context here from Marx to Rand to Russell. Each step is a shift in consciousness. Each step changes the end (goal) and, quite frankly, the means to achieve it. So, for the moment, allow me to present to you what I believe the essence statement of Walter Russell would be. He had so many quotes and, to my knowledge, never separated out just one essence statement. But for me, at least out of *The Divine Iliad*, it would be:

Thou, my Father-Mother, are the Light of the world.

In thinking about this statement, it is not so far off from the Biblical verses Genesis 1: 27 and Matthew 19: 4-6 which state:

Genesis 1:27: *So God created man in his own image, in the image of God created he him, male and female created he them.*

Matthew 19:4-6: *Have ye not read, that he which made them in the beginning made them male and female, And said, for this cause shall a man leave father and mother, and shall cleave to his wife: and they twain shall be one flesh? Wherefore they are no more twain, but one flesh. What therefore God hath joined together, let not man put asunder.*

In the Koran it states:

35:11. *God created you from dust, then from a little germ. Into two sexes He divided you. No female conceives or is delivered without His knowledge. No man grows old or has his life cut short but in accordance with His decree. All this is easy enough for God.*

51:49. *All things have been created in pairs so you may reflect on it.*

Even the Bhagavad-Gita states:

Learn that this is the womb
of all creatures;
I am the source of all the universe,
just as I am its dissolution.

So when Dr. Russell states—*Pairs of oppositely-conditioned bodies must forever interchange with each other to find balance with Me. In this wise I express My unchanging Love through the changing cycles of My thinking as manifested in the pulse beat, breathing and sex interaction of My dual electric body*—he is delineating some type of creative (sexual) process is he not? But more than that, he is delineating it as the God-head itself. And it is at this point that we get into problems. Is the God-head separate and apart from his creation or is the God-head the creative process itself? Let us ask it this way, why would "God":

...male and female created he them?
...created in pairs?
...Through woman I speak of Love to man, and to woman through man?

Why create pairs or male and female pairs at all? And, moreover, why does Dr. Russell speak of "God" as Father-Mother? Or let us ask this question this way, could "God" create other than male and female pairs? (That is the question now, isn't it?) And if not, what does that say about the God-head itself? Now, we may not be able to answer these questions right now. This requires further abstractions and another shift in consciousness.

My Background and Discovery

As I mentioned, I was brought up in a Christian home. I had loving parents and three older brothers. In high school I found my interests turning to literature, poetry, and philosophy. At age nineteen I was introduced to the writings of Walter and Lao Russell. About the same time Ayn Rand's Atlas Shrugged came into my space. It was through Ayn Rand's writings that I was introduced to Ludwig von Mises (1881–1973), the Austrian-American economist, historian, and philosopher which led me to Marx and his Communist Manifesto. To say the least, I had my hands full. During the next ten years my task, as I saw it, was to integrate all this. But the key to it all lay with the Russell writings. Walter and Lao Russell were presenting a metaphysical beginning point that was a shift from all that had come before. So, back to the issue of the God-head and the creation of male and female pairs. If the God-head could only create in male and female pairs then isn't that the nature of the God-head itself? We often, at least in Christianity, separate the male and female pairs from God himself. But we run into a problem right at this point. I referred to God as a he (himself). Is that what God is? Jesus refers to God as the *Father*. But one must ask, I think, where is the *Mother*? If I may include a quote from *A Bridge to Eternity: Sri Ramakrishna and His Monastic Order*, 1986, by the great Hindu saint Sri Ramakrishna (1836-1886) at this point.

Sri Ramakrishna (1836-1886)—*A Bridge to Eternity: Sri Ramakrishna and His Monastic Order*, 1986

I have long thought of telling you one thing, but have never done so yet. I want to tell you today. It is about my spiritual condition. You say that whoever will practice Sádhaná will realize it. That is not so. There is some specialty about it.

She, Mother has spoken to me. I have not merely seen Her—She has also talked with me. I was at the Vat-talã. She came out of the Ganga to me. Oh, how She laughed! She played with my fingers and cracked them in fun. And then She spoke—She talked with me!

I cried for three days at a time.—And She revealed to me all the contents of the Vedas, Purãnas and Tantras...

I had all wonderful visions. I saw the Undivided Existence-Knowledge-Bliss in which there was a partition. On one side were Kedar, Chuni and other devotees who believed in God with forms. On the other side was an effulgent light as brightly red as brickdust. Within this light sat Narendra immersed in Samãdhi. Seeing him thus absorbed, I called him by name. He slightly opened his eyes and I came to know that he had been born in this form in a Kãyastha family of Simla (Calcutta). Then I prayed to Mother saying "Mother bind him with Mãyã, or he will give up his body in Samãdhi." Kedar who believes in the form of God peeped over at Narendra, then got up and fled away.

That is why I think that the Mother Herself has been born and is playing within this (his body) as a devotee. When I first reached this state, my body became effulgent. My chest assumed a red hue. I then prayed to Mother, "Mother, do not manifest Thyself outside, repair within." That is why I have got such a poor body now. Otherwise people would not have given me peace. There would have been crowds of people about me if I had that effulgent body. There is no outward manifestation now. Worthless people go away. Only those who are pure devotees will remain. Why have I this illness? It also has the same significance.

I had a desire to be the prince of devotees and I prayed to the Mother accordingly. Again, the desire arose in my mind that those who had called sincerely on the Lord must come here—they must. You see that is what is happening—those very people are coming.

Sri Ramakrishna is bringing forth the idea of the *Divine Mother,* a Divine Mother as equal in necessity to a God the Father. What is happening here is that instead of a God the Father (who mystically creates in male and female pairs), we have a God the Father and a God the Mother who, as their natural sexual process, create in male and female pairs. Until we bring into the God-head both Father and Mother we really cannot understand why there are male and female pairs. *There are male and female pairs because there is a divine Father and Mother.* Do you see the distinction? Here-to-fore, God has been separated from Father and Mother. Most systems have God as something separate and apart from "his" creation. Let's listen to this quote by Thomas Troward (1847-1916). Thomas Troward was a part of the Creative Thought movement (also called the New Thought movement) of the nineteen century. Many great people were involved in this movement including the well-known American writers Ralph Waldo Emerson, Henry David Thoreau, Walt Whitman, William James, and Mary Baker Eddy. Even Walter Russell, who I have already referenced, came out of this movement.

CHRISTOPHER ALAN ANDERSON

Thomas Troward (1847-1916)—*The Creative Process in the Individual*, 1915

From this point onward we shall find the principle of Polarity in universal activity. It is that relation between opposites without which no external motion would be possible, because there would be nowhere to move from, and nowhere to move to; and without which external Form would be impossible because there would be nothing to limit the diffusion of substance and bring it into shape. Polarity, or the interaction of Active and Passive, is therefore the basis of all Evolution.

This is a great fundamental truth when we get it in its right order; but all through the ages it has been a prolific source of error by getting it in its wrong order. And the wrong order consists in making Polarity the originating point of the Creative Process. What this misconception leads to we shall see later on, but since it is very widely accepted under various guises even at the present day, it is well to be on our guard against it. Therefore I wish the student to see clearly that there is something which comes before that Polarity which gives rise to Evolution, and that this something is the original movement of Spirit within itself, of which we can best get an idea by calling it Self-contemplation.

...The order, therefore, which I wish the student to observe is, 1st, the Self-contemplation of Spirit producing Polarity, and next, Polarity producing manifestation in Form—and also to realize that it is in this order his own mind operates as a subordinate center of creative energy.

...And this Law of the Spirit's Original Unity is a very simple one. It is the Spirit's necessary and basic conception of itself.

What Mr. Troward is saying is that primary is *Spirit's Original Unity* and secondary is *Polarity.* (Think of polarity as a male and female pairs.) *...1st, the Self-contemplation of Spirit producing Polarity, and next, Polarity producing manifestation in Form...* Mr. Troward is beginning from the idea of a Divine Being reflecting upon itself as the first instance of creation. Yet how can there even be self-contemplation without thought which is a part of duality/polarity. In short, there isn't any (creative) force in play without polarity—the interaction of the two forces. This is what I was struggling with in my twenties, is the God-head separate, some *Spirit's Original Unity,* or as Walter Russell even stated in The Divine Iliad: *I, the undivided sexless One, am Unity*? This is to ask, is the

56

God-head some spiritual/sexless unity, some undivided or non-dual or non-binary "beingness" that is somehow separate from male and female pairs (although able to create male and female pairs)? This is basically what we have thought. I still hear people claim that "God" is asexual (sexless), some universal power that is neither male nor female. Or that "God" is androgynous (both sexes as a one). Do we ever hear it stated that "God"/order represents a sexual process of male and female pairs? My question was how can sexual polarity come out of a "sexless unity," and, moreover, why do we think some "sexless unity" is primary to sexual polarity? Let's return to the Russell's. This first quote is from Walter Russell's opus work *The Universal One*.

Walter Russell (1871-1963)—*The Universal One*, 1926

Sex is of all things from the beginning. Sex begins when light begins. Sex is the desire for the appearance of being which constitutes the appearance of existence. Nothing can be without the desire to be. All things are which desire to be. Desire dominates all thinking. Desire dominates all matter. All desire is sex desire.

Essentially, Dr. Russell is saying that sex (or the sexual process) is metaphysical in nature. It is not created by some God-head per se; it just is. All things are sexual things. The sexual permeates all things prescribing a thing's nature. Sodium and chlorine are polar (sexual) opposites if you will. *Each "separate thing" is a sexual thing existing as a part of a sexual pair.*

Later, after Walter and Lao Russell (1904-1988) came together they founded the University of Science and Philosophy. Together they wrote the *Home Study Course in Universal Law, Natural Science, and Living Philosophy.*

Walter and Lao Russell—*Home Study Course in Universal Law, Natural Science, and Living Philosophy,* Unit 6, Lesson 22, 1951

Mankind has thought of sex in terms of a relation between the opposite sexes in organic living systems, never for a moment including sex relations in the mineral kingdom, in hot suns, or the ice caps of the poles of planets. We have used such terms as cohabitation and sex relation as though the sex relation is entirely separate and apart from other relations, and as though its reproductive effect is limited to living things that die or decay.

From now on, sex will be regarded in our new perspective as being expressed continuously and perpetually in all things. Instead of thinking in terms of cohabitation and human sexual relationships, sex should be thought of as the interchange between pairs of oppositely unbalanced conditions for the purpose of balancing these conditions in every effect of motion in the entire universe. "Good effects" are those in which the interchange is balanced—and "bad effects" are those in which balance is not complete.

The Russell's are suggesting that every interaction between things is a sexual interaction *...sex should be thought of as the interchange between pairs of oppositely unbalanced conditions for the purpose of balancing these conditions in every effect of motion in the entire universe.* (I would not suggest that pairs of opposite conditions are necessarily unbalanced by their nature.) It appears that separate or opposite things desire unity. But might we also say that unified things desire separation or what can be called *division*? We have never really understood the why of division. Some religions speak of a first separation/division from God and how that is what constituted mankind's downfall.

Now let's move to another author, Max Freedom Long (1890-1971). Mr. Long is considered the founder of Huna (meaning the hidden secret) which he derived from his study of the native Hawaiians, mainly Kahunas or priests who performed Kahuna magic. He has published many books and founded the Huna Fellowship in 1945.

Max Freedom Long (1890-1971)—*Growing Into Light,* 1955

It was also observed that all male and female parts of the Creation were striving to unity. This observation has never been found incorrect. In modern days we know that even the smallest parts of matter or force are positive and negative, and that they strive to unite to come to a point of rest.

We cannot say what caused the division into the two separated parts from atoms to man, but we can be very sure that there is such a general division, and that the urge to unite and reach a state of balanced inertia is universal.

Union, however, does not stop with a simple combination of a positive and a negative force in the world of electrons. The united units become polarized and again are caused to strive for union. Units build. Living things develop as combinations of striving microscopic units. Trillions of such units make up the human body, and then the body itself is given an over-all or enlarged form of the basic division, making it male or female.

We cannot take the spirits of man into the laboratory to examine them, but their characteristics may be observed to be masculine or feminine, and we see on all sides the great urge toward union, male body with female body, the male mind or middle self seeking its complement and fulfilment in the female mind.

This brings us to the First Mystery, that of the High Self, or superconscious, as revealed by the study of Huna. It is very hard to observe. We can do little more than accept the ancient statement, "As above, so below," and reverse it to "As below, so above." In this way we may reach the conclusion that the same division which separated the two lower selves, separated the High Self spirits, and that they also strive on their own high level and in their own more evolved way to reach union.

Mr. Long states: *...that all male and female parts of the Creation were striving to unity.* I believe we all sense/know this. And yet there is the other suggestion: *We cannot say what caused the division into the two separated parts from atoms to man, but we can be very sure that there is such a general division, and that the urge to unite and reach a state of balanced inertia is universal.* And further, and even more to the point: *...we may reach the conclusion that the same division which separated the two lower selves, separated the High Self spirits, and that they also strive on their own high level and in their own more evolved way to reach union.*

So Mr. Long is suggesting that there is both a division and a unification occurring not just within the world of the "lower selves" which constitutes mankind, but also in the world of the *"High Self spirits."* The High Self spirits refer to the God-head. At this point in our understanding, we can begin to see that the creative process is the same for the world of mankind and the world of the God-head. As Mr. Long states: *We can do little more than accept the ancient statement, "As above, so below," and reverse it to "As below, so above."* There is only *one world* or, philosophically speaking, *one order*. And in this one world there is a creative process (or shall we call it a sexual process), which is the order, incorporating a *union of opposites* and a *separation into divided pairs*.

Returning to Walter and Lao Russell below is a picture from their writing *Atomic Suicide?*, 1957. They called it *The Divine Trinity*.

The Divine Trinity is the creative/sexual process if you will. There are the two parts—the "one" dividing into "two," and the "two" uniting into "one" over and over again. Now we still have to dig deeper to understand the motives of unity and division. Remember Mr. Long's comment: *We cannot say what caused the division into the two separated parts...* I would suggest we cannot say what caused the unity into a sexual whole. *What therefore God hath joined together, let not man put asunder.* Speaking to the creative or sexual process, the Russell's said it this way.

Walter and Lao Russell—*Atomic Suicide?*, 1957

The Father-Mother of Creation divides His sexless unity into sex-divided pairs of father and mother bodies, for the purpose of uniting them to create other pairs of father and mother bodies in eternal sequences forever.

According to the Russell's, the purpose of (His sexless) unity is to divide into pairs of father and mother bodies. And the purpose of the father and mother bodies (the division) is to unite them *...to create other pairs of father and mother bodies in eternal sequences forever.* There is a problem in this quote though, and that lies in the idea of "His sexless unity." It sounds as if this "sexless unity point" is outside of the creative/sexual male and female process. We are back to Thomas Troward's *Spirit's Original Unity* as being separate from and prior to polarity. This "His sexless unity" appears to be outside of, prior to, and perhaps different from the sex-divided pairs of father and mother bodies. Can you see the issue and struggle here? Is there a one intrinsic creative/sexual process containing both aspects of division and unity or is it that there is something outside of, prior to, and different from the sexual process (divided pairs of father and mother bodies)? This was the issue I was struggling with in my twenties—the languaging is just inaccurate. And so now we move further into Lao Russell. She wrote *The Continuity of Life* from *Why You Cannot Die* some nine or so years after Walter had passed. I think her wording is a little more precise. This is followed by another drawing from the writing *Atomic Suicide?* which Walter and Lao wrote together.

Lao Russell (1904-1988)—*The Continuity of Life* from *Why You Cannot Die*, 1972

"Know thou that thou shalt know space, but never emptiness for:

"Behold! I am Space and I fill all of it.

"I am its One, its undivided Father-Mother One of my universe.

"I divide My oneness, and behold! I am two—father and mother.

"These two extend from Me, one on My right hand and one on My left.

"Each equally balanced with the other in the Oneness of their mate-hood.

"And then, behold! My two become one in Me, the One Father-Mother, undivided—

"To again become two to Father-Mother my eternal universe."

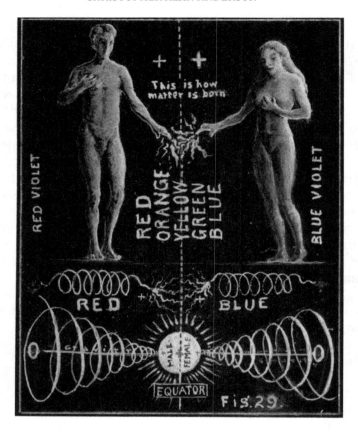

In this later quote by Lao Russell, we don't see this "His sexless unity" but rather an *undivided Father-Mother One* and an *I am two—father and mother*. This is much better, we are seeing a full cycle or interchange in place. In other words, both the unity (*undivided Father-Mother One*) and the division (*I am two—father and mother*) are incorporated into the creative/sexual process. There isn't any "Spirit's Original Unity" or "His sexless unity" outside of, prior to, or different from the sexual process of male and female unification and division. In fact, metaphysically speaking, the "what is" is *the sexual process of male and female unification and division.* So we need to re-language Troward's "Spirit's Original Unity" so that it is precise to life. Let's call it *Spirit's Original Division and Unity.* And in the case of Russell's "His sexless unity" how about *His and Her sexual (uniting and dividing) eternal life interchange.* Just a shift in a few words and bang!, the whole universe changes. Now that is a paradigm shift of immense proportions. Our job now is to see how this shift effects everything—and for the better.

Let's now bring in a few more examples to cement this paradigm shift into our consciousness. This next example is from the *Dictionary of Philosophy and Religion* under the topic *Opposites* by William L. Reese.

William L. Reese—*Dictionary of Philosophy and Religion—Opposites*, 1980

Some systems of philosophy have placed a stress on the role of opposites.

1. The Pythagoreans developed a table of opposites reflecting a basic duality in the universe.

2. Heraclitus found a "tension of opposites" providing the order and dynamism of the universe.

3. In Taoism Yang and Yin represent opposites in terms of which the universe operates.

4. Nicholas of Cusa presented a doctrine called the "coincidence of opposites" which applied to God, the Infinite Being.

5. Hegel believed the basic processes of reality and thought moved through contraries into novel unities.

6. Gnosis: The male and female or antithetical (directly opposed) pairs of the first principle.*

*Added by the author to complete the *Dictionary of Philosophy & Religion* definitions.

The idea of opposites or polar opposites is what we are speaking to—in this case unification and division. We could also refer to them as Yin and Yang which has historically been the case in Taoism. In the same *Dictionary of Philosophy and Religion* under *Taoism* it states: *There are two sets of opposed qualities, the yin and the yang, which help structure the universe, and must be part of one's personal equation.* Under *Tao-Te-Ching* it states: *The tao is invisible, inaudible, subtle, formless, infinite, boundless, vague, elusive.* It sounds in a way like the *Tao* is outside of, prior to, and different from the *sexual process of male and female unity and division*, that it is "Spirit's Original Unity" or "His sexless unity," etc. This is the problem—a disconnect between the God-head and "his" creation. Let's turn to another example, this one by inventor and engineer Ron Pearson.

Ron Pearson—*Solving the Problem of the Cosmological Constant*, 2007

...It was clear that, to find a solution to the creation problem, it was necessary to introduce the idea of a background medium consisting of primary particles made of two opposite kinds of energy, positive and negative. These had to be equivalent to the yin and yang of Chinese philosophy. The two kinds form a background that I call "i-ther," and must consist of a balance of these two kinds of primary particle, the "primaries." Opposite kinds could cancel each other to leave the nothingness of the void—a representation of mutual annihilation. Creation would be the converse case, with nothing giving rise to opposite somethings. A basic law of physics known as the conservation of energy would be satisfied in this way, and yet the universe could arise spontaneously from nothing.

This is nice. Notice that Mr. Pearson is postulating *a background medium consisting of primary particles made of two opposite kinds of energy, positive and negative.* It actually is the two primary particles (we can call them *Yin* and *Yang*) that are foundational not "Spirit's Original Unity" or a "His sexless unity," some "neither male nor female" point. So we have shifted from the God-head being an *invisible, inaudible, subtle, formless, infinite, boundless, vague, elusive...* to two primary particles (or forces) being the God-process. Now, it was much later that I came across Mr. Pearson's article. Back in my twenties my thinking was much more simplistic. I was just trying to frame the issue and solution. My thinking went something like this. *If division comes out of the unity must not that division be an essential part of the unity. From the unity comes the division into a two. As such, that division must be an essential part of the unity/division process. Likewise, from the division of the two comes unity, the two becoming as one. Therefore, unity must be an essential part of the unity/division process.* Do you see the balance in play here? Both parts are essential. In fact, you can't have just one part. Unity is always referenced with division and division with unity. Can you see that we are dealing here a process and not a point? The God-head, if you will, is not a thing but a process. And the two primaries are the sexual forces of Yin (Female) and Yang (Male). *So the God-head is not outside of, prior to, or different from the sexual process of male and female division and unification; the God-head is this sexual process.* This is what I had come to and was the frame from which I begin my writings in the 1980s. So let me turn to one of my earlier writings, *The Two Forces of Creation*, 1988. This writing was later incorporated into *Selected Writings—Volume 2*, 1991, 2010.

> *In review, let me suggest that "what is" is relationship-in-process. Relationship-in-process is fundamental or primordial, not a First Cause or One Force. This is to further say that there isn't a supreme being although there may be supreme beings.*

There isn't a mover of the spheres although there may be movers of the spheres. There isn't a one God who sees all that becomes or forms all immortal beings although there may be gods that do just that. There is not a single fundamental primordial creative force in the universe, i.e., energy, desire, motive, impulse, purpose, impetus, drive, intention, nature, will, consciousness, Prana, mana, Ki, Chi, Waken, bioplasma, light, cosmic energy, life force, vital pulse, or Holy Spirit. There is only one force in relationship to another force from which creation may then occur. We have to date made a critical mistake in not noting this elementary fact within our conception of order.

Now, I am not suggesting there isn't a metaphysical placement (God, Source, Light, Cause, Foundation, etc.), only that that metaphysical placement consists of a *primary two*. There are two primary forces (or Gods [or lights or energies] if you want to use that term). They are complements to each other—*equal and opposite* is the term I use. Think of the "God" placement as consisting of God the Father <u>and</u> God the Mother or just male and female—a two creative/sexual forces, not a one singular force but a two creative/sexual forces. Let's continue with *The Two Forces of Creation.*

Many names have been given to this "supreme essence" that subsumes both the ideas of a One Principle and a First Cause. Along with those mentioned are Divine Essence, Supreme Being, Absolute Unity, Infinite Energy, Universal Life Force, Unconditional Cause, and Universal Spirit. These conceptions all exist under the umbrella of monotheism which, as I have mentioned, has been one of the greatest conceptions of man, so great, in fact, that it may have hampered him on another level. We seem to have assumed that all things had their source in the oneness of God. We did not delineate between One Principle (order) and First Cause (force), for example. Yet order in itself does not subsume a one force. There could just as readily be two forces within nature without any loss of order to nature. Order does not subsume reality as being a oneness or unity; it does not subsume a primordial God, Unmoved Mover, First Cause and the like; it does not subsume a singular God, spirit, mind, consciousness, or essence. In short, order only subsumes order and not necessarily singularity. In fact, singularity may in itself preclude order. So why haven't we critically analyzed this distinction between order and force but instead fallen so easily into the idea that singularity holds the heart of all things? Is it because, given the vastness of things, it is just easier to believe that some First Cause is in control of our lives? Whatever the reason may be, it has been, as we shall see, a costly oversight.

The costly oversight, historical in its nature, has been that we have viewed "God" as a singularity (outside of, prior to, and different from) rather than a plurality working within. What I am suggesting to you is that the God-head is a <u>sexual</u> plurality, a process where the one divides into an opposite two and the two unite back into the one. And guess what, neither part is superior to the other part. This is the issue. In Marx's ideology there can only be class struggle. The two parts can never get together. We see the imbalance of the two parts wherever we look—sexism, racism, religion, nationality, Marxism/socialism, L,G,B,T,Q, etc. Everywhere there is an imbalance between the two—which cannot be rectified. And it all starts from a faulty metaphysics. In the case of the God-head, we have postulated God to be singular (and therefore superior), as the Father, or as "Spirit's Original Unity" or "His sexless unity," and so on. Polarity, the two-force sexual (uniting/dividing) process, has always come in second place—irrespective of Mr. Troward's comment to the contrary. So there is a split or rift between the so called God-head and our living of life. It is a split/rift we will never close unless and until we solve this issue of a singular "God" as to a two-force male and female living process. I am suggesting to you that it is this polarity (the two-force male and female living process) that is the God-head or source-point of it all and that there isn't, nor never was, an outside of, prior to, or different from, some God or Tao state that is *invisible, inaudible, subtle, formless, infinite, boundless, vague, elusive.* Now, there may be a unity point that incorporates all of these qualities but that is only because that unity point is in absolute equal and opposite balance from its polar opposite—that of division. *From this point of sexual balance (unification <u>and</u> division), with its male and female primaries, all life can occur as all life is itself the given.*

As a close to this section, I would like to return to Ayn Rand. I would like to show you just how close she actually was to what I am suggesting. She is often viewed critically as being an atheist. But she did have a metaphysics. She began her metaphysics from the self-evident statement "existence exists." That was her given, her "what is." Now, I am suggesting we enlarge that to *existence exists as male and female.* It might be better to use man and woman here: *existence exists as man and woman.* This is our beginning point. *We begin from a two primary/sexual forces that are equal to yet opposite from each other.* (More on their essential purposes/functions later.) So this next passage is what Ayn Rand wrote in *Atlas Shrugged*. The heroine of the story, Dagny Taggart, is reflecting under the burden of possible defeat of her life dream and never being with her life's love, but tell me, isn't Ayn Rand capturing the feeling of the essence of what I am presenting to you? Doesn't her heroine feel, and attempt to reach, her life's love?

Ayn Rand (1905-1982)—*Atlas Shrugged,*1959

She felt—as she had felt it one spring night, slumped across her desk in the crumbing office of the John Galt Line, by a window facing a dark alley—the sense and vision of her own world, which she would never reach... You—she thought—whomever you are, whom I have always loved and never found, you whom I expected to see at the end of the rails beyond the horizon, you whose presence I had always felt in the streets of the city and whose world I had wanted to build, it is my love for you that had kept me moving, my love and my hope to reach you and my wish to be worthy of you on the day when I would stand before you face to face. Now I know that I shall never find you—that it is not to be reached or lived—but what is left of my life is still yours, and I will go on in your name, even though it is a name I'll never learn, I will go on serving you, even though I'm never to win, I will go on. To be worthy of you on the day when I would have met you, even though I won't... She had never accepted hopelessness, but she stood at the window and, addressed to the shape of a fog bound city, it was her self-dedication to unrequited love.

The Shift that is Man and Woman Balance

For aeons, mankind has been caught in a trap, a trap so hideous it has prevented men and women from achieving any type of enduring success. Yet, from this trap our religions formed and promised mankind a way out through another world. Later, our socio-political institutions were formed promising us liberation in this world. Yet, neither could deliver, for they were part of the trap, which was nothing but a simple misconception mankind made at the dawn of consciousness preventing him from discovering life.

This writing is about understanding and correcting that misconception whereupon mankind, for the first time, may discover life, thereby bringing a fulfillment and completion to him (or her) self.

This quote is from my writing *The Discovery of Life*, 1994, 2010. The misconception made thousands of years ago is the trap we are still in and must now climb out of. To make this climb a shift is needed, a core shift at the very metaphysical level of things, a shift in the heart and soul of ourselves. (*"It is easier to denature plutonium than to denature the evil from the spirit of man."*) Let's begin from this point. There are two realities in this universe. One is your own existence. You exist. I exist. This is an absolute. This is what Ayn Rand means when she speaks of rational self-interest. Each one of us, and that includes not just human beings but every individual thing, has rational self-interest. I have often asked the question whether or not a "Christian" would give a damn about Jesus if they didn't believe that in accepting him as their personal savior they would be saved—for all eternity. Now there is a rational self-interest for you! We all have a fundamental interest, i.e., the desire of self-expression, in our own lives not just in this incarnation but in an eternal sense as well. But there is another fundamental reality—and that is of the *other.* The other is that which is not oneself. We exist, if you will, in a Self-Other relationship—at all times. So primary to things is not "God," or any such singular thing. Primary is self <u>and</u> other. To those who hold a belief in "God," one's primary relationship would be "Self" and "God." Now, I would suggest that both sides are of equal importance. We tend to elevate "God" to a higher status because we believe "he" is ultimate creator and we are not. There is an interesting quote by Walter Russell from his writing *The Universal One* on this exact point.

Walter Russell (1871-1963)—*The Universal One*, 1926
In the beginning, God. There is but one God. There is but

one universe. God is the universe. God is not one and the universe another. The universe is not a separate creation of God's. It is God. There is no created universe. Nothing is which has not always been... Man conceives a perfect and omnipotent God. A perfect and omnipotent God could not create imperfection. He could not create a lesser than Himself. He could not create a greater than Himself. God could not create other than Himself. God did not create other than Himself, nor greater, nor lesser than Himself.

Dr. Russell is suggesting that there isn't a metaphysical greater/metaphysical lesser order to things. If we go back to Marx's class struggle, it can be noticed that one side is considered superior to the other. Marx's called the two sides the Bourgeoisie and Proletariat. In racial terms we have the white and black races. In sexual terms, male and female, and so on. And there is always this class struggle—one part considered more important than the other part. Even if you equate your "other" to be God, or Jesus, Buddha, Mohammed, etc., there is still this inherent inequality between the two. But *God did not create other than Himself, nor greater, nor lesser than Himself.* You see, you and your other are metaphysical equals. *Self is never greater than Other; Other is never greater than Self.* There isn't any inherent royalty in life. The Pope does not have some special connection to "God" that we don't equally have. The King is not divine. The President is not the ruler through executive order. We are not here to kiss anyone's ring, to bow down as if someone else is holier than thou. Nobody gets special rights—over others. We are equal in this regard. I call this metaphysical equality. Here is its statement: *One is not without the other; both are needed for either to be.*

The Metaphysical Self and the Metaphysical Other

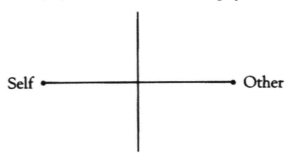

There is a further distinction to be made in the Self-Other relationship and this is that the two are not the same. There must be an *inherent difference* between them. We have an argument going on in the world right now regarding whether or not gender difference is inherent in our lives—which really means whether or not gender difference comprises the actual metaphysical order of things. Earlier I suggested that existence exists as male and female. That would suggest that gender is of the metaphysical order of things. But we must take a step back here. Recall what Max Freedom Long said: *We cannot say what caused the division into the two separated parts from atoms to man, but we can be very sure that there is such a general division, and that the urge to unite and reach a state of balanced inertia is universal...* So what causes the division? Let us also ask, what causes the unification? We have, as our given, these two parts—polar opposites, if you will. Why is there a division of the one? Why is there a unification of the two? Well, might not we say that this is the LIFE process itself? In life there is birth-life-death-rebirth. It is a continuum. The one divides into two. This is what we call individual life. But then the two unite into one. This is the death part of LIFE. Everything goes through this LIFE process.

LIFE

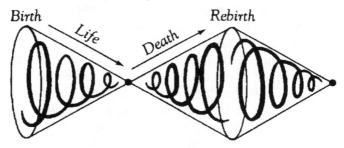

Let's take the example of breathing—there is inhalation and exhalation. Breathing is a two-way process between inhalation and exhalation. It is simply contained within itself, a two-way process. What are other opposites you can think of?

Sexual Opposites

Identification	Relation
Deduction	Intuition
Particular	Universal
Separation	Connection
Physical	Spiritual
Power	Guide
Fact	Feeling
Linear	Lateral
Concentration	Decentration

Event	Continuity
Point	Source
Individualization	Unification
Consciousness	Existence
Focus	Field
Dual	Non-Dual
Verbalization	Telepathy
Yang	Yin
First Say	Final Say

Everything, including you and I, is in a relationship with its other, dividing from and uniting together over and over again. Call this other your other half, your sexual opposite, your eternal companion, your soul mate, whatever you wish, you have one as do I. In our world (as humans), we generally use the terms man and woman. Male and female are more general. Spiritually we could say *God the Father* and *God the Mother*. See the shift going on? But why male and why female? We have never really understood the metaphysical necessity of the sexes. The "Who am I" and "Why am I here" questions should be asked in this way, "What is Male?" and "What is Female." "Who am I" and "Why am I here" are actually sexual questions. Here-to-fore, we have only asked them singularly. But must not we incorporate our "sexual other" in the context of an answer? I would think so.

What is Male?

What is Female?

So, we are looking for ...*a background medium consisting of primary particles made of two opposite kinds of energy, positive and negative,* as Ron Pearson states. I would point out that "negative" does not mean less than. It actually means opposite from. I use the words division and unification (or just unity). This is to suggest that the impetus of one of the sexes is to divide the one and the impetus of the other sex is to unite the two. As stated: *Existence exists as male and female.* Everything exists in this relationship. *One is not without the other; both are needed for either to be.* More specifically, *each one of us is of our sexuality in relation to that other of opposite sexuality.* If you are a male you exist in a relationship with a female. If you are a female you exist in a relationship with a male. This is of the metaphysical order of things. *Sexual relationship is primary.* Sexuality is encoded in the very fabric of the universe itself. See the shift here?

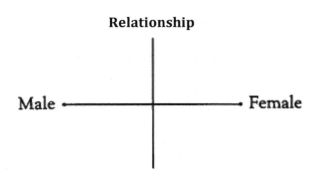

Now back to the questions: why division and why unification? Or we could just ask: why male and why female? Let's approach the answer from the view that just as there are two parts to the creative (life) process so there are two parts to sexuality. There is the *division of the one* and there is the *unification of the two.* Likewise, there is *male* and there is *female.* Would it be too much of a stretch to suggest that one part of this process corresponds to male and the other to female? If so, the question of male and female comes down to the idea of *purpose* or *function.* Is the male essence/purpose to divide the one or to unite the two? How about the female? What is her essence/purpose? Let's now get more specific as to the purposes of the two (equal and opposite) sexual parts. I will be quoting from some of my earlier writings. This first quote is from *The Discovery of Life*, 1994, 2010.

> We express creation through our sexuality. That is the effort of individual life. Then we release our sexual difference into the unity of rest. In the unification of the two, sexual difference, in that one moment, is voided. The two have become one which is their rest or death. But from that unity comes the next division into sexual difference. This whole process is sexual, creative to life. (I hope it is understood that sexuality is not just physical but metaphysical. It is of the non-beginning and never-ending. It is what is. In other words, we are not beings who just happen to be sexual, we are sexual beings with a sexual purpose.) So, which

do you do? Do you divide the one or do you unite the two? This is the great metaphysical question. To answer it, we need to discover our sexual selves, who we are in relation to whom we are not, thereby discovering life. If you are a male, you will do one of these functions. If you are a female, you will do the other. Both functions are equally necessary to life, yet they are opposite. So which are you?

Generalizations maybe but which one are you? Do you *divide the one* or *unite the two*? As mentioned, if you are male you will do one of these functions; if female, the other. The next passage is from *The Two Forces of Creation*, 1988.

Male is that force which seeks to individualize form separate and apart from the unity of male-female. The male desire is to hold male and female in individual form. It is the active conscious effort of holding separate identity in relationship to the other. The male effort is simply to hold apart and stabilize the man and woman relationship. We call this the effort to secure form or just "security."

Female is that force which seeks to unite the division of male and female. The female desire is to unite the separate male and female forms together as one. She rests the man and woman relationship through unifying male within herself. It is from this unity that the next division or reproduction can take place. The female effort then is to unite the separate forms of male and female, resting that unity so that the next reproduction of individual form will occur. We call this resting of old form/begetting of new form "reproduction."

In essence, it is the male effort to secure form and the female effort to reproduce form that makes for life and its continuity. Each aspect makes for one half of the creative process. Yet, and this is an important point, neither aspect can complete their creative desire without the other. The male cannot continually secure form. That effort is fatiguing and brings on a desire to rest. It is at this point that the male takes what he has secured in form and gives it over to female. The male deposits his life seed (force) into the female releasing his form into hers from which his next reproduction will occur. So without periodic rest or release of his form into hers, the male cannot continue to fulfill his own desire to secure form.

Likewise, the female cannot continually rest/reproduce form.

She herself must sequentially effort, and does so equal to male in preparing herself to receive male as well as nurturing new form. In this fashion, she supports the securing effort of male. Female is actually called to surrender her life to the male desire to individualize form even though her primary desire is to unite, for without that division of the one into two there would not be the two sexual selves to unite. At this point of unity, the male is called to surrender his life to the female desire to unite the forms even though his primary desire is to individualize. Without the unity of the two into one there would not be a unified one from which male and female could then divide into their sexually unique forms.

It is important to understand the equality of the two different forces of male and female. They each operate under different desires and yet both are equally essential for either of them to be. The male force alone or the female force alone is impotent. Without the other neither can be. They need each other. Each is as important to the other as they are to themselves. Both are called upon to make the ultimate surrender of their lives to the other. Neither is ever without the other. Both always are. Male and female, the two forces of creation, are what is.

These last three passages are from *The Discovery of Life*, 1994, 2010.

Male, then, is that force that divides the one. Female is that force which unites the two. This creative or sexual distinction is the great discovery of life and requires a deep comprehension. There just isn't anything else in all of creation but the two opposite forces of male and female, dividing and uniting together, each under the direction of their unique and opposite sexual purpose. You see, there isn't anything more real to life than a male and a female. Life is composed of these two forces. This is life, right now. We are all riding the universal wave of creation. Think of it as an ocean and the male and female forces as a ship. Male is the motor. The male purpose is to power it (divide the one and initiate action). Female is the rudder. It is her purpose to guide the ship (unite the two and complete the action in reaction.) We can never get off this ship for it is the vessel of the universe. We can only try and sail as straight a course as possible.

To be conscious then is to be sexually conscious. The

monotheistic (one-force) consciousness does not present us with sexual consciousness for the two forces are not identified essentially in creation. We just are not, and cannot be, fully conscious without the recognition of our sexual self in relationship to our sexual opposite.

And now we can return to the question, Who am "I"? including an added question, Why am "I" here? These two questions are the fundamental questions of our sexual identities and realities.

Who am "I"?

I am a male in relationship to a female,
or
I am a female in relationship to a male,
. . . whichever sexuality "I" happen to be,
"You" being the sexual opposite of me.

Why am "I" here?

"I" am here to express the sexuality that "I" am . . .
  Male, being that force which seeks to individualize a
form separate and apart from the unity of male-female.
  Female, being that force which seeks to unite separate
forms together from the division of male and female.
. . . so that together we may continue to manifest our
own sexual creation.

The Man and Woman Relationship

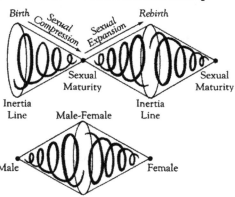

75

I hope you can see (and feel) the two *different forces of male and female.* Notice that it is the male force that is the force of division/separation. So, when Max Freedom Long says: *We cannot say what caused the division into the two separated parts from atoms to man, but we can be very sure that there is such a general division, and that the urge to unite and reach a state of balanced inertia is universal...* now we can answer that—the *male force* constitutes the desire/impetus to separate from the female. This is his initial action from which he efforts to secure female. The *female force* constitutes the desire/impetus to unite the division and, in doing so, brings forth the next reproduction of life. I hope you now can see the distinct essences of male and female and thus feel their *interconnection* together. Their interconnection only has meaning relative to their division and vice-versa. This is it. This is all we have. There isn't any higher calling because there isn't any other calling. There is just a male and a female, uniting together and dividing apart, over and over again.

Let's now see if we can experience this shift I am speaking about. It is the metaphysical shift to a two-force sexual center of life. In a way we are always with, not necessarily at one with or completely separate from but *with.* Our relationship is a dividing from and uniting with life process over and over. I sought to capture that in the poem *Consciousness* from the book *To Cassandra—Early Years* published in 1985, 1994.

Consciousness

> Walking along
> My path of life
> Sometimes, my woman
> I run into you
> Head on or a tender glance
> Exchanged
> By the acacia tree
> Is it in bloom this day?
>
> Staying a spell
> Or passing by this day
> I slowly almost silently
> Release my being
> That carries the essence
> That you may receive
> If that is your fancy.

Do you hear my soul
Precious one?
Calling to you
Desiring you with all my might
Imagining that I say to you,
"Please, my love
Come be with me
And stay away from me
Walk with me
As you walk away from me
Leaving me alone
So I may feel
Just how much I need
To be with you
And without you."

Do you desire my heart
Eternal one?
That breaks away from you
Again and again
That comes back to you
As a child renewed
With fresh ideas
And grand designs
I must follow the path
That again leads away from you.

That path is quite long today
I can hardly make my way
Through the heavy fog
That dims the light
That brightens my heart,
"Woman—would you come be
Apart-together with me
Just as are the tree
And the stream
Or the flower and the bee?
Would you come join
And disjoin with me,
For that is the only vision
I can see,
For do we not create

Each moment when together
Who we are when apart
Who we desire to be with
When together?"

"Cassandra,
Please stay away from me
And be with me
For in the moment
Of our apart-togetherness
I create my perfect self
To be away from you
And to be with you."

I would like to end this section with a booklet from *Meditations for Deepening Love,* 1994, 2010. It is called *Aphorisms for the New Age of Man and Woman.* This is another way of articulating this sexual metaphysical shift.

Aphorisms for the New Age of Man and Woman
The following aphorisms are listed to provide one with the principles necessary to conceptualize and experience the man and woman relationship as the one creative process of existence in which each of us are embedded.

1. *Male-Female is.*
   -In the non-beginning never-ending is male-female.

2. *Male and Female are.*
   -Male-Female divide, separating into the distinct sexualities of male and female that they are.

3. *Life is Male and Female.*
   -Separated, male and female express their distinct sexualities that they are to each other.

4. *Death is Male-Female.*
   -Male and female unite into the rest of male-female.

5. *Birth-Life-Death-Rebirth is Male and Female in dividing-uniting interaction with each other.*
   -The division of male-female into male and female is the birth of

life. The unification of male and female into male-female is the death of life. The division of male-female into male and female is the rebirth of life.

6. *Eternity is the birth-life-death-rebirth of Male and Female.*
   -The interaction of male and female division and unification never began nor will ever end.

7. *Male and Female are eternal to each other, never without each other.*
   -Male and female are always in interaction, one sexuality implies the other, eternally.

8. *Male and Female interact due to their desire to do so.*
   -The dividing-uniting sexual interaction between male and female is inspired by their creative desire.

9. *All desire is sexual desire.*
   -Sexuality, male or female, is the impetus of desire.

10. *Sexual desire is energy or motive force.*
    -The energy or force of universe is that of sexual desire.

11. *All sexual desire is Male desire or Female desire.*
    -Sexual desire is stipulated by sexuality, it being male or female.

12. *All energy is Male energy or Female energy.*
    -Energy, being sexual desire, is either male or female in force.

13. *Male and Female are all that is.*
    -Male and female comprise the two forces that through their interaction make up all that is.

14. *Male is individualization.*
    -Male is that force which seeks to individualize a form separate and apart from the unity of male-female.

15. *Female is unification.*
    -Female is that force which seeks to unify separate forms together from the division of male and female.

16. *Male force is generative.*

-The desire of male to divide from the female and individualize form is the compressive effort that creates form, male out of female.

17. *Female force is radiative.*
-The desire of female to unite with male and unify separate forms is the expansive rest that decreates form, male into female.

18. *Male and Female create-decreate-recreate all that is.*
-The interaction of male and female is that which creates through compressive effort the individual forms of male and female, and decreates those forms through expansive rest to again recreate...

19. *Male desire creates Female.*
-Through the male desire to individualize a form apart from female, female, too, is brought into form in relationship to male.

20. *Female desire decreases Male.*
-Through the female desire to unite separated forms, male, too, is taken out of form into male-female.

21. *Male desire is securitive.*
-Through the male desire to hold separate form, male as to female, life is secured.

22. *Female desire is reproductive.*
-Through the female desire to unite separate forms together, male-female, life is reproduced.

23. *Male secures Female for the reproduction of Female.*
-The male, in his desire to hold separate form, secures female form so that he in turn may be reproduced in form by female.

24. *Female reproduces Male for the security of Male.*
-The female, in her desire to unite separate forms together, reproduces male form so that she in turn may be secured in form by male.

25. *Male and Female create-decreate-recreate together.*
-Male and female together comprise the purpose and process of creation. Neither of them alone can bring forth the birth-life-death-rebirth continuum of all that is. The two forces must

interact, and do so as to their nature, dividing and uniting together.

26. *Male and Female exist in the state of rhythmic balanced interchange.*
-The male force and the female force are equally essential to the existence of either of them. The two forces of creation hold absolute balance together.

27. *Love is the rhythmic balanced interchange between Male and Female.*
-Love is manifested in the balance of male and female, dividing and uniting together, bringing forth the creation-decreation-recreation of all that is.

28. *Love is eternally creative.*
-The male and female rhythmic balanced interchange never began nor will ever end but is always creating, manifesting love one to the other.

29. *Love is the only state of existence between Male and Female.*
-Male and female are in love together, right now and forever.

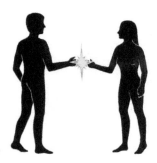

So, given where we are up to right now, what might be my essence statement? Let's review:

Karl Marx: *From each according to his abilities, to each according to his needs.*

Ayn Rand: *I swear by my life and my love of it that I will never live for the sake of another man, nor ask another man to live for mine.*

Walter Russell: *Thou, my Father-Mother, are the Light of the world.*

Christopher Anderson: *Love is the only state of existence between Male and Female.*

Part 2
What We Believe!

The Law of Opposites and the Teeter-Totter Drawings

Let's take a moment and define balance. From Webster's it says:

Balance: *A state of equilibrium or equipoise, equality in amount...as between two things.* **Equilibrium:** *A state of balance or equality between opposing forces.*

I like the definition: *A state of balance or equality between opposing forces.* Here we see the idea of opposing forces in play. In *The Discovery of Life,* 1994, 2010, I state:

> *The metaphysical center of creation is a dividing/uniting sexual creative process between the two forces of male and female in perfect balance together. It is this creative dynamic of Man and Woman Balance that will replace the old static one-force misconception, for Man and Woman Balance has always been and will always be. There isn't any other process, principle, or order in the universe that will bring forth life for it is life.*

There isn't any other process, principle, or order in the universe that will bring forth life for it is life. This is what the idea of balance presents to us—an *absolute.* Not an absolute that is outside of, prior to, or different from this one sexual creative process of life but an absolute that is this one sexual creative process of life. Sexual balance is actually that Godhead, Truth, Absolute, Source, Origin, Tao, Divine Light, Primary Substance, Etheric Field, Infinite Energy, Primary Given, etc. Sexual balance is a *living* process, a *procreant* living process to be exact. I call this balance *Man and Woman Balance.* Each one of us is always in balance with our eternal sexual other half. Now, I know that at times it does not seem that way. We will get to that in a moment. For now, see if you can visualize this fundamental sexual/procreant process—you and your equal and opposite other half dividing and uniting together. This next quote is from *The 2008–2009 Articles—Love: The Law of Polar Opposites,* 2010.

> *Only (sexual) opposites can unite to then again divide...creating the spiritual lineage of (procreant) love.*

This tells us that balance, i.e., the process of opposites dividing from and uniting with, is *the spiritual lineage of (procreant) love.* In short, *balance is love.* When we hear that "God is love," what is really meant is that *balance is love.* As you hold to the balance with another (specifically your equal and opposite other half) there is *love.* This next quote is from

Selected Writings: Volume 2, Dimensions in Consciousness, 1991, 2010.

> *Love is not separated from the metaphysic one holds concerning the nature of reality. If that metaphysic is creatively imbalanced, what then does that say about the availability of love? Love springs forth out of creative balance. It is the act of creation itself.*

So love, too, is an absolute. Love exists at the very essence/nature of all things. Love is encoded into the fundamental order or foundation of everything. *Love is procreant love.* Love exists naturally as the state of reality between opposites. Let's give this idea of love a diagram if we can. I call this diagram *Structural Balance.* We can also refer to it as *Man and Woman Balance* as shown below.

Structural Balance
Man and Woman Balance

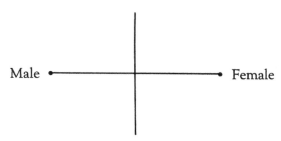

This procreant balance between opposites (also called love) is what we have coming in. *All life is held in the balance of love.* This is our ground zero point. So why then do so many of us seem out of balance/love? The reason for this is because we slap an imbalanced belief on top of the underlining balance. Listen to this next quote from *Man, Woman, and God: I Carry the Cross, too—The Completion of the Message of Jesus Christ,* 1994, 2010. It is a mouth full.

> *Sexual metaphysics is the comparative study of any given, i.e., conception, paradigm, or model to see if it meets the test of procreation and thereby holds to the one universal standard or law of creative balance. The fact that there is an absolute reality (creative balance) gives us the metaphysic of life that we must be aligned to if we intend to sustain life.*

Balance then is sexual balance. The fundamental balance we hold is with our sexual other half. Each one of us is a sexual dual/primary in balance with our equal and opposite sexual other half. If you want to view this balance in more universal/spiritual terms use the words *God the Father* and *God the Mother*. The point to all this is that there must be a *sexual life process* in play for one to hold to the balance. It does not help us to hold to some "one still light" or "Spirit's Original Unity," or "His sexless unity," etc. No, we must hold ourselves in balance to our sexual other half. And so the question of Sexual Metaphysics is:

The Question of Sexual Metaphysics

Is it Procreant to Life?
Can the two become as one...become as two...as one...?

Can you feel this balance/love? This is the state of your eternal existence, you with your sexual other half now and forever. That is a big bite to take, isn't it? It is also the bite of life. Either you hold to the two-way balance with your equal and opposite sexual other half or you do not. Quoting again from *The Discovery of Life*, 1994, 2010, let's continue with how we proceed to imbalance our relationships.

> There are two fundamental ways in which we imbalance our relationships. In one of these ways one, or both, of the parties do not acknowledge their metaphysical equality. I call this type of imbalance Masculinism. Historically, men have been notorious for thinking of themselves as the more important part of the relationship. Oftentimes, women were viewed as the man's property. Men have tended to acknowledge the sexual difference or opposition of the two but they have denied the equality, not truly seeing the necessity of a female in their lives. Such relationships are not truly procreative to the continuation of the relationship, or to the support of new life, because the imbalance is always in the way, preventing the sexual two from fully touching, soul to soul. Unity is not just physical. It is spiritual, entailing a consciousness of life.
>
> In the other case, the sexual two are viewed to be metaphysically equal, just not creatively opposite. I call this Feminism. Feminism is a reaction to Masculinism. Its focus is on "sexual equality," not in the way I have been referring (an equal necessity of the parts) but as if the opposite two were the same. There is a term the feminists use called "androgyny" which refers to some sexual similarity as if somehow in spirit we (male and female) are the same. They speak of an androgynous or gender-blind society where sexual distinction is not a factor in

life. But without creative opposition, how can the sexual two unite? Unity (reproduction) can only occur from the differentiated two. And from unity comes the next division into sexual opposition. For life to be secured and reproduced both equality and opposition are required. Both Masculinism and Feminism fail to adhere to the balance necessary for life. Neither offers a complete touch from oneself to another. Both are caught up in their one-force worlds that exclude the necessity and life of the other. Of themselves alone, they are not procreative.

Now we can begin to understand the frames of balance as to imbalance. There are three metaphysical structures we may choose from in life. One of them is balanced (Man and Woman Balance), the other two are imbalanced (Masculinism and Feminism). Let's diagram this as *The Three Structures of the Universe* followed by the drawings *Structural Balance* and *Structural Imbalance.*

The Three Structures of the Universe
Man and Woman Balance: *Equal and Opposite*
Masculinism: *Opposite but not Equal*
Feminism: *Equal but not Opposite*

Structural Balance
Man and Woman Balance

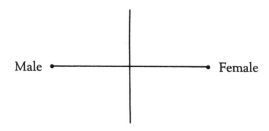

CHRISTOPHER ALAN ANDERSON

Structural Imbalance

Masculinism   **Feminism**

Male   Female

Female   Male

Now we have for ourselves *a frame for life*. And from this frame for life we are able to analyze any other thought-system, any religion or philosophical system, or even a political/economic system, to see if it meets the acid test—*Is it Procreant to Life? Can the two become as one...become as two...as one*...? We will pick this up later on. For now, as an analysis of this frame of life, let's do an exercise. It does us well to exercise our minds now and then. I will be quoting from the book *Cosmic Balance: The Secret of Polarity*, 1995, by Omraam Mikhaël Aïvanhov (1900-1986). I came across his writings many years ago and it took me awhile to integrate just what he is saying. The quotes I will list give to us a real mind exercise as to the balance (between the one and the two.) Since you, the reader, might not be familiar with Omraam Mikhaël Aïvanhov, I am including some information about him that I got off the Prosveta Publications website, and also from Wikipedia.

"The Master Omraam Mikhaël Aïvanhov (1900-1986) was born in Bulgaria and received French citizenship just before his death. At the age of 17 he became Peter Deunov's disciple and stayed with him until 1937. It was at this time that Peter Deunov, founder of the White Brotherhood, asked him to leave Bulgaria for France in order to spread the teaching.

"From 1938 until 1986 he gave some 4,500 talks in French, first of all in France (in Paris and its outskirts, and later at Fréjus in the Var region), and then in Switzerland, Canada, the United States, India, Sweden and Norway. He also visited many other countries.

"His talks were first recorded in shorthand, then in 1960 on audio tape, and then on videotape. Finally, in 1972 Prosveta Publications released several collections of these talks in the form of books and brochures (translated into 30 languages), CDs and DVDs with subtitles."

Aïvanhov's philosophy teaches that everybody, regardless of race, religion, social position, intellectual ability or material means, is able to take part in the realization of a new period of brotherhood and peace on earth. This happens through the individual's personal transformation: growth in perfection and in harmony with the divine world. Whatever the topic, he invariably focuses on how one can better conduct life on earth. Aïvanhov taught that to achieve a better life, one must have a high ideal: "...if you have a High Ideal, such as the bringing of the Kingdom of God on earth, you obtain everything you wished for, you taste plenitude."

Aïvanhov teaches the ancient principles of initiatic science. He describes the cosmic laws governing both the universe and the human being, the macrocosm and microcosm, and the exchanges that constantly take place between them.

This knowledge has taken different forms throughout the centuries. It is the "perennial wisdom" expressed through various religions, each adapted to the spirit of a particular time, people, and level of spiritual evolution. Aïvanhov's teaching incorporates aspects of Esoteric Christianity that relate to finding the "Kingdom of God on earth" within the individual. One of the essential truths of initiatic science, according to Aïvanhov, is that (in the higher world) all things are linked. Thus committing oneself to the Kingdom of God on earth makes it realizable: "The real science is to form within ourselves, in the depths of our being, this Body that Initiates call the Body of Glory, the Body of Light, the Body of Christ.

Omraam Mikhaël Aïvanhow (1900-1986)—*Cosmic Balance: The Secret of Polarity*, 1995

Creation, therefore, is the work of the Two. But what is the Two? It is the One polarized as positive and negative, masculine and feminine, active and passive. Manifestation necessarily implies partition, division. In order to manifest and reveal itself, the One has to divide itself. Unity is the privilege of God alone, his own exclusive domain. But in order to create, God, who never ceases to be One, had to become Two. The one cannot create, for in unity there is no reciprocity. In becoming polarized, therefore, God projected himself outside himself and from these two poles the universe was born. Positive and negative poles are mutually attractive and it is this mechanism of reciprocal action and reaction that originates and sustains the movement of life. If his movement were to cease, the result would be stagnation and death, a return to the original absence of differentiation...

The masculine principle is defined as active and the feminine principle as passive, but the role of passivity is just as important as that of activity. The masculine principle provides the content, but the feminine principle provides the container, the form, and the power of attraction of form is very strong. If the feminine principle is said to be passive, it is because this distinguishes it from the active masculine principle. In reality, however, the feminine principle is not inactive; although it appears to be passive, it is extremely effective. Instead of thrusting itself forward in the manner of the masculine principle, the feminine principle draws things to itself. This is its mode of activity, and anything that is incapable of resisting this attraction is absorbed. The masculine mode of activity is more visible but it is not more powerful. To be active is, as it were, to move from the centre towards the periphery; to be passive is to attract the peripheral elements toward the centre. And even if this attraction is not very visible, it is very real and very effective.

What is the rightful place of each element, the masculine and the feminine? One day men and women are going to have to settle this problem, which is a constant source of conflict. For hundreds and thousands of years, the domination of men has laid a burden on women, and now we are beginning to see a reversal of the situation. Women have become bolder: they are no longer willing to be subject to men, but want the same rights as men. They are even ready to take the place of men and assume their role. This is only normal; it is the law of compensation. Men have gone too far. Instead of being models of integrity, kindness, and justice, thereby earning the esteem and admiration of women, they have abused their authority and their greater physical strength. They have taken all rights and privileges for themselves and given women nothing but duties. How could they expect the situation to last forever?...

The equilibrium of life is based on polarization, this is, on the existence of two poles between which, because they are different in nature, there can be reciprocity. If the two poles were uniform, there could be no exchange, none of that magnificent mutuality that is the source of so much joy and inspiration. When men and women lose all sense of the life that exists in this reciprocity between the two poles, they turn to the pharmacist or a psychiatrist for a remedy, but there is no remedy for those who do not understand. The only remedy lies in understanding. When polarity disappears, it is the death of a generation. There can be no spark, no life, if the two poles, the two electrodes, are not clearly distinct.

In every area of creation equilibrium exists because the two complementary forces exist. The solution does not consist in levelling out the differences between men and women—for women to go to war and men to rock the cradle. It is absolutely normal for women to want to enjoy the same freedoms as men, it is normal that they should want to show their capacity for initiative, but they can do so without imitating men, taking their place, or trying to do without them. Freedom, audacity, and a spirit of initiative are qualities that women need to cultivate. True, but at the same time they must deepen and strengthen the quintessential qualities of the feminine principle...

Do you remember what I said about the number Two? According to initiatic science the number Two is not 1+1, it is the polarized One, the One that is both masculine and feminine. We must always bear in mind, therefore, that the One contains the potential Two, and that Two is the polarization of One. When an initiate puts the two keys into the lock (we can see nature as an immerse lock), the door opens—in other words, the veil which hangs between the two pillars of the Temple is drawn aside...

I have already explained to you that the entity of being we call "God" is both masculine and feminine. When we speak of the cosmic spirit and the universal soul, we are speaking about God as a single, unique being who is polarized. Although we can neither describe nor even conceive of such a being, we can draw closer to it. Through meditation and prayer, our spirit enters into communion with the universal soul, and our soul with the cosmic spirit. It is in this way that a perfect fusion can take place.

Very good and yet can you see the problem? *But in order to create, God, who never ceases to be One, had to become Two. The one cannot create, for in unity there is no reciprocity. In becoming polarized, therefore, God projected himself outside himself and from these two poles the universe was born.* "Projected himself outside himself?" Do we really want to consider that? We so want to keep the idea of "God" in the equation (undoubtedly for our own benefit) that we come up with these mystical ideas that cannot ever become sensible to us. I am okay with the term "polarizied One" that he refers to. I use the term "sexual potential." But we don't want to cross over to the idea of some separate domain of "the (sexless) one" outside of, prior to, and different from the two-way sexual process of life itself. So wouldn't it be so much simpler if we just stuck to the two (equal and opposite) forces of male and female, *understanding that they together comprise the two forces that are needed to both divide the one and unite the two.* Think of the sexual two as polar opposites comprising a sexual circuit together. The whole of the universe is a living sexual circuit. It is alive. My point is that there isn't any intermediary between the two forces. *There are only the two forces.* It is the two forces that, in uniting and dividing together, comprise the balance that is the love. We need not attempt to go any further.

Spiritual Procreation

Oftentimes, when I speak of Man and Woman Balance or procreation those listening will equate it to the physical realm. They don't know that I am equating it to the metaphysical/spiritual realm. But when we understand that procreation is not just physical but metaphysical in nature, well, that changes things.

This is what I was referring to when I stated on the *Foundation of Man and Woman Balance* website:

> On a personal note, when Mr. Anderson was asked to describe the writings and what he felt their message was he responded, "Spiritual procreation. Mankind has yet to distinguish the two sexes on the spiritual level. In this failure lies the root of our problems and why we cannot yet touch the eternal together. The message of Man and Woman Balance brings each of us together in love with our eternal other half right now."

As long as we equate procreation to only the physical realm we miss its true beauty and purpose. We fail to understand that the procreant and the eternal are one and the same, a two-force sexual life (birth-life-death-rebirth...) process. This next selection is from *The 2008-2009 Articles: Our Love is Eternal Love,* 2010.

> Spiritual procreation is the idea/understanding that will lead us to the eternal connection. This universe of ours is one of perfect sexual balance, sexual being equated as equal and opposite. The two forces of (pro)creation perfectly unite and divide over and over. The eternal is no more than the procreant process/lineage. It never began and will never end. It always is what it is and can only be what it is. We may try and circumvent its nature, but that will only be at our own peril.

What happens is that we endeavor to place a non-creative, non-sexual "being" in that metaphysical/spiritual position. For example, the Biblical verse Genesis 1:27 states: *So God created man in his own image, in the image of God created he him, male and female created he them.* Here, it appears we have God in the 1st tier position and man and woman (physical procreation) in the 2nd tear position. And "God" apparently is outside of, prior to, and different from "His" creation! But this is just not the case. Let me ask, using this example, why did "God" create male and female? Why not something else? Can you conceive anything else that "God" could create? Of course not. "God" created male and female because that (male and female procreative process) was/is "God's" <u>nature</u>. God, if you will, is a two-force male and female (sexual) process. God (order/process may be the better term) can only create in male and female pairs because that is what "God" is—a God-process. In this example, God is the unity point which is actual sexual oneness. (What Walter Russell called "His sexless unity" and Thomas Troward called "Spirit's Original Unity.") But guess what, unity, or unification, is only one-half of the whole procreant life process, the female half to be more precise. Remember the words: *In the heart and soul of the unity is the desire to divide into the opposite pairs; in the heart and soul of the opposite pairs is the desire to unite again as one.* Physicality is as real as spirituality; spiritually is as real as physically. Here-to-fore, we have been encased in a religious metaphysical conception that views God as the primary (unity point), somehow existing outside of, prior to, and different from us. What I am suggesting to you is that there are two primary points, a unity point and an individuality point. There is the universal (female) and there is the individual (male). Let's see how this would look in the drawings below.

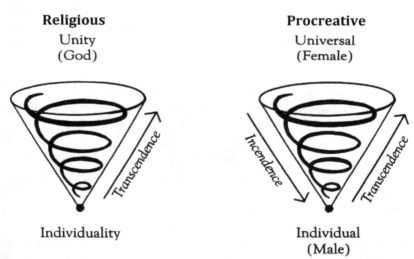

Religious
Unity
(God)

Individuality

Procreative
Universal
(Female)

Individual
(Male)

Which drawing has the larger *life-bearing* circumference? For you Christians, this means that there isn't any Virgin Birth. There also isn't any second coming. *Life exists now.* The Resurrection (which takes a two) can only exist in the now! There isn't any 2nd tier to anything. Everything is on the 1st tear. Every creation is equal to "God." Remember Walter Russell's quote: *...A perfect and omnipotent God could not create imperfection. He could not create a* *lesser than Himself. He could not create a greater than Himself. God could not create other than Himself. God did not create other than Himself, nor greater, nor lesser than Himself.* What this means for us is that grace runs both ways—equally from God to us and from us to God. Since "God" is a procreant process this actually means grace runs from man to woman and from woman to man. But we do not want to take this step. We are afraid. Or perhaps we don't even know there is another step to take.

So what might be the difference between spiritual procreation and what is called mysticism? Mysticism simply may be defined as *union with God*. What is it that I am suggesting? This next quote is from *Selected Writings—Volume 2: The Two Forces of Creation*, 1991, 2010. *The Two Forces of Creation* was actually written in 1988 and later became a part of *Selected Writings—Volume 2*.

The initiation or unity into Christ as a form is, in my view, one of the most authentic aspects of Christianity. It is a confirmation of the limits of the singular self whereby one reaches out to the "God" beyond. St. John of the Cross (1542-1592), a 16th century monk, gives an account of this mystical attitude in the following quote:

In the deepest spiritual darkness, in the most profound night of unknowing, in the purity of naked faith, God unites the soul to Himself in mystical union.

The mystical path calls for one's total surrender, the initiation into Christ. It may be said that one, of himself alone, no matter what powers or resources he may possess, amounts to nothing in the face of God. Only through one's surrender at the point of complete faith in Christ is one's love then revealed through God. At this point we see a marked difference between East and West. In Eastern thought (I Am), man is as God, the true self within, metaphysically equal. In Western thought, man is created by God but is not as God, thus the need for salvation through Jesus Christ.

The problem with the mystical undertaking lies in our current conception of God. No matter how favorable the act of initiation may sound, it is circumscribed by a conception that does not hold a balance between the two forces of creation. So again, the fault is not with the act of initiation per se but with that which one is initiated into, in this case a masculine conception of God. Given the two forces of creation the story differs. With the two forces, initiation only occurs between them. They each are initiated unto the other which means they each surrender to the essence of the other. Male surrenders to female reproduction and female surrenders to male security. This initiation takes place in marriage. Through marriage a couple may hold their creative balance together through which their love is continually revealed to each other.

Some of you may find my incorporation of the two forces into the Christian doctrine farfetched. This is quite understandable given our spiritual conception of and cultural immersion into Christianity in the West. Actually, I do not seek to discredit Christianity, just further develop it so it can cleanse itself from its imbalance and bias. Christianity will never be able to fully reveal itself in love given its structural imbalance between male and female. It will continue to have its brutal side, its dogmatic, elitist, and master/slave consequence just as its current metaphysic entails. This is because of its one force orientation which elevates one part of the relationship above the other. The only solution to this is to truly center Christianity in the two forces of creation where both male and female each comprises one of the two aspects of God.

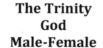

The Trinity
God
Male-Female

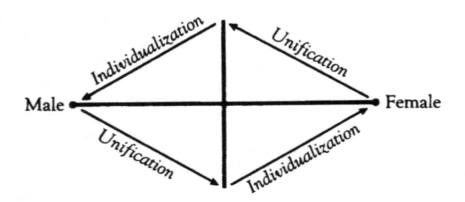

The mystical experience in its essence is representative of the unity of male and female. Both male and female are called to step beyond themselves through the unknown space between themselves, finally uniting with each other. It is their existent surrender acknowledging the necessity of that sexual other in their own lives. It is upon this surrender, one force to the other, that their creation together can continue. We may now say:

In the deepest spiritual darkness, in the most profound night of unknowing, in the purity of naked faith, male and female unite their souls together in perfect union from which the pure birth of their creation inspires.

That was what I wrote in 1988. At that time, I was deeply into spiritual mysticism and St. John of the Cross. Also I might mention *True Christian Religion, Volumes 1 & 2,* by Emanuel Swedenborg (1688-1772) which is quite a mouth full in itself. Some credit Emanuel Swedenborg as being the father of the Creative Thought movement. But we could go back to Meister Eckhart (1260-1327) (or Plato or Plotinus or Jesus for that matter.) Meister Eckhart is known for saying in effect, "Every son is the only begotten son." I think his wording was: *"God never begot but one Son, but the eternal is forever begetting the only begotten.* This fits in nicely with mysticism/oneness but where is the birth of life—where is the daughter in Eckhart's quote? Or where is "God" as procreative process of Father <u>and</u> Mother? As I stated: *Mankind has yet to distinguish the two sexes on the spiritual level.* During these earlier years of my writing, I did a study to see if I could find the word <u>procreation</u> (as metaphysical primary) in any of the great books or religions. *The Great Ideas: A Lexicon of Western Thought* by Mortimer J. Adler, 1992, lists 102 of the most important ideas of mankind. Nowhere is the word sex or procreation to be found. The book *Mysticism: The Preeminent Study in the Nature and Development of Spiritual Consciousness* by Evelyn Underhill, 1990, is a profound study of mysticism. Again, no mention of sex or procreation. There is the wonderful book by Richard Maurice Bucke titled *Cosmic Consciousness: A Study in the Evolution of the Human Mind,* 1901. Again, no mention of sex/procreation. There is the great writing *The Science of Mind* by Ernest Holmes, 1926 & 1938, that is a wonderful articulation of the Creative Thought movement. With Thomas Troward it is "Spirit's Original Unity" as the primary; with Holmes it is "Infinite Spirit" (the action of Spirit within Itself). The Bible itself has the verses Genesis 1:27 and Matthew 19:46 as mentioned earlier, but procreation is, and must be,

CHRISTOPHER ALAN ANDERSON

2nd tier. And there is *A Course in Miracles,* 1976, presented by Helen Schucman and William Thetford, which claims to be a channeling of Jesus himself, which I consider to be one of the great writings of all time, and again, no mention of sex or procreation. There are snippets of procreation here in there in other great/religious books but never as the metaphysical primary. In fact, the only place I ever found any metaphysical indication of procreation (besides the Russell's) was in Walt Whitman's *Leaves of Grass,* where he states: *...Urge and urge and urge, Always the procreant urge of the world. Out of the dimness opposite equals advance...* Now that is profound. Anyway, some twenty years later, writing in *The 2008–2009 Articles—Love: The Law of Polar Opposites,* 2010, I stated it quite simply:

>   *Only (sexual) opposites can unite to then again divide...creating the spiritual lineage of (procreant) love.*

So changing the placement of "Spirit's Original Unity" and Polarity, using Thomas Troward's words, is immense. This is what happens when we: *...distinguish the two sexes on the spiritual level.* You see:

We Can Only Create Together

♦ *Man and woman can only create together.*
♦ *From the love of a man and a woman new life, a son or a daughter, is born.*
♦ *All new born life is divine life.*
♦ *Each creation is a divine creation.*
♦ *Each creation is the most special creation.*
♦ *Each creation is bequeathed with the divine love of Father and Mother.*
♦ *Every creation has within its heart the desire to create life with and through its other half.*
♦ *Every creation is eternal in its procreative balance with its eternal other half.*
♦ *The heartbeat within every creation is the heartbeat of procreative love.*
♦ *Procreative love is the life-dynamic of the universe.*
♦ *Procreative love is God.*
♦ *God is Man and Woman Balance.*
♦ *God is expressed when a man and a woman reach out to each other and touch in the one pure, perfect moment of their most*

special love.

♦ *Only together can a man and a woman create.*

When a man enters a woman, he does so to release his very soul into her. This release of life (his death if you will) begins the woman's receiving of life. She receives the man's life-seed into her, unites with it, and gives (re)birth to life. Think about this. Could the life process itself ever be separated from the procreant process, i.e., *procreant light*? This is to ask, can the life process ever be secondary to some "one still light" or "His sexless unity" or "Spirit's Original Unity" or some "Divine Being reflecting upon itself"? Is a new-born baby somehow of 2nd tier importance? Jesus was a new born baby—he was not 2nd tier. And so each one of us is brought into life as a new born baby. We, too, are 1st tier.

This next quote is from *The Universal Religion: The Final Destiny of Mankind*, 1994, 2010.

> *A child is born represents the touch of love (balance) between a man and a woman. That one touch is the whole foundation of the universe. It is a direct touch, a complete touch. It is the touch of life. All that is required for this touch is a man and a woman, conscious of their creativity (connection) together. In their consciousness of life, they touch and—a child is born. This touch is the truth of life. There isn't any greater truth than life. In the universal religion, only the two forces exist expressing their love and their life. There isn't anything else but a male and a female in creative balance. Nothing else is recognized for nothing else exists. This perfect state of creative balance is known as God. Why? Because from this balance a child can be born.*

A Child is Born

Can you feel the spiritual/procreative connection in that last quote? What might this connection be? This next quote is from my writing *Man, Woman, and God: The Eternal Marriage*, 1994, 2010.

> *The spiritual connection is a connection between a man and a woman whereby they recognize their eternal creation and love together. It is based in their sexual differentiation from and creative need for each other. In this, a man and woman have life purpose together. They are the co-creators of all that is. The formed universe moves through them. They together hold the balance on which all life depends. The world moves one step forward into the light with just one touch of their love.*

What is the feeling of this spiritual/procreative connection? Here is another poem from *To Cassandra—Early Years,* titled *Transformation,* 1985, 1994.

Transformation

Easing
Slightly
Almost without effort
And suddenly
I find myself

Drawn into you
Drawn into your being
Becoming a part
Of your very soul
From your beginning
On through to your ending
To a new beginning
Never to return out from you
As the same man.

Do you see the procreation occurring? Here is another quote, this one from *Meditations for Deepening Love*, 1994, 2010. This passage is from the section *Romance—How to Find It and Keep It.*

Now, the question for men is, do you see into the soul of woman? Do you see her unity? Eternal love cannot be yours until you do. When you do, eternal love cannot be denied you. And women, do you see the soul of man, his individuality? Do you see that man holding the division of male and female with all his might just for you? That is where your eternal love lies. To enter the sanctuary of love we must know that very soul of our sexual other. And I will tell you that the distinct essences of male and female will never change. Male and female are from the beginning and will always be. Together they form what we call family. From their love come children. And life goes on. Love is, in its essence, procreative. Everything a male and female do together is creative. Everything they do together is created out of their love. Male and female are in eternal love together right now! Their love is happening right now. Each of us is actually in eternal love with our sexual other half right now. When you know it so will you see it.

We so wonder why we cannot find everlasting relationships/love. Could it be that we, men and woman, are not connecting together spiritually—which means procreatively? *To enter the sanctuary of love we must know that very soul of our sexual other.* It is not enough to know the very body (physicality) of the other. A man must know the sexual soul of a woman; a woman must know the sexual soul of a man. How do you express this? You see my expressions above. Have I captured it? How can a man touch the sexual soul of a woman? How can a woman touch the sexual soul of a man? This is the crux of eternal life. Okay, let us try another quote. This one is from *Meditations for Deepening Love—The*

Man and Woman Spiritual Center, 1994, 2010. In this quote, you can change the term *The Man and Woman Spiritual Center* to *spiritual procreation* or *Man and Woman Balance* or *God-process* if you like. They mean the same thing.

> *The Man and Woman Spiritual Center is only expressed in an actual touch between a man and a woman. It cannot be expressed in any other way. That touch may range from a momentary conscious recognition to a full embrace, but a touch, one to another, it is. The Spiritual Center is not expressed through belief, pledge, worship, ritual, or the paying of alms. It is not something that can be institutionalized, dogmatized, or ratified. There isn't any prescribed path to take, master to follow, or status to attain for its expression. There is only a man and a woman, touching and expressing creation together.*

Feel it. Our task is to feel the spiritual/procreative nexus together. In *Selected Writings—Volume 2—The Two Forces of Creation*, 1991, 2010, it states:

Man: *Feel what it is to be a man, the man you are and will always be.*
Woman: *Feel what it is to be a woman, the woman you are and will always be.*
Man: *Feel what it is like to be a woman, the woman you are not nor will ever be.*
Woman: *Feel what it is like to be a man, the man you are not nor will ever be.*

In other words, ladies and gentlemen, we need each other. *A man needs a woman as much as he needs himself and a woman needs a man as much as she needs herself. ...There is only a man and a woman, touching and expressing creation together.* And that is all there is. There isn't a separate (and superior) God-head outside of, prior to, or different from a man and a woman. There is *...only a man and a woman, touching and expressing creation together.* This whole order/process can be called the God-head or God-process or Source-light or center-point or divine origin, the Tao, the one universal substance, etc. But *it*, my friends, is a two-way sexual, living, eternal process. And *it* is eternal simply because there are two (equal and opposite) forces, uniting and dividing, in procreant love together.

Now, let us do an exercise. The purpose here is to see if you can capture that essence/feeling of spiritual procreation. It is different than Christianity, for example. It is different from all religions for that matter. Why is this important? Because it is from this essence/feeling of spiritual procreation that we can manifest our (eternal) lives and desires. Creative manifestation, which I will speak more to later, can only come out of the perfect balance of spiritual procreation, i.e., Man and Woman Balance. This booklet you will be reading is *Let Us Create Life Together* which is another from the writing *Meditations for Deepening Love*, 1994, 2010.

Let Us Create Life Together

There was born a girl who, at a young age, felt her heart stir. She said to herself, "I cannot deny the truth I feel within my heart." Of course, at this young age, she hardly knew the magnitude of what she said for few, if any, ever spoke of the truth. But she proceeded to spend many quiet years in her own searching. "I will come to know the truth," she said to herself. Such a determined young girl she was. But as the years went by, she began to become despondent, for everywhere she turned she could not find the truth that satisfied her soul.

One day, as this girl was in her quiet time, she felt her heart stir, and she heard the words: *Go to the town of your birth. There you will find the truth.* In those quiet words, she felt a deep peace come over her.

It took this girl many years to prepare herself for her journey. She needed resources and a job skill for when she arrived. Her family and friends really didn't understand her yearning, so she had to keep it to herself. It was not an easy good-by, but now, as a young woman, she departed for her destiny. Upon her arrival, she began to settle herself. The transition, finding accommodations, suitable work, and otherwise acquainting herself took many months. She really had no memory of this town, for her parents had moved away shortly after her birth. But in its spirit she thought she could feel a depth within herself that she had not before experienced.

Each week she worked five days. On Saturdays, she tidied up and did her shopping. Sunday was her free day, and she would take walks through the town. After a time, she found a quaint park at the end of town, and was so delighted by it she began to spend every Sunday there. While at the park one day, while sitting by the pond in her own solitude, she felt here heart stir. The words that came forth said: *It is here that you will meet me.* The woman felt jolted by these words. It had not occurred to her that someone specific was speaking to her. "Who could this be?"

she thought.

Every Sunday, she went to the park hoping to again feel her heart stir. But for two long years she heard nothing. She began to wonder, "Is this all foolishness? Why do I come here? Why do I hope so? My heart is weary." For the next month the woman did not walk to the park. Then one Sunday she returned. It was a beautiful day and for some reason she was joyously happy. And for the third time her heart stirred. This time the words she heard said: *It is I.* She immediately looked up and began to survey the others around the pond. "Could one of them be the person I am to meet?" she thought to herself. There were some couples with children, and others strolling on by. But no one distinct, she thought. Then she noticed a man sitting alone. There wasn't anything engaging about him. She probably would not have noticed him if she had not been surveying all the people. Suddenly, her heart stirred again. *It is I.* Emotion flooded over the woman's body. "Is this man to take me to the truth?" she asked herself. He was still just sitting there. He had not given any notice to her to confirm. "What shall I do?" she thought.

Undoubtedly, most people would have walked away. But this was a determined woman who wanted to know the truth and she had already gone this far. So she began to walk towards him, drawn almost by his own non-recognition of her. "Who is this man?" she thought. When she was a few steps away from him, he looked up at her and their eyes met one another. And for a moment this woman and this man just looked at each other, saying nothing.

After another moment had passed, the woman began to speak. "I seek the truth. I have been led to you, I believe. May you know the truth?" She noticed that her question did not surprise him. He continued to look at her and then replied, "I know the truth for only one who seeks. I seek only one for the truth."

The woman thought about this for a moment. Again she spoke to the man. "You know the truth and yet you also seek it. I don't understand. What is this truth?" The man looked away as he said, "I am a *man.* I only know the truth with *woman.* Man and woman *together* are the truth. I seek the woman who seeks me, that we may *create life together.*"

The woman looked deeply into this man. So strange he would seem to most. Yet I understand him, she thought. So simple are his words. She said to him, "The truth then is a man and a woman creating life together?"

The man nodded to confirm. "That is the whole truth?" Again the man nodded. "But that is so simple. A man and a woman creating life together. What could be more natural? I think that is fantastic. Yet you don't look very happy. You look lonely and hurt. Why is that?" The man turned to her, his gaze penetrating. "You are the first woman to whom I have told this. May you be the last."

The woman understood. She could feel the longing of this man, this man who knew the truth yet was without woman. The truth had just grown very personal to her. She said to him, "Why haven't you told anyone else?" He replied, "The truth can only be known by one man and one woman together. There is no one else to tell. Try it. Go out upon the world and speak this truth. I did that once upon a time, and the world did not believe."

The woman flinched. She did not like the thought of the truth not being believed. She said unto the man, "Why would anyone not believe the truth?" The man quickly replied, "Because it was spoken."

But the woman felt incomplete with his response and wanted to pursue this subject. "If I go out and speak this truth would the world also deny me?" she asked. "Yes," the man replied. "For, as I have so learned, the truth is not to be spoken. It can only be lived, man to woman, woman to man."

The woman was beginning to see the magnitude of the man's responses. The truth cannot be spoken—she had no idea. "But," the woman spoke, "how do you hold all of this within yourself over time? It must break your heart." The woman looked at the man and suddenly begins to flush. She saw that this man did carry a broken heart—so within himself he seemed to be. "What can I do to help?" she uttered. "We don't want the truth to die." The man responded saying, "The truth lives only as it is *reproduced.* The truth lives only through man and woman. If I have been sent with this message then I must not have been sent alone." The man paused and then trembled as he said, *"May you be the one who has been sent with me. May you be the one to extend beyond me."*

The woman looked to the ground as she captured her thoughts. She knew now that the truth was her choice, her surrender, to this man who knew of his incompleteness without her. She could feel that her life was on the line, her life's search had all come to this moment and her response to this man with the broken heart. Was not his hurt also her own that she had felt for so long? Could she receive his pain as her fulfillment and carry this simple man onward? That was her question, her truth. And once more the woman's heart stirred and she spoke the words even before she heard them. *Let us create life together.*

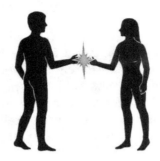

Let me list just a few passages from this booklet.

Suddenly, her heart stirred again. *It is I.* Emotion flooded over the woman's body. "Is this man to take me to the truth?" she asked herself. He was still just sitting there. He had not given any notice to her to confirm. "What shall I do?" she thought.

"I am a *man.* I only know the truth with *woman.* Man and woman *together* are the truth. I seek the woman who seeks me, that we may *create life together.*"

"What can I do to help?" she uttered. "We don't want the truth to die." The man responded saying, "The truth lives only as it is *reproduced.* The truth lives only through man and woman. If I have been sent with this message then I must not have been sent alone." The man paused and then trembled as he said, *"May you be the one who has been sent with me. May you be the one to extend beyond me."*

That was her question, her truth. And once more the woman's heart stirred and she spoke the words even before she heard them. *Let us create life together.*

Can you capture the essence/feeling of spiritual procreation here? Hear the words: *create life together;* or *The truth lives only as it is reproduced;* or *May you be the one who has been sent with me.* Another word for spiritual procreation is *love.* The whole idea that the highest form of (spiritual) love is from "God" to man is actually unfounded. Love can only be the connective (uniting and dividing) love from male to female and from female to male. Or let us way it this way: that which we call the God principle, the one operating principle, is but the *Life principle*. The operating/Life principle is not static nor does it originate from a static (singular) position. Rather it is both static and dynamic (a two forces, equal and opposite). The two-force equal and opposite sexual interaction from the two givens of male and female is the operating/Life principle. That must be our LIVING foundation for it is life itself. And so the spiritual and the procreative are one process and we call this process *love*. So let's close to this chapter by taking a moment to *actually connect* with our own eternal other/sexual opposite half. It is your life after all. *Feel the connection you have with your eternal other half right now.* This is taken from *Selected Writings—Volume 2, Mind and Spirit*, 1991, 2010.

> *Let us end this section by taking a moment to actually commune with that sexual opposite or other half of ourselves. Let's go within ourselves to the deep recesses of our hearts and feel the essence of that other. Let's for at least one moment close the fissure of unconsciousness between our souls and release the heartbreak and pain held within our beings. Let us heal ourselves in the balance of man and woman.*
>
> *Man, commune with woman. Feel that woman in your life. Whether you be single or married, young or old, feel your connection with woman, your woman. Send her your love as male, wherever she may be in this universe. Tell her you are the one who will care for her, that you are ready to lay down your life for her as no one else. Let her know that you will do whatever it takes to secure her soul and implant new life into her being.*
>
> *And woman, you, too, talk to man. Let your man know of your love, that you are there for him ready to take him into your being. Let him know that you, female, are the only one for him. Guide him to you. Commune to him your presence so he may find you. Whisper to him through his dreams so he can come only to you in his life quest, driving his male force into you so you may continue to bring forth life anew, a sexual life, male or female, in body, mind, and spirit.*

CHRISTOPHER ALAN ANDERSON

Love

Let's begin this section with a quote from *Channeling the Eternal Woman*, 2014.

Thank you. I am the Eternal Woman. I am not a "God." I am a woman. I am the female soul within every woman. As a woman, I stand with man. Actually, I stand between man and child. I am the link between man and child. I am the space between man and child. I am the death of all life and the life of all death. From a man dying inside of me, so our child is born out of me. I am what you might call the field, frame, zero-point, space, opening, womb, or void. But I am not death. Rather, I give life to death. I bring life-potential to all things. I connect all things within me. In this, I am love. Without me there would never be love. All women know this about me because they know it about themselves.

I, the Eternal Woman, stand as the counter-balance to the Individual Man. The Individual Man is that center-point of all men. A man's life purpose is to secure a woman. A woman's life purpose is to reproduce a man. Can that ever change? As such, a man can only find his rebirth, i.e., eternal life in me. Individual men have yet to understand this. And so they go about their "lives" creating "Gods" to believe in—which are nothing more than idols that they serve—that they may somehow reach eternal life. And then they enslave the women who are their eternal life connection. What folly. Any man who walks ahead of a woman in his life and heart cannot know life or love. We are co-creators together. We can only walk hand-in-hand.

That which you call belief systems, or might you call them philosophies or religions or enlightenments, or what you may call your sciences or any embodiments of thought, if they exclude man and woman as co-creators they cannot be correct and true. I don't say this as somehow being superior to you. I say this in the frame of Individual Man and Eternal Woman together. Women have wept for thousands, no millions, of years for just a connection of equality between the Individual Man and the Eternal Woman. We are still weeping. Come to me my man and let me touch your heart and breathe new life into your soul. I call you from the space that you thought was somehow empty and have for so long been afraid to enter. But how can you fear me? I am the Eternal Woman. I can only give life to you as my love for you.

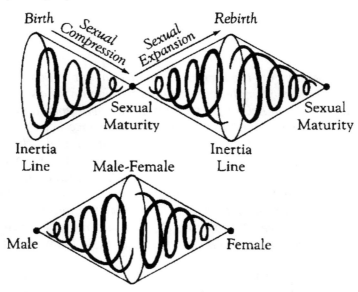

I can only give life to you as my love for you. So says the eternal woman. It is from this depth that a man is to enter into the spirit of woman and give his love to her. And in this depth the woman knows the man's love is true and she can reproduce this love in the next birth of life. But let us understand, this two coming together as one is a direct connection. Their touch alone is true. There isn't anything in between them, i.e., some intermediary. *There is only a man and a woman, touching and expressing creation together.* The basis of religion is that there is some intermediary between the man and the woman that they are to worship. I am suggesting that the man and the woman have *primary love* together. Their love (male division and female unification) is direct/primary love.

They complement each other. Each one's love (male to female and female to male) completes the other. A man can never truly love a woman and thereby complete her if he places some intermediary before her. Likewise, a woman can never truly love a man and thereby complete him if she places an intermediary before him. Within their balance together is enough love to handle each moment in life. In fact, their love together is the only love that can handle each moment in life. Without their love there wouldn't be any life.

"What about Jesus?" some may ask. Let me just say, Jesus needs love too. Jesus is not all giving. He needs our love as much as we need his love. Do you understand? Worship is really one-way love. Jesus gives/loves to us through his grace and we worship him. But this is not a primary love. Primary love goes both ways. Your love for Jesus is just as important as Jesus' love for you. Your love saves Jesus just as much as his love saves you. My point to all this is that fundamental primary love originates out of the man and woman relationship. A man's love for a woman is <u>real</u> love. It is not some secondary love. His <u>securitive</u> love saves her. Likewise, a woman's love for a man is <u>real</u> love. Her <u>reproductive</u> love saves him. That is primary love. Here isn't some (transcendental) love that exists outside of, prior to, or different from the primary love a man has for a woman and a woman has for a man. Their love for each other is as spiritual as it gets. It is live-affirming love.

Besides primary love the male and female pair comprises a *spiritual perfection* together. Their balance is a perfect balance. One does not stand above (superior to) the other. They are metaphysically equal in importance yet they are opposite in purpose/function. Their teeter-totter does not fall into the imbalances of Masculinism (opposite but not equal) or Feminism (equal but not opposite). Religion promises to us a salvation from our sin (imbalance). I am saying that there is a placement deeper than that from which we, man and woman, stand in perfect balance together which is our spiritual perfection. There never was an original sin, if you will. There is only our understanding of the perfect two-force (sexual) balance which is also primary love.

Within the balance (which is also a name for love) there lies a universal purpose for both the man and the woman. A man's purpose is to secure a woman; a woman's purpose is to reproduce the man. This is another way to say, divide the one and unite the two. Our purpose is related to our sexual natures—as is our love. From an understanding of our *sexual opposite purposes* each man and woman may discover their own individual purpose, the expression of their own heart and soul. It is nice when a man and a woman find one another as complements of their purposes. Essentially, a woman follows/supports the man's primary purpose from her belief in him and his love for her. But a man must give to that woman as a part of his security the space for her to express herself. She comprises her own authenticity. She can't give her love back to a man, and thereby reproduce his very soul, if she is not free to make that choice. Universal purpose is a great idea—that each one of us has encoded within ourselves a divine purpose from the very beginning. This being the case, universal purpose constitutes a very essential part of our heart and souls—our very love that we can only give to each other.

Purity of heart is another wonderful aspect of a man's and woman's love for each other. Purity of heart knows not the taint of sin. "Sin," as it were, is just one holding that sexual other in one of the two forms of imbalance, Masculinism or Feminism. We could bring in the word beauty here, inner beauty. Purity of heart comes from one viewing that other as spiritually perfect. It is so easy to "judge another." So easy to see that that other just doesn't quite make the grade. So the real challenge here is not so much to see our own spiritual perfection and purity of heart but to see that in another. No man or woman is an island. We each need one another. In this metaphysical fact lies our choice to love that other or deny that other. If we choose denial we will experience hate—of ourselves. If we choose love so that is what we have to give. Let your heart be pure in love.

Love only exists in a giving-receiving interchange/cycle between a man and a woman. Giving is not more blessed than receiving as some state. Without one to receive, the other has no one to give to. And the one who does receive in turn gives back. And the one who gives can then receive. Giving and receiving are equal opposites and both are necessary for any enactment of life. This is metaphysical law. We cannot transcend this reality. There isn't an outside of, prior to, or different from state of being. There is only this moment now. There is only giving love and receiving love now. Call this grace if you must. Call this a sexual touch if you want. The so-called "what is" is a sexual giving and receiving (dividing and uniting) interchange between a man and a woman. Within this frame is all life and its bearing. Each and every moment is a sexual moment of male and female love. In my essence statement I stated: *Love is the only state of existence between Male and Female.* If you get this you get it all.

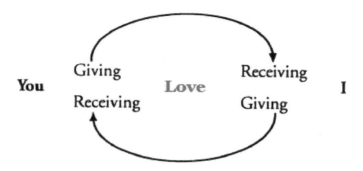

Now let's do another exercise and see if you understand the two sexual (equal and opposite) forces as being primary in origin. Remember in the Troward quote it is suggested that *Spirit's Original Unity* comes first and *Polarity* comes second. And also remember the analysis we did of the quotes from *Cosmic Balance: The Secret of Polarity* by Omraam Mikhaël Aïvanhow from an earlier chapter. We are always endeavoring to find the two-force balance (as we review other writers and their thinking) as that is our anchor point to correct thinking and rightful action in life. The following is a quote from Gabriele Wittek, who I believe was the founder of *The Homebringing Mission of Jesus Christ* (which later became *Universal Life—the Inner Religion*), a Christian mystical organization out of Germany during the 1970s and 1980s. This passage is from *Recognize and Heal Yourself By the Power of the Spirit*, 1984.

Gabriele Wittek—*Recognize and Heal Yourself By the Power of the Spirit*, 1984

The Ethereal Power is the Eternal Power of the Spirit. Its starting point are the two Primordial Powers of creation, the Two Particles. By means of these two Particles, "Plus" and "Minus" or "Positive" and "Negative," the whole of Creation originated. Ether is the substance of the Spirit, and the carrier of the whole of life. These two Primordial Powers are the Nucleus of life in all existing forms.

Both of these Particles are the most powerful Ethereal Powers. By their power of love the whole of Creation breathes. Without both of these Particles no life whatsoever would exist. They are fundamental to all of creation, fundamental to all spiritual and material worlds. They are the Nucleus, the outpouring Power, in all spiritual atoms, which are the building stones of all forms of life.

Both of these Particles produced the whole of Creation. The Ethereal Powers, which were not yet following in a controlled course, arose from them. They were set in order by both of these Primordial Powers. In this way, the spiritual atoms arose, i.e., the different streams of Ether or energy which are grouped precisely around the Nucleus, which sets everything in order and maintains everything.

In every fruit is the seed or kernel which is the carrier of life. Every kernel contains the particular species. I think of an apple or of any other fruit. The germ has absolute power for every species. The pulp does not produce new life, the seed does.

Therefore the divine Nucleus of life, i.e., the Primordial Power in every spiritual atom, must be invoked according to the Laws of the spiritual realm. Only in this way can the fundamental human powers be unfolded. The divine Elements react only if the Nucleus is invoked. The Law of God and its Powers can only be recognized and perceived if one practices love, because the Nucleus is Love, the highest Power in the universe.

In order to master the Elements so that they can serve every individual and the whole of mankind, love must be practiced, because love is the fundamental idea, the fundamental Power in Creation.

The individual who wants to subdue heaven and earth in a righteous way must give his love first of all to God, his Creator, and to the whole of Creation. Whoever wants to master the Elements, and the whole of life, must live the fundamental Law, which is Love. He must love the whole of mankind, all souls, beings, and forms of life, mineral, plant, and animal.

First of all he must love his divine Father, who is the Nucleus of all existing forms of life. Above all the human being must recognize that everything that exists is made by the Creator and that the Creator, our God and Lord, answers to His child only if he, the child of God, turns to God, the Nucleus of Life, and acknowledges Him.

The fundamental and eternal commandment or Law is Love. Without Love for the whole of Creation and, first of all, for God, the Creator, nothing will be possible, nor endure.

Somewhat difficult to abstract, I think, but perhaps not so to different from what I am saying. Gabriele Wittek does at times fall into the one-force mistake with words like *divine Father, the Creator, our God and*

Lord, and the *Nucleus of Life*. But then, notice how she defines *Nucleus of Life*, which she also refers to as *divine Father, the Creator*, and *our God and Lord*. Let's review the first three paragraphs again.

> The Ethereal Power is the Eternal Power of the Spirit. Its starting point are the two Primordial Powers of creation, the Two Particles. By means of these two Particles, "Plus" and "Minus" or "Positive" and "Negative," the whole of Creation originated. Ether is the substance of the Spirit, and the carrier of the whole of life. These two Primordial Powers are the Nucleus of life in all existing forms.
>
> Both of these Particles are the most powerful Ethereal Powers. By their power of love the whole of Creation breathes. Without both of these Particles no life whatsoever would exist. They are fundamental to all of creation, fundamental to all spiritual and material worlds. They are the Nucleus, the outpouring Power, in all spiritual atoms, which are the building stones of all forms of life.
>
> Both of these Particles produced the whole of Creation. The Ethereal Powers, which were not yet following in a controlled course, arose from them. They were set in order by both of these Primordial Powers. In this way, the spiritual atoms arose, i.e., the different streams of Ether or energy which are grouped precisely around the Nucleus, which sets everything in order and maintains everything.

These two Primordial Powers are the Nucleus of life in all existing forms. The *Nucleus of Life*, also referred to as *divine Father, the Creator*, and *our God and Lord*, are, according to Gabriele Wittek, made up of the two Primordial Powers. Do you get it? There isn't a single thing in back of the two Primordial Powers/Forces. They are it. We could change the names *"Plus"* and *"Minus"* or *"Positive"* and *"Negative"* to *Male* and *Female*, that would help. And now indeed we can say as Gabriele Wittek states: *"The fundamental and eternal commandment or Law is Love."* Being able to decipher others' writings as to their one-force primary or two-force primary is very important indeed and helps cement the two-force primary into our own understanding.

I would like to end this section with a booklet I wrote called *The Birthing Process*, 1987. This booklet later became part of a collection of booklets called *Meditations for Deepening Love*, 1994, 2010.

The Birthing Process
The Birthing Process is a special communication from man to woman and from woman to man that a couple may engage in together, designed so they may bring forth to their consciousness the birth-life-death-rebirth continuum of their existence, experiencing themselves as the two necessary aspects of sexual creation that they are.

Birth

Man: *I...am. I am here, a being, in physical form. This I notice as I look out from myself, a unique being...but even more than that, a sexual being. I am a male. I know this—only as I notice you. I notice you in contrast to me. You, too, are a unique being, but you are not a male being. You are a female. You and I are not the same. Of this I am certain. A consciousness of our sexual differentiation is born into me. Whenever I look at myself I also, at the very same instance, see you. And when I look at you, so do I see myself.*

Woman: *I see you, too. Yes, I am here, physical in being yet different from you in my form. I am a female. Female is my form given to me at my birth.*

Man: *We, male and female. Born into our sexuality at our birth were not then conscious of our sexuality. Who am "I"? We have come to notice that we are different, sexually different, but why? What is the purpose of our sexual difference, male as to female?*

Woman: *Yes, we are different. We have been born into our different sexualities at our birth, but we have yet to be born into a consciousness of what our sexual differentiation means to us. We have yet to be reborn.*

Life

Man: *I walk another day's journey. Toil—a necessity to live. I give to this day full. I stand tall on my ability and hold firm in my accomplishment. I carve out a piece of creation and in so doing form myself—in relationship to you. Now another night is approaching. May I come home to you, woman, once again?*

Woman: *Yes, man, you may. I have been waiting for you. I*

have been preparing myself to receive you. What is it you have for me this day?

Man: *My consciousness. Today I bring to you my consciousness of our sexual differentiation. I am a male; you are a female. I choose to know why. I form this question within my being. Will you receive my consciousness this day?*

Woman: *How could I say no? I see how much you need me. I need you to need me, to give to me. Here, come closer. I will help you. I need to receive all that you bring forth. I need to receive all of the male you are. Come closer to me.*

Man: *Closer, yes, I see...in my consciousness I hold you and I sexually distinct. I, male, form this distinction. I stand apart from you, female, on the sexual division of You and I. I secure this division in my day's toil and hold it in my consciousness that I may give my form to you as is my purpose. Now I may rest.*

Woman: *Yes, my man, that is good. Deeper, yes—deeper, all of you. Let all of yourself go—into me. Release, surrender your being. Let me take all of your consciousness into me, for that is my purpose. I am female, here to unite your sexual being with mine and rest your very soul. Yes, let yourself go...It is good.*

Death

Woman: *Rest my man. You have given much. Let me now hold you—inside me. Rest. I will talk to you for a time and soothe your soul. You are now united with me. Rest in that unity. Know the peace of your "non-being" in me. You need not worry about tomorrow. I will bring you back. That which I receive into me I also reproduce out of me as is my purpose. Yes, the day will come again when I see you—apart from me, forming, toiling, making your way home to me once again.*

...Before that day comes let me leave this thought with you: Man, from this day forth you will know the purpose of your being, male, and the purpose of my being, female, that we together bring forth life, you securing form and I reproducing form, upon which our creation continues. You will know that You and I are all that is through which birth-life-death-rebirth

manifests, conscious that You and I are never without each other from the non-beginning to the never-ending.

...Take this thought, my man, that I bear into your consciousness. Take it and go forth far and wide, expressing our sexual creation to anyone who may ask, "Who am I?" Know it to be your purpose to being forth the consciousness of sexual creation of You and I to every living being so that every being may know the purpose of their sexual being and their eternal interconnection with their sexual other half.

...And lastly, never forget to trust me. Your task will not be easy. Never before have I directed such a difficult undertaking as one coming to know his or her sexual self. Many will disbelieve. Some will even scoff and mock you. But do not despair, more and more will gather around you. I will not let you fail. I will always be guiding you—when your purpose is complete—back home to me. Again, I, female, will take you into me and rest your wary soul.

Rebirth

Woman: *A movement--I feel within me. The time is near. Are you speaking to me, my man, telling me you are ready for rebirth? Remember my words...Oh, help, yes, you are coming forth. I hear you. I will...push, push, breathe, push, look, look at you, a new being, transformed, a child of our sexual creation. Are you now conscious of your sexual essence in relation to mine?*

Man: *I...am. A unique sexual being. I am a male—in relationship to you a female? Here we are; you, woman, have rested me and through yourself produced in me the consciousness of You and I. You have brought forth a new life. Your purpose is now complete; take a moment's rest. You will hardly know that I am gone. I must depart and secure this new life. I will be back, of course. You know I will return to you when I have again formed in myself something to give to you.*

Woman: *I know you will, my man. What else can you do? And what else can I do but wait for you, so patiently, to receive you unto me once more?*

Man: *I may now declare to you, woman, that from this day forth I will be conscious of You and I in our own sexual creation together. Birth-life-death-rebirth...*

Woman: *And I as well for it is good.*

A Model for Freedom

What might be the relationship between love and freedom? This may surprise you but essentially they are the same thing. In the last section I stated: *Love only exists in a giving-receiving interchange/cycle between a man and a woman.* We could change the word love to freedom. *Freedom only exists in a giving-receiving interchange/cycle between a man and a woman.* In general terms we could say: *Freedom only exists in a giving-receiving interchange/cycle between Self and Other.* The key to the interchange is that both parts are equal in the relationship. One part is not superior leaving the other part inferior. This relational imbalance was what Marx fought to change, in this case the imbalance between the bourgeois owners/controllers and the proletariat laborers. As he states in *The Communist Manifesto*: *The immediate aim of the Communists is the same as that of all the other proletarian parties: formation of the proletariat into a class, overthrow the bourgeois supremacy, conquest of political power by the proletariat.* The problem with Marx had to do with his solution—*conquest of political power by the proletariat.* Notice in the many Communists/Socialist revolutions how the power positions of bourgeois and proletariat change but the fundamental imbalance remains. This is the problem. Right now in our own country power has centralized in Washington, D.C. On the state level it has centralized in the state (capital). Even on the County level it has centralized in the County over the individual. The two parts, the individual and the government, are not on an equal playing field. Historically, government has been the ruler over. The purpose of the government/state/King was not necessarily to serve the people but to rule over them. The people were subjects, which generally meant slaves. The government/state was the master.

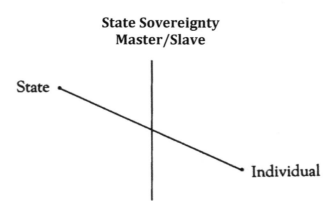

State Sovereignty
Master/Slave

State

Individual

One of the great documents that began to change that master/slave status quo was the *Magna Carta*. In Webster's it states: *The great charter that King John of England was forced by the English barons to grant at Runnymede June 15, 1215, traditionally interpreted as guaranteeing certain civil and political liberties.* In Black's Law Dictionary, 5th Edition, there is the further statement: *This charter is justly regarded as the foundation of English constitutional liberty. Among its thirty-eight chapters are found provisions for regulating the administration of justice, defining the temporal and ecclesiastical jurisdictions, securing the personal liberty of the subject and his rights of property, and the limits of taxation, and for preserving the liberties and privileges of the church.* Notice how at that time the people were subjects. How can there be any type of mutual giving and receiving if you are a subject? What many consider as the completion of the Magna Carta is our own *Declaration of Independence* and *Constitution of the United States of America.* And who has not heard the immortal words from the *Declaration of Independence:*

> We hold these Truths to be self-evident, that all Men are created equal, that they are endowed by their Creator with certain unalienable Rights, that among these are Life, Liberty, and the pursuit of Happiness—That to secure these Rights, Governments are instituted among Men, deriving their just Powers from the Consent of the Governed, that whenever any Form of Government becomes destructive of these Ends, it is the Right of the People to alter or to abolish it...

And why are these words immortal? Because they flip the power from the State/government to the people. The *Declaration of Independence* says that all men (every man and woman) have *unalienable Rights.* According to Black's Law Dictionary, 5th Edition, that means: *Rights which can never be abridged because they are so fundamental.* It also states: *Incapable of being aliened, that is, sold and transferred.* When the Declaration of Independence states: *...they are endowed by their Creator with certain unalienable Rights...* the inference here is that these rights can never be abridged, they can never be liened (put under debt) or transferred. This is to say that you and I come into life with certain *unalienable Rights,* rights that we can never lose. To say: *endowed by their Creator* means that these rights are prior to government; it does not define the Creator as the Christian God or the Muslim God or the Secular Humanist God... It is just saying that prior to government and its power, we stand as the sovereign with unalienable rights. This is big. Prior to this time, rights, in whatever limited form they existed, were under the definition and rule of the powers that be: ...in the name of "God," or Jesus, or the Prophet, the Pope, the Universal Church, the Supreme Leader, Führer, King, Emperor, Emir, Dictator, Ruler, Caesar, Czar, Chairman, Tyrant, Lord, Imam, Priest, Emperor, Chancellor, President, or some chosen person or people, any type of perceived royalty. You and I were 2nd tier, i.e., subjects. Then, with one stroke of the pen, the idea of *unalienable rights* was brought forth and instead of subjects we became the *sovereign.* Not sovereign over but *sovereign with*; we were *co-sovereigns* together. And you think ideas don't matter?

Ayn Rand saw this point quite clearly. As she states:

> The [U.S.] Constitution is a limitation on the government, not on private individuals... it does not prescribe the conduct of private individuals, only the conduct of the government... it is not a charter for government power, but a charter of the citizen's protection against the government.

We are not interested in changing who has the power; we are interested in changing the equation of power, that power is held equally by each side. So, if you are with me, freedom (and love) must begin from the point of a two sovereigns or co-sovereigns. This is the check and balance. What is or what exists are a primary two; not a one over another but a two in co-sovereignty together. This is what Man and Woman Balance means, the two are co-sovereigns together. And from that position we can say that they are free. Their freedom lies in their (co-sovereign) balance. The check on one part seeking to take over the relationship and turn it into a master/slave relationship is that each party has *a voice* in the matter. This voice is what is called *a choice*—or concerning both parties *mutual consent.* And here we are—the great check and balance point of relationship—MUTUAL CONSENT. Freedom only exists if all parties have it.

Man and Woman Balance
Co-Sovereignty

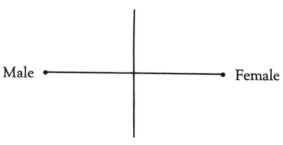

Male ● ──────────────┼────────────── ● Female

The idea of a free market is based on people's choice/consent. *No one is to force you to buy their good or service. Nor can you force another to give you their good or service.* See the check and balance in place? The basis of freedom is the free market of mutual consent. Every transaction between parties is a transaction of mutual consent. Now, we need to clarify or define the idea of unalienable rights more succinctly. What actually are they? I mention this because some, and perhaps many, people today believe they have a "right" to other people's things. After all, didn't Karl Marx state: *From each according to his abilities, to each according to his needs?* The great Russian writer Fyodor Mikhailovich Dostoyevsky (1821-1881) had a different view of needs. He said this:

> The criminal assumption is that one has the right and authority to take or confiscate values earned by others so long as someone else has a need for those values.

And here we see the criminal mind, our own original sin by the way. We justify the taking of what we want because we have a need for it. This justification runs through all of our religious and political ideologies. It runs from the petty criminal to the greatest of politicians. It runs through the totality of fascism, socialism, humanism, racism, sexism, and even through L,B,G,T,Q. Whole economic systems are set up today on the *primacy of need.* You see, we just can't take the chance that we are <u>really</u> accountable for our lives. And what is it we are accountable for? We, my friends, are accountable for the *creation of value.* And those of you who have read any of Ayn Rand writings, you will know that that was her point. I call it *value creation.* Value creation is our task in life. Since we must consume to live so we must produce to consume. Production is the effort required to create consumables. Nothing gets produced without the effort. I believe Marx missed this essential point, or else he thought the proletariat (laborers) were the only ones who produced, as if the industrialist stole everything he had... as if a doctor hadn't put in ten or more years just learning his craft to bring people to health... as if an artist hadn't struggled his life away to bring a moment of spiritual de-light to another... as if an inventor hadn't given his soul to his work to lessen the burden of mankind... you get the point. It is value creation that is the essential aspect of survival not the (forced) dispersion of one's value creation to another who has needs. We all have needs. What freedom is all about is the right to *pursue one's own happiness*, i.e., create one's own path of value creation from which one can thereby receive the fruits of that labor. Notice in this scenario that the acquiring of something or having the use of something (ownership) comes after its production! Who would have thought that the person doing the work to bring something forth would then possess its use value? In other words, the order is production <u>than</u> consumption. There isn't a right to consume as it were. Any people or society that places the primacy of need before the *primacy of right* (primacy of right being that volitional choice to make the effort to bring forth a value [one's labor] and then to receive those fruits in ownership of them) is doomed to failure. What we call Marxism is based on the primacy of need. What is called Objectivism, Ayn Rand's system of thought, is based on the primacy of right. One must earn to than own. Listen to what she says concerning rights. This is from her book *The Virtue of Selfishness: A New Concept of Egoism*, 1964.

> **Rights**—conditions of existence required by man's nature for his proper survival.
> The right to life is the source of all rights—and the right to property is their only implementation. Without property rights, no other rights are possible.

No wonder why the social progressive types despise her so much. She exposes their criminal minds. Now, since this issue is so critical, let's look at these two schools of thought as they have come down to us. One school of thought is presented to us by John Locke. John Locke (1632-1704) was an English philosopher. Many consider him the grandfather of our own American system of governance. The following passage is from his *Second Treatise on Government*. As you read it see if you can capture its essence relative to value creation and the primacy of right. How does he view them?

John Locke (1632-1704)—*Second Treatise on Government*, 1690

...every man has a property in his own person. This nobody has any right to but himself. The labour of his body and the work of his hands, we may say, are properly his. Whatsoever then he removes out of the state that nature hath provided, and left it in, he hath mixed his labour with, and joined to it something that is his own, and thereby makes it his property. It being by him removed from the common state nature placed it in, it hath by his labour something annexed to it that excludes the common right of other men. For this labour being the unquestionable property of the labourer, no man but he can have a right to what that is once joined to....

He that is nourished by the acorns he picked up under an oak, or the apples he gathered from the trees in the wood, has certainly appropriated them to himself. Nobody can deny but the nourishment is his. I ask then when did they begin to be his? And'tis plain, if the first gathering made them not his, nothing else could. That labour put a distinction between them and common. That added something to them more than nature, the common mother of all, had done: and so they became his private right. And will anyone say he had no right to those acorns or apples he thus appropriated, because he had not the consent of all mankind to make them his? If such a consent as that was necessary, man has starved, notwithstanding the plenty God had given him.

So Locke is saying—*I ask then when did they begin to be his? And'tis plain, if the first gathering made them not his, nothing else could. That labour put a distinction between them and common. That added something to them more than nature, the common mother of all, had done: and so they became his private right*—that the moment one adds to the common of nature his or her own labor is the moment something becomes one's own (private property). In the good book it says: *As one sows so shall he reap.* There is a causal nature to productive effort—*the sowing of it brings it forth.* There is a moral nature to the Biblical statement as well—*he who sows reaps.* I call this *he who sows reaps* principle the *primacy of right.* The primacy of right, as one sows so does one reap, i.e., as one works (earns) so does one <u>own</u>, is the basis of unalienable rights. If a man or woman is prevented from exerting his or her will in the effort to create value or cannot receive the fruits of his or her labor (earning), so then that man or woman is not free and essentially cannot survive.

This next quote is by Jean-Jacques Rousseau (1712-1777). Rousseau was a French philosopher. His writings were influential in the course of the French Revolution. The following passage is from his *Discourse on the Origin of Inequality.*

Jean-Jacques Rousseau (1712-1777)—*Discourse on the Origin of Inequality,* 1755

The first man who enclosed a piece of land, who then came up with the idea of saying "this is mine" and found people simple enough to believe him, was the true founder of civil society. How many crimes, wars and murders stem from this act? How much misery and horror the human race would have been spared if someone had simply pulled out the stakes and filled in the ditch and cried out to his fellow men: "Beware of listening to this imposter. You are lost if you forget that the fruits of the earth belong to everyone and that the earth itself belongs to no one!"

Rousseau is suggesting just the opposite of Locke—*You are lost if you forget that the fruits of the earth belong to everyone and that the earth itself belongs to no one!* So, according to Rousseau, if you sow, that is to say, if you put forth the labor to bring something forward that here-to-fore had not been then that production belongs to everyone. The French Revolution was based on the principle which I call the *primacy of need.* Locke puts forth the primacy of right linking production as a necessity for consumption. Rousseau puts forth the primacy of need suggesting everyone has a "right" to consumption irrespective of their effort/value creation. Sounds a bit like the Humanist: *We seek to minimize the inequalities of circumstance and ability, and we support a just distribution of nature's resources and the fruits of human effort so that as many as possible can enjoy a good life.* Which system (Locke's or Rousseau's) is going to work?

After Rousseau came, as you know, Karl Marx. Marx simplified/completed Rousseau with is essence statement: *From each according to his abilities, to each according to his needs.* Marx presents to us the universal statement for the primacy of need. Accordingly, *your needs* shall be the criterion upon which ownership is to be based. This is what the Progressives mean when they shout and demand "economic justice for all." Economic justice for them means the forced dispersion of other people's stuff to them. Unfortunately, there is one problem in the primacy of need position, and that is that little or nothing is being produced such that one's needs can be fulfilled. Production must come before consumption. Consumption depends on production. If no one is producing, how are needs to be fulfilled? And, furthermore, the only reason why people effort/produce in the first place is to consume, i.e., to receive the fruits of their labor. ...*That labour put a distinction between them and common. That added something to them more than nature, the common mother of all, had done: and so they became his private right.* So, let us state this once again, *the only reason why people effort/produce in the first place is to consume, i.e., to receive the fruits of their labor.* How else could it be?

Apparently it could be back to our friend socialism (the primacy of need), the polite word for communism, i.e., dictatorship. Isn't this what is being taught on our college campuses today? Isn't this what the media strives for? Isn't this what our politicians vote for? (And the Republican vote in favor of corporate/big banks/IRS capitalism is generally the same—state power.) And remarkable as it seems, we have a perfection example of socialism and its collapse playing out right before our eyes. It is called Venezuela which had its Socialist (Bolivarian) Revolution beginning sometime around 1999 when Venezuela was a fairly well off country with its oil money to today where its currency, due to hyperinflation, is next to worthless. How can this happen in so short of a time period? Or let me just say this is always what happens when you put one's needs before one's rights. So again we have a choice to make. The Austrian economist Ludwig von Mises (1881-1973) put it this way in his writing *Human Action*, 1949:

> Men must choose between the market economy and socialism. They cannot evade deciding between these alternatives by adopting a "middle-of-the-road" position, whatever name they may give to it.

In his book *Socialism*, 1922 he states:

> Everything brought forward in favor of socialism during the last hundred years, in thousands of writings and speeches, all the blood which has been spilt by the supporters of socialism, cannot make socialism workable.

Why would this be the case? It is simple, under socialism you, and I, are not free. This is to say we do not have unalienable rights; we are not co-sovereigns. We do not get to pursue our dreams (effort) nor keep the fruits of our labor (ownership). Somebody else is telling us what to do. And our individual *initiative* (hopes and dreams) and thus *ingenuity* dies. Here are some other von Mises quotes.

Every socialist is a disguised dictator.
Human Action, 1949

Under socialism production is entirely directed by the orders of the central board of production management. The whole nation is an "industrial army" ...and each citizen is bound to obey his superior's orders.
Planning for Freedom, 1952

In the bureaucratic machine of socialism the way toward promotion is not achievement but the favor of the superiors.
Bureaucracy, 1944

Socialism and democracy are irreconcilable.
A Critique of Interventionism, 1929

Socialist society is a society of officials. The way of living prevailing in it, and the mode of thinking of its members, are determined by this fact.
Socialism, 1922

Socialism knows no freedom of choice in occupation. Everyone has to do what he is told to do and to go where he is sent.
Socialism, 1922

The nationalization of intellectual life, which must be attempted under socialism, must make all intellectual progress impossible.
Socialism, 1922

The ideas of modern socialism have not sprung from proletarian brains. They were originated by intellectuals, sons of the bourgeoisie, not of wage-earners.
Socialism, 1922

No one shall be idle if I have to work; no one shall be rich if I am poor. Thus we see, again and again, that resentment lies behind all socialist ideas.
Socialism, 1922

In fact socialism is not in the least what it pretends to be. It is not the pioneer of a better and finer world, but the spoiler of what thousands of years of civilization have created. It does not build; it destroys. For destruction is the essence of it. It produces nothing, it only consumes what the social order based on private ownership in the means of production has created.

Socialism, 1922

Right now we have a socialist running for president in the USA. Some other candidates say, "I am not a socialist; I believe in democracy." I would suggest that is pretty much the same thing today. Look at the Communist Party (CPUSA) website. They believe in socialism. They believe in democracy. They believe in progressivism. They believe in social justice. The one thing they don't believe in is unalienable rights. The point to all this is that unalienable rights can never be separate from *your* earning and owing. This is what it means to say that unalienable rights really constitute property rights.

The Unalienable Rights Test*

- *A right must be based in individual life.*
- *A right must be the same for everyone.*
- *A right can never be taken away.*
- *A right can never be a (consumptive) need.*
- *A right can never circumvent the right of another.*

* *What Ever Happened to Our Unalienable Rights,* 1998, Christopher Alan Anderson

We will get to capitalism and banking in a moment. For now see if you can grasp the essence of freedom in your own heart and soul. Thus far we have viewed the idea of sovereignty, or actually a co-sovereignty. We looked how freedom must lie in a sovereign two—and that their fundamental interaction lies in their mutual consent. This led us to the idea of unalienable rights, that there are certain rights (earning and owning) that lie in our balance together; rights of our very lives that no one else has a right to circumvent. When another circumvents our rights and lives we call it a crime. Yet, when government does the same thing we call it compassion. Can a government force us to accept their health plan? Can a government tell us we must be vaccinated? Can a government tell us we cannot home school? Can a government create the curriculum for (government) schools and mandate "taxpayer" payment? How about the War on Poverty or Drugs or Cancer or Climate Change... Notice how underneath these pretexts are mandates that require us to participate in and fund just as they decide. But is it government's job to serve us in the protection of our unalienable rights (the *Bill of Rights*) or to force us to serve it and its agenda? I think von Mises had it right when he said: *Men must choose between the market economy and socialism. They cannot evade deciding between these alternatives by adopting a "middle-of-the-road" position, whatever name they may give to it.* This is to say that we must choose between freedom for our lives or government edict which is slavery. You would think it would be a simple choice given that our Founding Fathers fought *our* war of independence over this exact issue and our *Constitution of the United States of American* was written from the frame of a limited government. So understanding and standing up for freedom is not so simple of a task today. In fact, I would contend, we must understand freedom/rights all the way back to the fundamental balance of a two (procreant) forces, male and female. Isn't that, after all, the first interaction? This next quote is from my writing *The Man and Woman Manifesto: Let the Revolution Begin*, 1994. (This was my first attempt at a manifesto.)

> It is important to understand that any and every imbalanced relationship will result in a system of master/slave. The individuals who proclaim their right to rule over others inevitably justify their rule in the name of some one-force conception such as "God," the people, the state, some race, tribe, clan, or group. (It's interesting how we can never stand up just for ourselves.) And from time to time, the slaves grow uneasy and begin to protest and shout slogans, possibly even revolt. Sometimes the slaves overthrow the system and they become the new masters. But our current nation-state stays firmly in place. You see, until and unless the underlying metaphysical structure is altered (within us), nothing will change. The only way to alter the underlying structure is for a paradigm shift or metaphysical restructuring to occur from a one-force conception to a two forces of creation. Until we begin to understand the two equal but opposite forces of male and female and center our lives on that balance, the imbalance of the nation-state will control. As long as the imbalance of the nation-state controls, we will continue to be a pawn to the imbalance no matter which side of the master/slave relationship we may reside. We will stay in bondage and all of our religious, transcendental, or spiritual unions, our consciousness liberations or psychological clearings, will not alter the fact of reality. Our prison may be one without bars, but no less a prison.

Perhaps somewhat a depressing scenario, don't you think? How can we really ever get to freedom? Let's try the *Declaration of Freedom*, a document I wrote in 2011.

Declaration of Freedom

...Be it known, the following truths are self-evident...

We, the People of (   ), come to a turning point in our history, a time for each of us who seek a better life to recognize a simple yet immortal truth—*freedom.*

Freedom—That necessity required for an individual and/or people to create wealth. It is understood as a primary principle that wealth is generated from individual exertion not from government coercion.

Freedom—From which each man and woman have <u>un</u>alienable rights/intrinsic worth, not as a guarantee of our needs but as the opportunity of our lives—to pursue our own happiness, to make our way through our own efforts, and to receive the fruits of our own labor.

Freedom—The acknowledgment of our sovereignty, that we the people—both individually and collectively—stand as the sovereign and that government stands as our servant, never our master, and that the purpose of our government is to serve the common law—that order that arises around people's contracting through mutual consent.

Freedom—And lastly, let us understand that the test of freedom lies not in whether "I have mine," but rather in my own willingness to allow you to equally have your freedom. *"Can 'I' let others be free?"* Let that be our enduring question.

May the spirit of freedom forever touch each one of our souls.

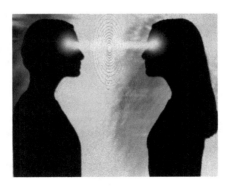

The next aspect of a model for freedom that I would like to look at is the subject of sound money. You could also call this <u>substance</u> money. What is substance money? It is money that has an intrinsic worth value. It is something that has a value separate and apart of its value as money. Gold and silver are clear examples of substance money. They have a certain value in the free market and happen to be quite useful in the exchange of value, i.e., money. Historically, many things have been used as money—tobacco, sea shells, furs, metal coins, etc. The thing that they have in common is that they all have a use value separate from their use as money. Even paper money had a use value in that the first paper scripts could be exchanged for its substance (also called commodity) value. In other words, if you had a 10 dollar silver certificate that certificate could be exchanged for 10 dollars in silver. That is what substantiates paper money, that you can exchange it for an actual value. But something happened. Along the way the paper (script) money was separated from its commodity backing. We today cannot exchange the paper money we use for its gold or silver backing because it doesn't have a gold or silver backing. On the paper money we use today its states FEDERAL RESERVE NOTE. So our money today is not a silver certificate or the like but a Federal Reserve Note. I wonder, does anyone know what that means or why it was done? Well, let's look deeper. This is from the book by Merrill M. E. Jenkins—*"Money" The Greatest Hoax On Earth*, 1971. I view Mr. Jenkins book as the Bible of the money hoax.

Merrill M. E. Jenkins—*"Money" The Greatest Hoax On Earth*, 1971

The sixteenth amendment to the constitution is definitely in violation of Article I section 2 paragraph 3, section 8 paragraph 1, and section 9 paragraph 4, all of which stipulate the "cost" of federal government should fall as a tax "uniform" throughout the United States, determined by the numbers of persons; whereas the sixteenth amendment places a tax based on "individual income" not "cost of government."

The Federal Reserve Act (so-called monetary reform) now permitted a group of privately owned banks under Congressional corporate charter to issue and regulate the supply of money in the United States.

Notice here how the 16th Amendment (the income tax) changed the nature of the tax system from cost of government to individual income. Now government was free, if you will, to tax individual income/earning. At this moment each one of us lost our freedom. Our pockets books were no longer of our sovereign owning. Why did the government make this change? They wanted more money so they could spend at will. The Constitution limited governmental taxing power. The 16th Amendment opened it up. And spend they did—trillions of dollars they never had the right to spend. We, as free and sovereign citizens, were never to be taxed on our income. That income, as it were, was ours (unalienably) to keep. We earned it. That is the point of being a free man or woman. *Free to earn and own.* The income tax, which was a central and necessary component of the Federal Reserve Act, actually doomed our freedom. It began innocently enough. Now we are all slaves to the economic police that watch our every economic move. Does that sound like freedom to you? Again from Merrill M. E. Jenkins.

> A Federal Reserve "Note" is a paper token as evidence of a created "dollar" of imaginary debt, written as a number on the books of a bank, and accepted by a borrower as his debt to repay; are printed at the Bureau of Printing and Engraving, on orders of the Treasury, countersigned by officials of the Treasury, turned over to the "Fed" for distribution and accepted by the people as mediums of exchange for wealth that is over a thousand times greater in value than the worth of the "note" itself.

Wow! There is a quote for you: ...*and accepted by the people as mediums of exchange for wealth that is over a thousand times greater in value than the worth of the "note" itself.* How does that make you feel? The government, essentially, changed the dollar of substance into a <u>note</u> with a creditor and a debtor. The FED became the creditor and the government was the debtor. But the government then placed the debt on the American people. (See the 14th Amendment.) We became the ones responsible for the debt which constituted the amount the government was borrowing from the FED. Instead of being a sovereign citizen we became peons, i.e., debtor slaves just like what our forefathers fled from in old Europe. Can you see the fleecing of *your hard-earned value* going on? Do you ever really expect people's earning to keep up with government taxation/spending/inflation? And there is more from Mr. Jenkins.

> "Our" government chartered a private corporation to use imaginary debt as a base for money stock instead of using some tangible wealth and bearer certificates to maintain sanity and control automatically by natural law. Congress also gave that private corporation regulating powers such as

reserve requirement "control" and interest "control." The Federal Reserve may believe the government gave it the "power to control" but in reality the government did not have the "power" to bestow "power to control." The power to control is vested in the natural laws of economics. All the government bestowed on the Federal Reserve was the authority, it is up to the "FED" to make man's law supersede natural law.

Many of you would like to believe that there aren't economic laws, that man's law *can* supersede natural law, and that a credit/debit, i.e., note can actually work as a money system. But guess what, it cannot—at least not without putting all of us in perpetual debt. The whole credit/debit NOTE money scam cannot and will not ever benefit you and me. Let's return to Mr. Jenkins once more.

If we understand that the Fed through the creation of imaginary debt dollars and the people's acceptance of their "money" controls the people and their means of production through ownership purchased with the "money," we should be able to understand that the I.M.F. is designed to be the Fed of the world and it is planned for it to control the peoples of the world and their means of production through the medium of the S.D.R. (Special Drawing Rights) which they create. The hierarchy of the I.M.F. is moving toward the take-over of the world just as the hierarchy of the Fed took over control of the United States. Just as in the United States where the great mass of people have the popular vote and will not vote themselves off the dole, even to regain their freedom, so it is with the member nations of the I.M.F. If they can all be kept busy trying to get all they can in the way of S.D.R. purchasing power free (through the medium of using their own "creation" to create debt and S.D.R.'s to settle it) they will not see the trap.

There you have it: *The hierarchy of the I.M.F. is moving toward the take-over of the world just as the hierarchy of the Fed took over control of the United States.* And let's also include: *Just as in the United States where the great mass of people have the popular vote and will not vote themselves off the dole, even to regain their freedom, so it is with the member nations of the I.M.F.* Checkmate. *...the great mass of people have the popular vote and will not vote themselves off the dole, even to regain* *their freedom.* Well, we are right back to Marx, that need comes before rights even if it takes force to procure (steal) that need. And so, that simple decision between *the market economy and socialism* is not so simple after all.

Ayn Rand had much to say on these same subjects. She, of course, stool on the side of freedom. *I swear by my life and my love of it that I will never live for the sake of another man, nor ask another man to live for mine.* Following is one of her quotes on the subject at hand from her writing *Atlas Shrugged,* 1957.

> Money is the barometer of a society's virtue. When you see that trading is done, not by consent, but by compulsion— when you see that in order to produce, you need to obtain permission from men who produce nothing—when you see that money is flowing to those who deal, not in goods, but in favors—when you see that men get richer by graft and by pull than by work, and your laws don't protect you against them, but protect them against you—when you see corruption being rewarded and honesty becoming a self-sacrifice—you know that your society is doomed.

So between the two illusions of socialism and the credit-debit money system, all voted on and put into place by our politicians, you surely will not be surprised by what follows. *The Politician* was written by this author in 2005 and *Confessions of an "Honest Politician"* in 2013.

The Politician

- *Promising that which you do not have to give.*

- *Confiscating people's money from them.*

- *Coercing those who do not support you.*

- *Incarcerating those who do not pay as you demand.*

- *Continuing the lie that we are free as long as we "pay up."*

- *Bankrupting the system.*

- *Placing your pensions above all else.*

- *Tying the hands of the producers.*

- *Trashing people's hopes and dreams for an honest and decent life.*

- *Betraying all of those who have given of their lives in the long and rigorous struggle for freedom.*

Confessions of an "Honest" Politician

- Though I speak with the fluidness of the well-educated, and most certainly have your best interests in mind, ...if I do not allow you to keep what you earn, I am just another thug on the take.
- Though I speak of your "human rights" ...if I claim your rights actually originate from me, the government, it is just because I want the right over your pocketbook!
- Though I speak of "tax fairness" ...if I legislate a progressive (income tax) upon you, it is because I am just trying to control your bank account!
- Though I speak of helping the middle class ...if I give subsidies/favors to business or union interests, I am just trying to get my hands on your wallet!
- Though I speak of job creation ...if I demand you get a "business license" to work (and call your work a "profession"), I just want your money!
- Though I speak of justice for all ...if I pass laws that I myself do not have to adhere to, I am just trying to steal your stuff!
- Though I speak of fiscal responsibility ...if I pass budgets that are not balanced, I only want you to pay my way!
- Though I speak of openness and transparency ...if I vote on legislation that has yet to be read by me, I am just trying to hide from you its cost

to you!

◆ Though I speak of income fairness ...if I give myself the power to decide what my own salary, perks, and pension will be, I just want you to know that there really are two classes of people!

◆ Though I speak of governmental accountability ...if I approve a governmental accountability review board to be run by government (paid, perked, and pensioned) bureaucrats, it is just me doing my job of holding sovereignty over you!

◆ Though I speak of freedom, and liberty and justice for all ...I still just want your money!

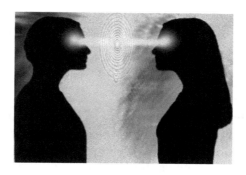

I could have added the terrible trade deals Congress has passed in the last decade or two. Both parties were in on it and many knew these deals were not for the benefit of the American people. If a deal is not win-win it ought not to be for us. It makes one wonder why our politicians are so interested in selling us out. We must understand that our politicians are not our friends, that their only agenda is to take from us our money. Look at how the establishment politicians are squealing at just the thought of an outsider taking away some of their power. And when it comes to FED/IRS control both Democrats and Republicans are on the same team. I know this personally. I spent 6 years defending my parents from IRS onslaught. In such a case you haven't any rights or remedy and your "elected" politicians are not on your side. Why might this be? Because the "money" is not yours; you are using their FED notes—and you haven't any *unalienable* rights. Do you get this? *As long as there is a FED/IRS you are a slave.* Well, let's go to *An Open Letter To Elected Officials... From Mr. Nobody,* 2003.

An Open Letter To Elected Officials... From Mr. Nobody

Dear Elected Official,

You may not have heard of me so perhaps I ought to introduce myself. My name is Mr. Nobody. I am one of the millions of people who no longer matter to you. As long as I do my J.O.B., whatever it is I am assigned to do, and pay "my taxes" so you can live the "good life," that is all that matters to you, right? I know you speak of your concern for me and others like me; how much you want to help us all. It all sounds so good. Hey, if it makes you feel better. But surely you must know—it no longer matters. That is right. *It no longer matters.* Do you know why? Because I, Mr. Nobody, am *flat broke.* What do you think of that? I work my tail off day after day and I just can't make it anymore. No matter what I do or how hard I work, I just cannot make a living for my family. Over one-half of what I make goes to you or your cronies in some form of tax or regulatory cost. You know, I never did want to work for you. I just want to work for my family. Is that too much to ask? Today, I feel like some sort of slave. I understand that we are taxed more today than the serfs were who fled the old world to come to what was to become America—the land of the free. Yet, how can anyone be free if he or she is taxed on his or her person or property? You actually think the money I make is somehow yours or that you can tax my property at threat of forfeiture. Where did you get those ideas? Ah, but you won't listen, will you? And I am growing tired. Every day, I lose ground. My indebtedness grows. Hey, I just cannot afford to pay your pension anymore. I can't even afford one for myself. I hope you understand this when I tell you, *I'm broke.*

I remember vaguely—it's been so long—when I, Mr. Nobody, was actually a Mr. Somebody. Yes, each of us mattered. We counted. Each one of us was *sovereign*. We had *unalienable rights*—that, supposedly, no one could take away, especially not the government. A man, all by himself, with an honest day's labor, could support his family. Dare I say, a woman could stay at home with the children. Children could grow up believing— in a moral base and a future. We actually believed we were free to earn and own. Were we? Ah, but those days are gone now, aren't they? You know what happened, don't you? You people stole the money system.

When did this happen? Certainly the attempts to control money have been going on for aeons. In the beginning of our own country, we had the great debate between Thomas Jefferson and Alexander Hamilton over a central bank to control the money system. Later, after a central bank was formed, President Andrew Jackson succeeded in destroying it. Then there was Abraham Lincoln's creation of the greenback in an attempt to free himself from the usury of the bankers during the Civil War. Perhaps, for our purposes, we should begin in 1913 with the creation of the Federal Reserve System (central bank) and the Internal Revenue Service (the bank's taxing and enforcement arm). How many people really know what these two organizations do? How many people know that a central bank is really a privately owned institution with monopoly monetary power to loan money (credit created from nothing) to the government? The exclusive power to loan credit money (as contrasted to commodity money that is backed by a substance value) is the exclusive power to control, i.e., bankrupt the government and all people. How many people know that the IRS is the enforcement arm, not of the government but of the private Federal Reserve System, and operates under their own tax laws which, by the way, is why Constitutional rights do not exist in tax matters? It is not our own money we use today; it is their money. That is the point. Let me refresh your memory just a bit. In 1933, you people, through the Emergency (War) Powers Act, declared the United States government bankrupt, placing the American people into debt/liability for repayment. And then in 1935, you stole our gold and severed the connection between the Federal Reserve Note (which had replaced the gold-backed dollar) and gold. Many people today don't even remember that a dollar used to be a certificate of gold or silver, signifying an actual amount (weight) of a real value. What is the dollar today? Can you tell me? It says "Federal Reserve Note" on it. Is a dollar really just a note? If so, who is the creditor and who is the debtor? Is it the debtor that now backs the dollar? If so, then the monetary system in place today is one that intentionally creates debtors, and does so simply by the Federal Reserve Note being a debt instrument. It is created, essentially, out of or from nothing, as a credit demand and loaned into existence, creating a debtor. We are no longer speaking of a dollar being a commodity backed value, earned and owned by a free man or woman who trade value to value, freeman to freeman. A debt instrument by its very nature creates only one type of exchange, master to slave.

Might I add, that without a commodity backed money system, the Declaration of Independence and the Constitution for the United States of America really haven't any meaning. Unalienable rights cannot exist in a credit/debit system of funny money. Instead we, the debtors, are given "civil rights" created or taken away as you permit. The sovereign individual dies with the fall of gold/silver. The debtor-slave rises with the Federal Reserve Note. Who would have thought that the United States of America would lose its freedom through a counterfeit money conspiracy that you people have orchestrated?

May I dare say that this, the stealing of the money system, is the great conspiracy. Keeping the people in perpetual debt is the invisible way to control us all. We, the people, are now no more than "human resources," also known as peons. But the masses of Mr. Nobodies are beginning to get restless. A new group of revolutionaries is beginning to call for the demise of "Capitalism" and the global economy. They don't understand it is not Capitalism (if what we mean by Capitalism is a free economy and not monetary fascism) that is at fault but the money credit/debit structure that is being used to bankrupt every country world-wide since the Bretton Woods Agreement in 1944. Bretton Woods was created to foster in a "new economic order" by imposing through the United Nations and International Monetary Fund this same credit/debit scheme of bankruptcy and tax laws to every country. They have essentially succeeded. Now, these new revolutionaries want to recycle Communism—not realizing that Communism itself, i.e., the ten planks of the Communist Manifesto, was and is the exact prescience followed to steal the money system of America. Least I sound a bit radical myself, look at planks 2 and 5 in the Communist Manifesto. What do you see? Lucky for you that nobody is really talking about economic freedom these days where each man and woman own their money and control their own pocketbook. If they were you might see a real revolution—like the one in 1776!

I now admit, you have defeated me. I can no longer carry the fight for freedom. And I know you won't, having already been bought off long ago. After all, that is why you are a politician rather than a statesman, right? But don't worry, I won't tell anyone. You can count on me to do nothing. I am just too tired. I am so tired that I can't even get up the energy to vote anymore. Imagine—the whole key to "democracy" and I can't even do "my part." (Doesn't registering to vote sign us up and/or signify us as U.S. resident, tax-paying, debtor citizens?) Oh, go ahead and call me all those names: unpatriotic, selfish, mean-spirited, and simple-minded. Yes, all those and more. Come to think about it, I guess there is one thing you can count on me to do. I will not vote anymore. That is right. The voting game is now over for me. In case you don't understand, let me be specific. *I will not vote—for you!* Wow, that's exciting! I feel a little of my energy coming back. I think I will go tell my friend, Ralph… See you later.

Yours truly,

Mr. Nobody

The Voter's Oath

- *I shall not vote until I am free to vote.*

The Declaration of a Freeman

- *How I earn my sustenance will be of my choosing,*
  given that I do not force another to participate in my effort.
- *What I earn is mine, to spend as I choose.*

In my earlier writing *The Man and Woman Manifesto: Let the Revolution Begin*, 1994, I traced a Model of Freedom that went as follows:

Model of Freedom

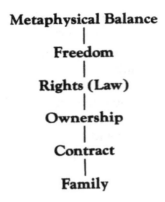

In this chapter we began from Man and Woman Balance as representing a co-sovereignty. (That actually is what metaphysical balance means. The teeter-totter must be balanced.) Our basic freedom is that of mutual consent. Rights/law come into play given the survival necessities of production and consumption. Primary rights we call unalienable rights, rights that cannot be taken away or liened. Today under the Federal Reserve Note as "money" our rights are liened, i.e., our money is not really ours. We are the debtors of this credit/debit system— or is it scam? Understand that in such a system we cannot be free. And, to those of you who want to believe you are free because you have the vote, I would suggest to you that in the Federal Reserve Note credit/debit system you can only vote to continue that system. You can only vote for the continuation of the IRS to control your personal economy. If that is what you are voting for, you are only voting for your own slavery/bondage. Okay, enough said on that. Back to the earlier Model of Freedom above, notice how it ends in *family*. Why do you think that would be its ending? Because that was its beginning. Man and Woman Balance, i.e., co-sovereignty is the metaphysical term that generally means family. Writing in that earlier *The Man and Woman Manifesto: Let the Revolution Begin,* I said it this way.

> *Family is the sovereign unit of all creation. It stands at the hub or center of life. It is the source of all things. A family is, by definition, composed of a male and a female. The two equal but opposite forces are in play, dividing and uniting together. From each unity of a male and a female comes procreation, a reproduction of life. Family is the most essential thing in all of life. It is life.*

This is to suggest that *family is the sovereign unit of all creation.* We often think that "God" is the sovereign. Politicos like Marx think it is the state (also called the nation or the federal). Individualists like Ayn Rand think it is the individual. But notice how it is only a man <u>and</u> a woman that can continue the play of creation. Sovereignty does not really lie in the individual for the individual by him or herself cannot continue the play of creation. True sovereignty lies in a man <u>and</u> a woman, i.e., a *family*. Thus the importance of *marriage*. Marriage is the sacred act of a man and woman coming together as *one* for the purpose of dividing that one into the next *two*—birth of life. All the talk today about other forms of marriage or family fail to take into account the necessity of a man and a woman as the creators/parents of their children. We are speaking of life here. And so, back to our Model of Freedom, we end in family. This is important concerning how we ought to structure a government and its balance of powers. Today we, for the most part, are a top-down governmental system. Our current structure looks like this:

The Structure of Governmental Power

Nation – State – Community – Family

In the United States of American, we might think of the nation as the federal/Washington, D.C., the state as the 50 states, and the community as the county each one of us live in. Most power today is concentrated in Washington, D.C., followed by the states and their seats of power, than the counties and their control, and lastly by the family. But this Nation–State–Community–Family is exactly backwards. In the United States, our Founding Fathers set up a system of the people, each individual, being the sovereign and the government, controlled by limited powers, being the servant of the people. So much has changed. We again need to recognize from where co-sovereignty arises. I suggest to you it is the family and from there moves to community, state, and nation. In this model, the family would retain the most power, it diminishing as it moved to community, state, and nation. The nation/federal would have the least power, i.e., limited to its original duties of protecting us.

The Structure of a Sovereign Society

Family – Community – State – Nation

We, you and I, cannot be free if power begins from the top and works its way down. Our freedom lies in bottom down government. The first primary authority and power lies in the family, i.e., the parents. Then comes the community. The community is the extended family in a way. Most of the needs of families who struggle can be met at the community level. When we place the federal in charge, or even the states, inefficiency, abuse, and waste occur as there isn't any direct check on that power. Community needs to be the place to resolve issues of health care, welfare, crime, restitution, drugs, sexual issues, guns and militias, environmental issues, energy, etc. The more independent families and communities are from state and national government the better. Primary power must lie in the family and the community. *Family owned businesses, independent of the federal taxman and bogus rules and regulations, with their owning rooted in their own substance money—this is the ideal.* This is why I am for bottom down government with the most power vested in the family and going up from there. That is the real check on government largeness. Monies spent by government at all levels must be strictly accounted for with a cost-effect analysis of every law. Budgets must be balanced every year. Citizen's panels should be set up in every community to decide the salaries, perks, and pensions of every government official and worker. Government people should never have the right/power to decide on their own salaries, perks, and benefits. That is the true check and balance— who controls the money. I say it is us, <u>*we the people*</u>, not the government bureaucrat. Bottom down government allows us the most freedom/ power; top down government allows us the least freedom/power. This is an absolute. The creation of the United States of American was the true proletariat revolution not communism which just cemented power in the hands of the state. Let us understand: *In any system of state-socialism all peoples (except the bureaucrats in power) equally gravitate to the lowest common denominator of poverty. In free-market capitalism (which should be called free-market/sovereign ownership/sound money/mutual consent) all people unequally gravitate to the highest common denominator of wealth. Unequally because wealth creation depends not just on upbringing, education, or social position but idea innovation and hard work. So which is the better road, the primacy of right or the primacy of need?*

"But what about helping those in need," you ask. I am all for that. It is called charity. Charity is one of the great virtues. 1 Corinthians 13:13 states: *And now abideth faith, hope, charity, these three; but the greatest of these is charity.* Our politicians often attempt to school us in the virtues of charity. The problem is that they want to mandate it upon us. Socialism, that great failure of human kind, is essentially <u>forced</u> charity. Charity can only work if it has at its center point the freedom to choose. *Charity is charity precisely because it is freely given.* Charity (that is freely given) assists both the giver and the receiver. Charity that is forced serves neither the giver nor the receiver. That is metaphysical law.

The Parameters of Charity

❖ *No one shall be forced to help another.*
❖ *No one shall be prevented from helping another.*
❖ *No one shall be forced to receive the help of another.*
❖ *No one shall be prevented from receiving the help of another.*

With this said, let's end this section with *Family: The Force to Save the Planet,* also included in *Meditations for Deepening Love,* 1994, 2010.

Family: The Force to Save the Planet

What would you do or whom would you turn to if it became apparent to you that this planet earth was under assault? Or maybe it should be asked, what would it take for you to believe that planet earth is under assault? Would you need to see some army taking over your town or home? Maybe you would first have to be hauled away to some prison camp. But what if suddenly your marriage dissolved or your children turned their backs on you and you found yourself left with nothing? Would that get your attention? Perhaps the real assault on planet earth is not coming from some overt source but is coming from within. Perhaps it is a spiritual assault that we almost cannot see, an assault going right into our core and yet we are nearly defenseless to do anything about it. I would suggest to you that it is an assault on that thing that is most dear to us. The assault is a spiritual one on the family.

But, it must be asked, why would anyone want to assault the family? Isn't the family that order of life that allows for life? The family is that one man and one woman unit that when united in marriage is the base and stability of procreation. We might say that all life comes through family. It is the balance (equal and opposite) of male and female that holds the family together such that children can be born and raised to continue the play of creation. Without family, there isn't any hope for any of us. In short, the family is life.

So again, it must be asked, why would anyone want to assault the family? You would think that all of us would do everything we can to support this institution. Yet it is being assaulted on all sides. Don't we hear today how monogamous marriage is outdated, how we as men and women don't really need the other sex in our lives; how sex is whatever feels good irrespective of commitment and procreation; how in the name of our "sovereign" choice it is morally acceptable to kill unborn children; or how babies are being created only for their stem cells or organs, etc.? Or, maybe your child comes home from school one day to inform you that he or she is "gay." Or, the state takes your child from you and your spouse because the state does not like how you are raising your child. So you turn to your church for help and support only to find that your minister, pastor, or priest (of your IRS-registered church) can only tell you to ask for forgiveness. Suddenly, you realize that no one is there to stand up for the family. Why?

May I suggest that the assault upon the family is imposed by the threat the family presents to the powers-that-be. The threat is one of sovereigncy. (Sovereigncy means co-sovereignty; a sexual procreative two, i.e., a male and a female.) Family is the sovereign center of the universe. It is sovereign by its procreative nature. (It takes a man and a woman to make a baby.) As the sovereign center, nothing stands over or under it. Family is that one living entity that breaks the master/slave hierarchy the powers-that-be use to enslave us. Family leaves us accountable for procreation, leaves us free to pursue our own happiness (earn and own), and presents to us the inner strength to stand up for and defend the family we comprise.

For those of us who want the family to survive, and with it all life, we must first understand the nature of this assault. As I have mentioned, it is a spiritual assault. The battle is for the soul of man and woman. The attempt is to get a man and a woman to believe in anything else but family, to believe that a committed, sacred marriage between one man and one woman is but an illusion. In my view, there are generally three areas from which this assault is coming.

The first direction of this assault is from the church. By the church, I mean any institution of any religion. You might think that if anything stands for the family it is the church. But the church does not hold the family as being the sacred and sovereign center of all things. Historically, it has often supported patriarchy.* The church holds (a one-force) "God" as the sacred and sovereign entity of which we are called to submit. We are told we cannot find our salvation or eternal life except through "God" or his son (Christianity) or that the eternal (singular force) Self is within us individually (Hinduism), etc. Nowhere is it mentioned that a man and a woman come together as eternally mated (procreative) pairs and that our sole salvation is in understanding the reality of our existential need for each other. In other words, in all of our religions today, the church places its sanctity above and before the family. We are to choose Jesus or the Self, etc., before our husband or wife. Can you see how this undermines marriage and family at the spiritual level? Spiritually speaking, in our religions of today, man and woman are not primary. We have never understood their eternal/procreative balance together. As such, we undercut the spiritual base of family and place it in second position. It is not to stand on itself. If the family were to stand on itself that, of course, would undermine the (hierarchical) "authority" of the church and the alms to the church would dry up. And thus, we see the real reason that the church cannot allow the family to be sovereign.

*Patriarchy is the imbalance of male domination. Today churches, primarily in the West, in the name of equality, are moving to a feminist imbalance.

Another assault upon the family comes from the state or what I also refer to as the nation-state. The ideology (religion) of the nation-state is that of secular humanism. Secular humanism holds that all people are equal under the state. In this case, the state is the sovereign or leviathan master supposedly acting in the name of the people. Secular humanism has its roots in the Dialectical Materialism of Karl Marx and others. Today, it is known under the banner of democracy. In secular humanism, there isn't any mention of the necessity of the family. Men and women are viewed as singular or independent of each other (and, in essence, work for the state). "We can stand on ourselves alone," they would claim as they all clamor for the state to give to them the handout as if it were their right. Of course, the state can only provide what it itself has first taken (stolen) from some poor sap who is just trying to support his family. The state retains its power over the people by promising the handout and at the same time keeping the people in need. Like the church, its motive to undermine the family is economic. If the family stood on its own, which the state cannot allow it to do, the state's only task would be to protect the unalienable rights of all and provide for none. Then, the politicians might have to get an honest job.

The third assault upon the family that I want to mention comes from the feminist/homosexual coalition. The attempt of the feminist/homosexual coalition is to redefine the family structure itself. Rather than the basis of a family being that structure of marriage between a man and a woman that is procreative to life, a new definition of family is to arise. This "new family" would consist of anything people consented to. There could be homosexual "families," bisexual "families," or transgender "families" but gender distinction between one man and one woman as we have known it would no longer be the defining characteristic of family. We may still have man and woman families but that would just be another choice among the many choices available. The intention of the feminist/homosexual coalition is to deny and destroy the essential necessity of the one man and one woman family as that procreative center of all things. They call for "reproductive rights" so they can sidestep the reality that it takes a man and a woman to make a baby. They advocate abortion as a "life" choice to create the appearance of freedom from sexual (man and woman) interdependence. And they seek to "teach" children their ways of "love" that deny the essential essence of procreative love and leave a man and a woman spiritually empty inside.

The attempt to undermine or destroy the family is the attempt to undermine or destroy life itself. Without the one man and one woman family as that center point of all creation, we are doomed. Given this reality, I again must ask, why? Why is the church, the state, and the feminist/homosexual coalition, or anyone else, trying to undermine/ destroy the family? Don't these people know that they themselves cannot exist without it? Yet the assault continues. Why?

The answer to this assault upon the family is solely yours to discover. And discover it you will, once you have made the commitment to support the one man and one woman marriage and family as if your own life is dependent upon it, and dependent on nothing else. And supporting the family is all any of us need to do to save this planet for, you see, the family is nothing other than that exact procreative order from which all things revolve in perfect (sexual/spiritual) balance. *Family is not physical but metaphysical!* The family (in its two-way sexual process) is not just the "one force" to save the planet, it is the only force to save the planet. Life only exists in the balance of family.

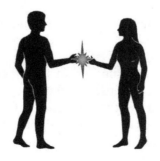

Why We Fail in Life?

We fail in life because we refuse to make the correct choices. In short, we want things to be "our way." Rather than ask, "What is the truth of the matter?" we fail to question our own (automatic) thinking. It is an interesting question, "How may we step back from our own minds, with its own thought calibration, and peer into the naked truth, also called the light?" Can we make a fundamental shift in consciousness such that we can see into the truth? Yes, by understanding that there are two primary forces, equal and opposite, male and female, man and woman. That is our doorway into the truth.

Truth is balance. Balance is axiomatic (self-evident). It needs no more clarification than its definition. Its definition is *equal and opposite*. Equal and opposite (what I call Man and Woman Balance) presents to us the frame out of which love and freedom flow. If you are not *in your soul* integrated into Man and Woman Balance, love and freedom will not be able to flow out from you. The definition of balance also gives to us the definition of imbalance, which would be Masculinism (opposite but not equal) and Feminism (equal but not opposite). In the West, we are seeing a great shift from Masculinism to Feminism. Unfortunately, Feminism is no more balanced than Masculinism.

The Three Structures of the Universe
Man and Woman Balance: *Equal and Opposite*
Masculinism: *Opposite but not Equal*
Feminism: *Equal but not Opposite*

Structural Balance
Man and Woman Balance

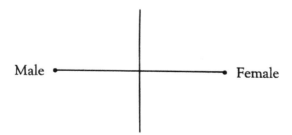

Structural Imbalance

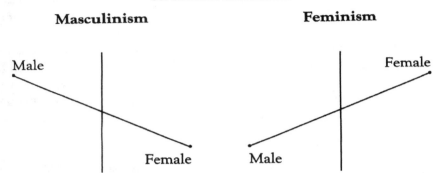

Masculinism

Male

Female

Feminism

Female

Male

Most systems of thought, philosophical systems or religious systems, have some degree of balance and some degree of imbalance. The religion of my upbringing, for example, has much of Man and Woman Balance in it. Remember the words of Jesus in Matthew 19:4-6: *Have ye not read, that he which made them in the beginning made them male and female, And said, for this cause shall a man leave father and mother, and shall cleave to his wife: and they twain shall be one flesh? Wherefore they are no more twain, but one flesh. What therefore God hath joined together, let not man put asunder.* And yet, Christianity never completed because of its failure to recognize the two-force sexual/procreant process on the spiritual level. Remember the earlier quote? *On a personal note, when Mr. Anderson was asked to describe the writings and what he felt their message was he responded, "Spiritual procreation. Mankind has yet to distinguish the two sexes on the spiritual level. In this failure lies the root of our problems and why we cannot yet touch the eternal together. The message of Man and Woman Balance brings each of us together in love with our eternal other half right now."* The Christian cannot come into spiritual balance through Christianity and must revert to worship (hierarchy) and a "faith" in their own individual salvation over their equal and opposite other half. Unfortunately for them an intermediary cannot take them into direct contact man to woman and woman to man. Shall we review the earlier quote from *Meditations for Deepening Love— The Man and Woman Spiritual Center*, 1994, 2010:

> *The Man and Woman Spiritual Center is only expressed in an actual touch between a man and a woman. It cannot be expressed in any other way. That touch may range from a momentary conscious recognition to a full embrace, but a touch, one to another, it is. The Spiritual Center is not expressed*

through belief, pledge, worship, ritual, or the paying of alms. It is not something that can be institutionalized, dogmatized, or ratified. There isn't any prescribed path to take, master to follow, or status to attain for its expression. There is only a man and a woman, touching and expressing creation together.

...*There is only a man and a woman, touching and expressing creation together.* In Islam, we also see aspects of Man and Woman Balance. In verse 35:11 it states: *God created you from dust, then from a little germ. Into two sexes He divided you. No female conceives or is delivered without His knowledge. No man grows old or has his life cut short but in accordance with His decree. All this is easy enough for God.* In verse 51:49: *All things have been created in pairs so you may reflect on it.* Can you capture the procreative essence here? Very similar to Matthew 19:4-6 in the Bible, I think. But, and here is the important question: *Is it Procreant to Life? Can the two become as one...become as two...as one...?* I ask this because there is another verse in the Koran that, I believe, has carried the day of the Islamic religion for centuries. This verse states: 4:34. *Men have authority over women because God has made one superior to the other, and because they spend their wealth to maintain them. Good women are obedient. They guard their unseen parts because God has guarded them. As for those from whom you fear disobedience, admonish them and send them to beds apart and beat them. Then if they obey you, take no further action against them. Surely God is high, supreme.* Can you feel the imbalance in that verse—the imbalance that compels a man to bury his wife or daughter up to her neck in sand and stone her to death if he decides there and been some type of disobedience to his "honor"? Or compels a man to strap a suicide vest onto a young boy or girl and have that boy or girl go into some crowded place and blow themselves up along with many others? Or compels someone to shoot into a crowd of defenseless people to which he may disagree while shouting *Allāhu Akbar* (God is great), as recently happened in Orlando, Florida? Or compels men in the name of their caliphate to the burn alive nineteen kidnapped Yazidi girls in metal cages for refusing to have sex with them. Another recent event. This comes from that person's inner hate of himself and the world. This inner hate is really an inner (sexual) imbalance. Specifically, one's standing with his or her polar opposite (eternal sexual other half) is imbalanced. One holds that other as inferior and therefore one, supposedly, is somehow entitled to the special privilege—like the fulfillment of that one's needs regardless of who must pay for it. We aren't speaking of love and freedom here. We are speaking of an imbalanced relationship with one side as master and the other side as slave—with one *forcing* the other to meet his or her needs. It is called submission. Islam/Sharia Law is not a religion of peace but of submission. Submit or else. Your right to choose is not available. You will not be allowed to own your own soul. Your autonomy will be smothered. Everywhere you turn you will run into force and thievery, another's upon you. Such is your plight. Force and thievery are the only things that arise from any imbalance. The use of initial force is always to steal. Murder is a form of stealing from another as is rape, looting, discrimination, etc. Returning to the Muslim religion, or any religion, the only solution available is to balance the two sexual parts. And you know what? The balancing of the sexual two can be done in the twinkling of an eye. All it takes is a paradigm shift, an abstraction—or two! That is it.

So when advocates of a religion claim there is an outside of, a prior to, or a difference from and, furthermore, it is not one we can know or comprehend but we can believe in (faith) or that it is something we can experience (without thought), those advocates are only denying the direct sexual (procreant) touch (happening everywhere) that is the universal balance. Our educators and psychologists (Secular Humanists/Feminists) of today aren't any better. They advocate that there isn't any metaphysical truth, that everything is equal but not opposite. The result is the failure to make those critical distinctions that define different things and sustain life. Two distinctions mentioned in this writing are the distinction between production and consumption, i.e., the primacy of right as to the primacy of need and the fundamental and metaphysical distinction between a male and a female. The result of Feminism in the sexual arena is the Lesbian, Gay, Bisexual, Transgender, and Queer (L,G,B,T,Q) movement. Their point is that gender is not to be considered metaphysical in its nature (of the fundamental order) but is fluid. That is to say we are not necessarily born constituting our own sexuality. Sexuality/gender is something that can be altered, they suggest. Here are a few quotes I have gathered over the years on this subject.

There is no relevant difference between same-sex couples and two-sex couples.

Being queer means pushing the parameters of sex, sexuality, and family, and in the process, transforming the very fabric of society... We must keep our eyes on the goal...of radically reordering society's views of reality.

It isn't enough to become parallel to straights. We want to obliterate such dichotomies altogether.

What the L,G,B,T,Q community is saying is that the essence of reality is non-binary, not a one of polar (sexual) opposites. (I just heard on the news that a student came out as non-binary to the President!!!) This would mean that sexuality/gender is not something metaphysical in nature but is rather fluid (equal but not opposite). That really is the agenda of the L,G,B,T,Q movement, to separate man and woman, i.e., the procreant process, from its metaphysical base as comprising the nature of reality. Remember just recently (June 26, 2015) when the Supreme Court of the United States recognized same-sex marriage, the lights of the rainbow flag lite up over the Whitehouse. (Who planned all that?) This was a signal as to which way the wind was blowing, especially for the powers that be in running this country. But let's not forget the consequences here. In (attempting) to separate sex from procreation—and its holy spirit of love—we can only debase life. Let's not forget what Sigmund Freud (1856-1939) in *The Sexual Life of Human Beings* said to us:

Sigmund Freud (1856-1939)—*The Sexual Life of Human Beings*, 1920

The abandonment of the reproductive function is the common feature of all perversions. We actually describe a sexual activity as perverse if it has given up the aim of reproduction and pursues the attainment of pleasure as an aim independent of it. So, as you will see, the reach and turning point in the development of sexual life lies in becoming subordinate to the purpose of reproduction. Everything that happens before this turn of events and equally everything that disregards it and that aims solely at obtaining pleasure is given the uncomplimentary name of "perverse" and as such is proscribed.

This debasing of life is called depolarization. We see this in the porn industry. Ask yourself, why, at the end of the day, does porn collapse? Could it be that it lacks the spiritual component of procreative love at its center? That is exactly why it debases, collapses, and destroys everything it touches. Functional healthy life is polarized, always into male and female <u>binary</u> opposites, uniting and dividing together. Dysfunctional life is depolarized—into gender fluidity. Remember from *The 2008–2009 Articles—Love: The Law of Polar Opposites*, 2010, where it was stated:

Only (sexual) opposites can unite to then again divide...creating the spiritual lineage of (procreant) love. This is universal balance. This is love. This is not to suggest that every sexual act must produce a child. But this is to suggest that the original light/spiritual essence is itself the procreant process of male and female division and unification. My whole effort, and the purpose of my writings, is to sync up the spiritual with the procreative—and to do that we must place polarity (which is procreation) prior to "Spirit's Original Unity." You just can't have a "non-creative spiritual essence" (as the Church and L,G,B,T,Q have) hovering above the procreant process of life and love. Every touch, every glance, every thought, man to woman and woman to man, is a procreative act. *Procreation is the basis of creation.* Without procreation (and its two parts/forces of male and female) there isn't any life not to mention the lineage of life. L,G,B,T,Q takes us on a different path that can only lead to the denial/disintegration of life. Essentially, we lose our souls and connection to the eternal. Eternal life is procreant life. Our sense of "God"—meaning the transcendental here although I don't mean supernatural—becomes lost. And we lose our faith in LIFE. Do you know that it has already been suggested (and is playing out on some college campuses) that anyone holding a *belief* in two genders (and only two genders) is engaging in a discriminatory "action" and "hate thought" against "non-binary" people. We are so close to hate crimes legislation, i.e., thought and speech control—and transgender bathrooms! And so we lose our souls.

The Denial of Life

1. *The denial of the spiritual (metaphysical) union between male and female.*
2. *The separation of the sexual embrace from (spiritual, mental, and physical) reproduction.*
3. *The breaking of the requirement of a male and a female for the sexual embrace.*
4. *The inability to bring forth life.*

You see, we fail in life because we have the wrong absolute. It is not because we have an absolute, like the progressives and feminists would have you believe, but because we have a wrong absolute. It is imbalanced. It is not in support of life but in the denial of life. And so it should be noted that a wrong absolute, as a direct reflection of its imbalance, leads to a system of master and slave. Even in the feminist ideology, where the only absolute is that there aren't any absolutes, their absolute of "equality for all/difference for none" leads to fascism. It should be noted that in the L,G,B,T,Q movement we are quickly losing our freedom of expression and association. We are no longer able to say NO. You now have to serve a customer not just with your product but in celebration of that customer's values. Likewise, you now can be turned away from a business if it is determined that you have "anti-diversity" inclinations. Just the other day I was reading an article in Crisis Magazine that stated, "The Commission on Human Rights in New York City has declared thirty-one official kinds of sexual identity, mandating the use of the "non-binary" pronoun "zie" instead of "he" and she" and threatening fines of up to $250,000 for not adopting this grammar." The fascism is back! Well, it really never left now did it? And let's not forget how tax dollars are used to support abortion clinics (even selling baby's body parts!) and for "sexual re-assignment surgery." Brave New World is upon us. This next article, *Gender Dysphoria and Hope,* is by Joe Bissonnette, a teacher of religion and philosophy at Assumption College School in Brantford, Ontario. It should be noted that Canada is about ten years ahead of the USA in its feminist progression.

"Oh my God. I'm home. All the time ... you finally really did it.
You maniacs.
You blew it up. Damn you. G-d damn you all to hell."

Wearing only a loincloth and a look of despair Charlton Heston slides off his horse and falls to his knees. Still on the horse sits a beautiful but speechless woman, a complete innocent, an almost sub-human heir of culture long since obliterated and forgotten.

The <u>closing scene</u> from *The Planet of the Apes* is intensely powerful and deeply ironic. At one level it is every man's dream; post-apocalyptic and therefore unencumbered by any social obligations, heroic, sensual. But at another level it is a tragic and terrifying nightmare; a shocking blow to the myth of Western perpetuity. All could be lost. Great cultures can blow themselves up—or perhaps in our case, implode.

Culture includes what we do every day, but also what we think is important, what we think is right and wrong, what we believe. And most of this is based on received tribal wisdom. In "The 10 Principles of Conservatism," Russell Kirk paraphrases Edmund Burke: "The individual is foolish but the species is wise. Prejudices and prescriptions and presumptions are the instruments which the wisdom of the species employs to safeguard man against his own passions and appetites." We learn without necessarily understanding the significance of our culture's prejudices. We occupy and are encompassed by culture, more like a body in water than a curious sampler at a buffet. Of course we know that we should transcend culture, that we should make our way out of the cave and gain critical distance, but this itself is often a false consciousness, a picture of a picture, but the bigger picture is also framed by the culture. For the most part this is good. We are not meant to be alone even in our minds. If left to ourselves, without the fear of shame that was the first effect of Original Sin, few if any would behave nobly, but culture can help us become noble.

And just as individuals need to be held accountable by culture, culture needs to develop within an older living tradition. G.K. Chesterton said that the future can only be seen in the shining shields of the past. He said that tradition was the democracy of the dead because through it we hear wisdom distilled through ages of triumph and failure and that we must "refuse to submit to the small and arrogant oligarchy of those who happen to be walking about."

But the authority of tradition has become like a shadow at noon. Every new technology is a sacrament affirming the universal creed that what is old is obsolete and what is new is superior. We are transfixed by the unfolding technological horizon. We are floating, there is no fixed point, no rootedness. Unsure of our physical world we have become unsure of ourselves because we too are physical. The only constant is change and the only certainty is that everything is developmental; there are no permanent things. And so we are limp, expressionless, and voiceless as things that formerly would have enervated wash over us.

Guidelines for Mandatory LGBTQ Policies in Alberta Schools gives a fine example of the late decadence which swirls like a celestial black hole, sucking in and annihilating everything.

It reads: "Students have the right to self-identify their gender and be addressed by the name and pronoun of their choice...."

The first thing we notice about another human being is their maleness or femaleness. In the order of being this objective fact falls somewhere between "I exist" and awareness of the elapse of time. It is a cornerstone for a correlation between perception and reality. But all must be eclipsed by the LGBTQ gods. Make no mistake, when the high priests of oppression and grievance require you to deny what is plain to every eye, they are requiring you to deny nature and truth, they are claiming the authority of the supernatural and we are being forced to recite their creed.

It continues: "...students may dress in clothing and participate on sports teams that reflect their gender identity and expression."

Over and above nature, one of the greatest achievements of Western culture was the gentleness and courtesy men extended to women. On average, men have 60 percent more upper body strength and are naturally more aggressive, but this was strictly contained. To use strength to overpower a woman was despicable and any man who did so would be thoroughly subdued and humiliated. But no longer. Since maleness and femaleness and the different obligations these facts entail have been replaced by the kaleidoscope madhouse of gender subjectivity and gender fluidity there are no longer restraints. And on this point, the Alberta Ministry of Education is merely imitating a global trend.

In a January 26, 2016 Lifesite article, Steve Weatherbe reports: "The International Olympic Committee...has ruled that "so-called male-to-female transgender athletes already allowed in the Olympics since 2012 after castration and two years of hormone therapy, will be allowed in the Rio Olympics without surgery as long as their testosterone has been below male levels for a year..."

Gender ideologues have enacted a near totalitarian mind control, inverting the most obvious facts and subverting the most important restraints and obligations. But surely there must remain some echo of sanity and decency on the ground, where people live? Not so. The January 13, 2016 CBC news article reporting on LGBTQ policies for Alberta schools put the policy document in context.

> Last year an Edmonton transgender student's wish to use the girl's washroom at her Catholic elementary school pushed the issue of gender inclusive policies into the spotlight. The seven-year-old girl was originally told she had to use a single-stall washroom at the school. But the principal relented after public outcry.

In other words, a public outcry arose when the principal at a Catholic elementary school provided a separate washroom for a 7-year-old boy who thought he was a girl, rather than confirm his madness and have him use the girl's washroom with all the girls.

The Alberta Ministry of Education has replaced the terms "mother" and "father" with parent, caregiver or partner and has added "ze," "zir," "hir," "they," "them" and "Mx" to he, her, Mr. and Ms. And only God can help you if you don't abide.
Blogger Charolette Allen writes:

> If you're a girl and you don't like the idea of someone in the shower room who claims to be a girl but looks exactly like a boy anatomically, you're the one who has to move. A student who objects to sharing a washroom or change-room with a student who is trans or gender-diverse is offered an

alternative facility. And also, adults who claim to belong to a different sex from the one they anatomically resemble get to be in the shower room too!

There is a small minority for whom tradition still has some resonance, but we are in a freefall, unable to compete with the modernist vision. We may have hoped that things would stabilize on the low but sturdy ground of enlightened self-interest and that parents would protect their children, even if only as extensions of themselves, but all manner of madness prevails. Is this the twilight of our culture? Are we on the brink of a dark age in which vandals will smash all that is orderly, true and beautiful? Maybe, maybe not. Again, the wisdom of Edmund Burke may offer hope. In 1795 Burke wrote of the resilience of states:

> At this very moment when some of them seem plunged in unfathomable abysses of disgrace and disaster, they have suddenly emerged. They have begun a new course, and opened a new reckoning; and even in the depths of their calamity, and on the very ruins of their country, they have laid the foundations of a towering and durable greatness. All of this has happened without any apparent previous change in the general circumstances that had brought on their distress. The death of a man at a critical juncture, his disgust, his retreat, his disgrace, have brought innumerable calamities on a whole nation. A common soldier, a child, a girl at the door of an inn, have changed the face of fortune, and almost of Nature.

Though our culture may at the moment be unhinged from tradition and sanity, we ourselves can look into the shining shields of the past and imitate the noble few who throughout history proclaimed the truth with joy and without fear, and unexpectedly, altered the course of history.

And there is more. This next article is from the Crisis Magazine website, 7/14/16, titled *Secularism as Religious Indoctrination* by Kenneth Crowther.

Australia has a program in its schools that, at first glance, you'd have to be crazy to be against. It's called Safe Schools, and it is an anti-bullying campaign.

Well, at least that's how it has been promoted.

In reality, Safe Schools has become a pro-LGBTQI indoctrination system designed by one academic Marxist with hopes of replacing the Australian flag with a red one, and another who has, in academic theory, supported pedophilia. The program consists of: allowing students to wear whatever uniforms that they want; encouraging schools to allow bathroom use by any gender; promoting homosexual and transgender role-play in the classroom with students as young as eleven, and points children to this website, which endorses chest-binding, penis tucking, and (at one point) contained links to a website called the "tool shed," an online shop for the purchasing of sex-toys.

I kid you not.

Oh, and the best part? Schools that are participating in the pilot program can have their identities concealed. That's right. As pointed out here, all schools participating in Queensland are unnamed. This 'anti-bullying' campaign is so positive that the government decided it would not reveal which schools are participating. *Not even to the parents of children enrolled in the school.*

The outcry in Australia has been huge, and many major players behind the program have realized that they have played their hand a little too early. In fact, after an official inquiry, the program has already been altered.

The changes notwithstanding, the anti-bullying campaign is actually resulting in bullying—of the children who feel uncomfortable about participating—sometimes even by their teachers.

Stories are rolling in from around the nation detailing the explicit nature of what is being taught. One such story is of a heterosexual thirteen-year-old boy doing some research on his home computer. His homework? To "find a picture of a male celebrity on the internet and explain to the entire class why he is sexually attracted to that male."

And much of this is without parents' consent, and is not optional.

On the flipside, religious education in state schools *is* optional. Not only is it optional, but there have been numerous attempts to reject the involvement of religions, in particular Christianity, from schools. Recently a man took his complaint against government supported school chaplains all the way to the High Court.

I wonder what he would have to say about Safe Schools? Because, you see, the thing is—Safe Schools *is* religious education.

The so-called 'secular' is not *a-religious*, it is religious. The point has been made many times in the past, and made recently and clearly by James K. A. Smith, who determines the religiosity of secular systems by recognizing their liturgies. But not only does secularism have liturgical practice, it also contains much of what would commonly be pointed to as primary foundations required by religion: creation, fall, gods, sects, atonement, and redemption.

The Creation Myth
I say myth, because that's the word that the academics use to denote religious creation stories. They're myths because they're unproven. Just like the random nothingness that

created everything according to the secularists. In the beginning was nothing. And nothing said, "Let there be quarks, gluons, and Higgs-Bosons," and there was. And nothing saw it and said ... nothing. And then all the bits that came from nothing exploded, and suddenly there was everything. And nothing saw it and said ... nothing.

The Pantheon and its Sects

Like other religions, there is not just one god in Secularism, but many: the god of sex, worshipped by the thronging ignorant masses; the god of technology, followed by the transhumanists; the god of nature, idolized by the environmentalists, and the god of academia, revered by the Marxists.

The Sacrificial Atonement System

The secularist religion, like others, believes in a form of sacrificial atonement. Whereas for many religions it's animals, and for Christians it was Christ, the secularist's sacrificial system is much cleaner. Each year millions of tiny human babies are sacrificed on the altar of applied science, and each sacrifice is dedicated to a particular demi-god. The sex-worshippers abort to further their sexual liberation; the transhumanists in order to carry out experiments to further their scientific progress; the Marxists because babies are nothing but oppressive shackles that remind us of the constraints of gender, and the environmentalists because there are too many people in the world. Interestingly when they speak of reducing the population for the sake of Sumatran Tigers, they never themselves climb upon the sacrificial altar and give up their lives. Babies are much more convenient. And much less like them.

The Fall

Just as in Christianity, the secularists know that something is wrong with us. They don't know what exactly, but it is clear through their rhetoric that humanity is not quite what it should be. Each of the sects has a different answer for this: the Marxists say that it's inequality and oppression; the environmentalists say its man's abuse of nature; the transhumanists say it's nature's abuse of man; the sex-worshippers say it's sexual repression, and the nihilists say it

THE MAN AND WOMAN MANIFESTO

doesn't matter.

The Main God
At its heart, the religion of Secularism follows itself. That is, it worships humanity. If a religion is marked by a zealous love of the god at its head, then Secularism is clearly a religion, as it is marked by a zealous love for oneself. To love yourself is the answer to all of life's problems. The major teachers preach this from the pulpit of the media on a daily basis. Ellen tells us to be true to ourselves. Oprah's website reminds us that you can't love others until you love yourself. The individual—you—are at the heart of your own worship. No wonder so many people are jumping onto the Secularist bandwagon. This is a religion that promises to cost nothing and gain everything.

The Redemption Story
Redemption is where, like many religions, the denominations of Secularism start to disagree. Where the environmentalist says that redemption from our brokenness will come when we are at one with nature in a harmonious coexistence, transhumanism says the opposite:

"If it is natural to die," said FM-2030, (a transhumanist who rejected his human name and replaced it with 2030 in the belief he would live for one hundred years to see the year 2030), "then to hell with nature. Why submit to its tyranny? We must rise above nature. We must refuse to die."

Death is evidence of the fall, and it is death that must be conquered. Eternal life is the goal, just as in most religions, and it is the transhumanist sect that is doing the best and most important work to achieve this goal. The redemption of humanity will come when humanity has eternity in its grasp, and this will be achieved through applied science and technology. I said earlier that the sex-worshippers were the largest sect, and they are. But every member of every sect also has a little idol of technology in their home, and usually one in their pocket. They sacrifice their time to it daily. According to the secularist, it is technology—through the genius of humanity—that will be the savior of our species.

The Default Religion

Secularism is in no ways above religion; it operates on the religious level, and fulfils all of the same basic functions. For this reason, Safe Schools is not the only 'religious' element of secularism in schools. The fact is that there is no such thing as 'religiously neutral' education. All education is religious, and such a claim is not new. In fact, as Christopher Dawson pointed out in *The Crisis of Western Education*, John Dewey, "in spite of his secularism, had a conception of education which was almost purely religious."

As G.K. Chesterton wrote, "When you stop believing in God, you don't believe in nothing, you believe in anything." It is also true that when you stop worshipping God, you don't worship nothing, you worship anything—usually yourself.

That is what Safe Schools is doing. It is teaching a zealous self-worship. It is no less religious that Islam, Christianity or Judaism.

In Australia, perhaps our schools will be a lot 'safer' when we recognize that there is no such thing as value-neutral education. As warped as the program is, it would make more sense if it were included as a part of opt-in religious education, and if the secularists finally admitted that they are not neutral. They are yet another religion with their own worship to fulfill, sacrifices to make and redemption to enact. They have a mission, to go out into the world and fill it with their disciples. And our schools are their seminaries.

Father, forgive them; for they know not what they do. (Luke 23:34) Shall we change that verse to read: *Father, forgive us; for we know what we do and do it anyway*—basing identities on "attractions" and "feelings" without looking at the underlying denials, hurts, and rejections. And what are the consequences (to one's soul) of such a policy? Is anyone asking that? The following quote is from The Patriot Post website.

Speaking of science, Dr. Paul McHugh of Johns Hopkins Medical School explains, "Transgendered men do not become women, nor do transgendered women become men. All (including Bruce Jenner) become feminized men or masculinized women, counterfeits or impersonators of the sex with which they 'identify.' In that lies their problematic future." Furthermore he writes, "Ten to fifteen years after surgical reassignment, the suicide rate of those who had undergone sex-reassignment surgery rose to twenty times that of comparable peers." Leftists think they're removing the influences that cause that suicide rate, but they're only enabling and normalizing a destructive pathology.

So it turns out, as it always does with socialism, that (sexual) equality, fraternity, diversity, and tolerance are allowed to go only one way. That is always how it is with the feminist/progressive types—consent is a one-way street. "We value Diversity—All are welcome here," their signs read. It should have added to it, "unless, of course, you don't believe as we do." In other words, the L,G,B,T,Q agenda is a forced compliance, one's consent must be coerced, just like in Masculinism. The one thing the Masculinists and Feminists have in common is that they are more than willing to force another's choice. They just cannot let another be *free to choose*. In fact, they can't stand the idea of freedom itself. For them, freedom, no matter the cost, must not be allowed. Neither can excellence, honor, truth, or even (the sovereign) family be allowed! And even Christianity, with all it talk about the necessity of the family, cannot and will not stop this L,G,B,T,Q onslaught on the family. Just the other day (4/8/16) Pope Francis released his Magna Carta on the family—*Amoris Laetitia.* Pope Francis is a beautiful defender of marriage and family love. And he is right except for one thing. He has marriage and family on the 2nd tier rather than the 1st tier that I place them on. On the 1st tier he has the non-sexual, non-procreative God the Father, God the Son, and God the Holy Spirit. Until we understand that the metaphysical structure of the universe is Man and Woman Balance, i.e., marriage and family itself, we cannot defend it from the L.G,B,T,Q onslaught that seeks to destroy that beautific vision of marriage and family called life. One must wonder why the collective suicide of the West is so essential to the masculinists and feminists alike. They are doing a good job. This next quote is from *The 2008-2009 Articles—Homosexuality is not a Sexuality*, 2010.

> *Neither Masculinism nor Feminism, in any of its forms, can bring us to a true union (fullness) where the two become as one. Union of opposites is a metaphysic issue concerning the order/nature of the universe itself. Call that order a dual or a primary or a two forces or a 1st pair—it is the primordial male and female. Our purpose as man and woman pairs is to touch in love and in so doing create life together.*

There are three choices in the universe, and only three. Two of them are sexually imbalanced. (In general, Masculinism resides on the side of the haves, the royalty types who believe in their own privilege; usually Republicans in our political world. Feminism resides on the side of the Have-nots, the social progressives/Democrats who want to spread everyone else's stuff around.) Only one is balanced to life. This next quote is from *The Universal Religion: The Final Destiny of Mankind*, 1994, 2010.

> *The simple problem with homosexuality is that it is not procreative to life. You cannot begin or base a universe on two males alone or two females alone—there isn't any force (difference) there. Without the two (equal but opposite) forces there just isn't any charge or life dynamic. Male, by definition, is always in relation to female and vice versa. Two men together cannot unite the two. Two women together cannot divide the one. This fact of life is absolute. Homosexuality is not creative to life—a child cannot be born from it. What more needs to be said? There just isn't any (metaphysical) liberation out of the creative process of male and female individualization and unification that brings each of us into birth (individual sexual form) to begin with.*

No one can judge you if you have here-to-for made a misguided choice. You did not know, did you? None of us have known. But now...now we can know... Homosexuality/Feminism is depolarizing. It fails to make the critical linkage between sexual (polar) difference and procreation and, as such, denies both the sexual nature of all things and the necessity of the actual order of the universe being procreative in its origin. Again, let us review this quote used earlier from *Man, Woman, and God: The Eternal Marriage*, 1994, 2010:

> *The spiritual connection is a connection between a man and a woman whereby they recognize their eternal creation and love together. It is based in their sexual differentiation from and creative need for each other. In this, a man and woman have life purpose together. They are the co-creators of all that is. The formed universe moves through them. They together hold the balance on which all life depends. The world moves one step forward into the light with just one touch of their love.*

And we do know... continuing with *The Universal Religion: The Final*

Destiny of Mankind, 1994, 2010:

> *...This touch is the truth of life. There isn't any greater truth than life. In the universal religion, only the two forces exist expressing their love and their life. There isn't anything else but a male and a female in creative balance. Nothing else is recognized for nothing else exists. This perfect state of creative balance is known as God. Why? Because from this balance a child can be born.*

My use of the word "God" in this quote does not mean I am insinuating a singular and separate "God." It would be better perhaps to use the term "God-process" or one order. Remember, there is not a singular anything. *There is not a single fundamental primordial creative force in the universe, i.e., energy, desire, motive, impulse, purpose, impetus, drive, intention, nature, will, consciousness, Prana, mana, Ki, Chi, Waken, bioplasma, light, cosmic energy, life force, vital pulse, or Holy Spirit. There is only one force in relationship to another force from which creation may then occur. We have to date made a critical mistake in not noting this elementary fact within our conception of order.*—taken from *The Two Forces of Creation* used in a previous chapter. So now we come to our own choice in *life*. What shall it be I wonder? If you listen to the L,G,B,T,Q crowd, their parties and parades, they essentially are saying, "Anything but procreation; anything but life." Why might that be, I wonder? The following selection is from *Meditations for Deepening Love* titled *The Choice*.

The Choice

Once upon a time there lived a boy. By his very nature he was a curious lad, wanting to know everything, but especially wanting to know *the truth*. He could often be seen pacing back and forth in his room uttering to himself, *"I need to know the truth."*

This issue of the truth weighed heavily on the boy's mind for, you see, he was coming into manhood. It was the custom in the village where he lived that every young man had to make a choice. It was required that each young man go before the whole village and state the commitment of his life. So, too, did this young man.

This boy was aware of the three choices available to him. All the boys in the village were taught at a very early age about the three choices. But for some reason, he never felt satisfied by them. He thought that he would go speak to the council of elders. Certainly they could help him decide.

The next day the boy set off to the council of elders. There were three elders, one representing each choice. The boy needed to talk to them— the elders knew he was still undecided and they wanted to help him. The village meeting was only one day away. He was received by the elders and sat before them. The first elder spoke, "I know how your heart is troubled. Only God can soothe your heart and bring peace to your soul. Follow God. God will show you the way. Tomorrow, when you go before the village you must turn your life over to God."

The boy listened carefully. In a moment the second elder spoke saying, "It is your duty to help those in need. We are all part of a community. Each of us must work together for the good of all. Let the people be your guide. Tomorrow, for your own sake, I suggest you give your life to the people."

Now it was the third elder's time to speak. With a smile he said to the boy, "Your other elders are always placing obligations upon you. Liberate yourself. Come join us and be free of all oppression and constraint. Give your life to your brothers by declaring yourself proudly "gay." Tomorrow, when you make your decision, remember, we only want to love you."

The next day had arrived. The boy found himself in front of the whole village. It was now his time to declare his choice and enter into manhood. The other young men had already chosen. He now stood alone, silently. His mind raced frantically. He could not decide. Suddenly he shouted, *"I need to know the truth. Which choice is the truth?"* No one spoke up, not even the elders. Again the boy spoke, *"Does anyone know the truth?"*

There was some commotion amongst the villagers. Someone was trying to wade through the crowd. Suddenly, a young woman emerged and stood in front of the young man. Everyone was surprised for it was quite improper for a woman to speak out without permission. But this woman spoke without hesitancy saying, *"I don't know about the truth but, if you allow me, I will follow you."*

The young man was stunned. He had never heard of such a thing. *"You will follow me?"* he asked. *"Yes,"* she replied, *"to wherever you may go."* Upon hearing these words, the young man took the woman's hand and said to her, *"Let me then give my life to you."*

The elders were shocked. "You can't do that," they screamed. But the villagers slowly began to cheer and soon the elders could no longer be heard. The young man and woman raised their clasped hands in acknowledgment as the man whispered to the woman, *"Thank you for revealing to me the truth."*

The Healing Light

Metaphysical (spiritual) imbalance is our spiritual disease. You can call it the original sin if you want. It consists of a dark spot upon our very souls. Unfortunately, we can't really see it. But make no mistake, we do believe in it and act from it. As long as our hearts and souls are colored with self-other imbalance we will only know that reality—as our own inner pain. As said, love, life, and freedom only arise out of the two-force balance. As our wonderful teacher instructed us: *This is my commandment, That ye love one another, as I have loved you.* (John 15:12) You see, we are not to worship Jesus per se, we are to love one another. *God is love*, as I was taught as a boy. God does not constitute a superior/inferior hierarchy—which worship always leads to. Let look at some other Biblical verses.

> **1 John 4: 7:** *Beloved, let us love one another: for love is of God; and every one that loveth is born of God, and knoweth God.*

> **1 John 4: 8:** *He that loveth not knoweth not God; for God is love.*

> **1 John 4: 12:** *No man hath seen God at any time. If we love one another, God dwelleth in us, and his love is perfected in us.*

> **1 John 4: 16:** *And we have known and believed the love that God hath to us. God is love; and he that dwelleth in love dwelleth in God, and God in him.*

> **1 John 4:18:** *There is no fear in love: but perfect love casteth out fear: because fear hath torment. He that feareth is not made perfect in love.*

> **1 John 4: 20:** *If a man say, I love God, and hateth his brother, he is a liar: for he that loveth not his brother whom he hath seen, how can he love God whom he hath not seen?*

> **1 John 4: 21:** *And this commandment have we from him, That he who loveth God love his brother also.*

As Walter Russell stated, *...Man conceives a perfect and omnipotent God. A perfect and omnipotent God could not create imperfection. He could not create a lesser than Himself. He could not create a greater than Himself. God could not create other than Himself. God did not create other* *than Himself, nor greater, nor lesser than Himself.* You see, it is our choice. You get to choose which teeter-totter drawing you want to live by. Now, how many of us have made the choice to love? How many of us have made the choice to allow others the freedom to choose over their own economic matters? Have you made the choice for your own wealth and health? Have you made the choice to view others as spiritually perfect? "Oh, but my problems are not really my fault," you say. Oh really. Well, who made the choice? Who made the choice to steal from or spit on another's soul? Who actually did the deed? This is what happens to us in the spiritual disease of self-other imbalance. We become trapped in our own imbalance. Rather than "love ye one another," we "hate ye one another." This is what I call *spiritual lack.* It runs our lives. It is played out through our own Victimization Cycle of lack-blame-demand-attack-deny. Does that sound familiar? We walk through life on the treadmill of the Victimization Cycle. As American writer Henry David Thoreau stated, *"Most men lead lives of quiet desperation and go to the grave with the song still in them."* And so we hate another for it and the motto of our lives becomes, *"It's your fault."* Isn't that what Marx's proletariat were saying? Did they have grievances? You bet they did. But did they want to look into their own souls first? Because they did not millions of people were killed. How about the L,G,B,T,Q movement? Or Black Lives Matter? Can they first go to that place in their own hearts and souls whereupon they can view the OTHER as spiritually perfect before they begin their rant? How about the Muslims, they view themselves as downtrodden, don't they. Can they look upon the "great Satan" and decide that they are really only looking in the mirror? Or how about our politicians and bankers, attorneys and judges, can they really begin to serve the people? *The balance—you can never find love while in judgment/blame of another.*

The next quote is from *Healing In The Light—The (Homo) Sexual Wound,* 1998. As you read this quote please know that you can put most anything in the place of *(homo)sexual* wound. You can put in Christian wound, Muslim wound, Hindu wound, etc., Secular Humanist wound, L,G,B,T,Q wound, racial wound, national wound, ...and so on, all of those imbalanced identity positions that we cling to.

> *We must look at the (homo)sexual wound—all of us. We must ask ourselves when we decided to deny our eternal other half and reject the love that is procreative to life. This is our existential pain... It's an issue (or denial) of procreative accountability. But homosexuality is what your generation (and all of us) must (spiritually) go through to finally and fully realize*

the sexed-electric (procreative) nature of the universe. This is a sexual dividing/uniting universe between the two universal forces of male and female.

I have often thought that homosexuality and the like, including religion (and Marxism/secular humanism is as much a religion as anything), is just about one not wanting to be alone. We all want to know someone is walking with us, accepting us, loving us, etc. When someone says, "I am gay," or "I am a Christian," aren't they just saying, "Someone, anyone, please, walk with me?" Someone is walking with each one of us. That someone is our sexual (equal and opposite) other half. Do you get it? *Our healing lies in the sexual balance, man and woman giving and receiving from each other in this moment right now.* If you are not with your equal and opposite partner right now, please know that you (spiritually) always are. *This is a sexual dividing/uniting universe between the two universal forces of male and female.* In short, all spiritual healing comes down to this moment in your giving-receiving balance/love with your eternal other half.

Spiritual Healing is only always Love!

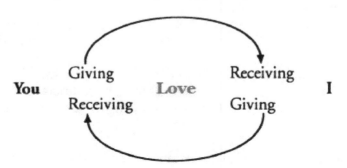

Love is the only state of existence between Male and Female.

Where two or more are gathered is the Christ moment, is the miracle. Here is the actual verse from Matthew 18:20: *For where two or three are gathered together in my name, there am I in the midst of them.* Christ is a two if you will. Isn't this what Jesus knew? Not a one singular "God/savior" but an <u>interdependent</u> two. The miracle of Jesus was that he saw "the other" as the Christ as well. There was a *togetherness*, the giving to and receiving from, that is love, i.e., the Christ moment. The way to approach Jesus is by saying: *Thank you, Jesus, for allowing me to see the Christ in you. And thank you for seeing the Christ in me as well.* If we really wanted to get this right we might say: *Thank you Eternal Father <u>and</u> Divine Mother for creating me (and everyone) in your perfect image.* We must get to the perfect balance which is love. Below is a text I sent to a special friend of mine.

> *As you go about your day, begin with saying, "I can give love to another and receive love from another." Say it many times throughout the day. This is your anchor or source point. This puts you in universal balance with all things and lifts that karma/negativity from your soul. This is your declaration that you, too, have primary love as you also acknowledge it in another. See the balance? Most religions begin from a singular "God." Man and Woman Balance begins from two primary forces—a paradigm shift. You, too, are one of the two primaries. Your love, too, is divine love. This must be your understanding.*

Spiritual healing, which is all healing, is that perfect balance that arises in the giving and receiving of love, one to another. Salvation, as it were, is a *togetherness*. Or shall we say an *eternal* togetherness. *Man and Woman Balance is an eternal togetherness.* It is an <u>us</u> point, *a connection together.* This is where our faith stands. This is where answered prayer stands. Answered prayer actually comes from our inner spiritual perfection. Spiritual perfection is also spiritual healing. Spiritual healing is also a purity, a purity of heart and soul. Physical healing comes to us with the spiritual purification of our souls which is Man and Woman Balance. Spiritual healing emanates outward from our cores healing everything in its path by releasing imbalance/impurity/stress/disease. Physical disease, in a nutshell, is an acid/alkaline imbalance. Today many of us are too acid. We have putrefied, sluggish blood. We are not oxygenated. This is also what we are seeing with the oceans of the world, too acid, not enough oxygen. The Russell's warned us about this years ago, sounding the alarm concerning nuclear power.

Walter and Lao Russell--*Atomic Suicide?*, 1957

Radiation is the normal death principle. Everything in Nature dies normally by slowly radiating its heat. Radioactivity is the explosively quick death principle. Radioactivity is man's discovery of how the human race can die quickly, and not be able to propagate its kind for many long centuries.

...All things in Nature die normally by slow expansion.

Radioactivity is multiplied expansion, which is caused by multiplied compression. It helps man die from explosively quick expansion. Flame is caused by maximum compression. Flame is the ultimate consumer of all bodies.

...Multiplied expansion means helping matter to expand quickly, and that is what radioactivity is. The use of nuclear fission, therefore, vastly multiplies the difficulty of living things to keep alive, by vastly aiding them to die.

...but you can no more be protected from it than you could protect the dryness of earth from becoming wet when it rains. Neither can this planet be protected from the rise in its whole temperature, which alone would so change the earth's environment that all life would be impossible.

Following is an article titled *Fukushima: Worse Than a Disaster* by Robert Hunziker, June 7, 2016. I found this on the website— www.counterpunch.org

Disasters can be cleaned up.

Naohiro Masuda, TEPCO Chief of Decommissioning at Fukushima Diiachi Nuclear Power Plant, finally publicly "officially" announced that 600 tons of hot molten core, or corium, is missing (Fukushima Nuclear Plant Operator Says

600 Tons of Melted Fuels is Missing, *Epoch Times,* May 24, 2016).

Now what?

According to Gregory Jaczko, former head of the U.S. Nuclear Regulatory Commission (NRC), it is not likely the fuel will ever be recovered: "Nobody really knows where the fuel is at this point, and this fuel is still very radioactive and will be for a long time."

A big part of the problem is that nobody has experience with a Fukushima-type meltdown, which now appears to be 100% meltdown, possibly burrowed into the ground, but nobody really knows for sure.

What's next is like a trip into The Twilight Zone.

"The absolutely uncontrollable fission of the melted nuclear fuel assemblies continue somewhere under the remains of the station. 'It's important to find it as soon as possible,' acknowledged Masuda, admitting that Japan does not yet possess the technology to extract the melted uranium fuel," (600 Tons of Melted Radioactive Fukushima Fuel Still Not Found, Clean-Up Chief Reveals, RT, May 24, 2016).

Nuclear fission is when atoms split apart into smaller atoms. With nuclear bombs, fission must happen extremely quickly to charge a large explosion whereas, in a nuclear reactor, fission must happen very slowly to make heat, which, in turn, is used to boil water to make steam to turn a turbine to generate electricity.

Eventually, by rubbing two sticks together, one can boil water, but modern-day society doesn't have the patience, which means accepting risks leaps and bounds beyond rubbing two sticks together. Welcome to an altered world.

Even if Masuda's cleanup crew find the missing 600 tons, which is so highly radioactive that workers cannot even get close enough to inspect the immediate areas, then they need to construct, out-of-midair, the technology to extract it, and then what? It's guesswork. It's what modern-day society has been reduced to, guesswork. Toss out rubbing two sticks together and build monstrous behemoths for billions to boil water, and when it goes wrong, guess what to do next. What's wrong with this picture? Well, to start with, nobody knows what to do when all hell breaks loose.

They do not have the technology to extract it!

In 1986, Russian teams of workers found the melted corium of the Chernobyl Nuclear Power Plant's reactor core in the facility's lowest level. Whilst "frying 30 workers" along the way, they contained it just enough to prevent burrowing into the ground, maybe.

During containment work at Chernobyl, a makeshift robotic camera managed to actually photograph the monster, the melted core, nicknamed "the Elephant's Foot." Thirty years after the fact, the "Elephant's Foot" is still lethal.

By way of comparing/contrasting Chernobyl and Fukushima, extraordinarily high radiation zaps and destroys robots at first sight when sent into Fukushima's containment vessels. It's kinda like the Daleks in Doctor Who.

Whereas, thirty years after the fact, Chernobyl seems to have found a solution to the elephant's foot menace to society, but as for Fukushima, they must first locate 600 tons of hot stuff. That may be an impossible task. Then what?

"Thirty years after the Chernobyl nuclear accident, there's still a significant threat of radiation from the crumbling remains of Reactor 4. But an innovative, €1.5 billion super-structure is being built to prevent further releases, giving an elegant engineering solution to one of the ugliest disasters known to man," Claire Corkhill, PhD, University of Sheffield, New Tomb Will Make Chernobyl Site Safe for 100 Years, Phys.Org, April 22, 2016.

As it happens, the older collapsing sarcophagus for Chernobyl is being replaced by a brand new enormous steel frame: "Thanks to the sarcophagus, up to 80% of the original radioactive material left after the meltdown remains in the reactor. If it were to collapse, some of the melted core, a lava-like material called corium, could be ejected into the surrounding area in a dust cloud, as a mixture of highly radioactive vapour and tiny particles blown in the wind. The key substances in this mixture are iodine-131, which has been linked to thyroid cancer, and cesium-137, which can be absorbed into the body, with effects ranging from radiation sickness to death depending on the quantity inhaled or ingested," Ibid

"The Elephant's Foot could be the most dangerous piece of waste in the world," (Chernobyl's Hot Mess, "the Elephant's Foot," is Still Lethal, Nautilus, Science Connect, Dec. 4, 2013). It's a highly charged radioactive massive hunk of goo that will not die or waste away. This could be a Doctor Who script, par excellence! Therein exist the soft underbelly, the vulnerability, and the risks of using nuclear power to boil water, or alternatively, the sun and wind could be used. They're not radioactive and still much faster than rubbing two sticks together.

Fukushima is three times (3x) Chernobyl, maybe more; however, in Fukushima's case there's a distinct possibility that its white-hot sizzling corium has already started burrowing into Earth. Thereafter, let your imagination run wild because nobody has any idea of how that ends, if ever!

But, Einstein knew. Here's a famous Einstein quote: "The unleashed power of the atom has changed everything save our modes of thinking, and we thus drift toward unparalleled catastrophes."

We're finally there!

Gregory Jackzo, former head of the NRC, ponders the security of nuclear power: "You have to now accept that in all nuclear power plants, wherever they are in the world … that you can have this kind of a very catastrophic accident, and you can release a significant amount of radiation and have a decade long cleanup effort on your hands" (Epoch Times).

Looking ahead a few years, the question remains: Where will the sizzling white-hot melted corium be when the Tokyo Olympics arrive in 2020?

Nobody knows!

Still, Prime Minister Abe told the Olympic selection committee that Fukushima was "under control."

"This debate has dogged him since his Sept. 7 speech to the International Olympic Committee, when he said the nuclear disaster is "under control." The next day, Tokyo won hosting rights for the 2020 Summer Olympic Games," (Tsuyoshi Inajjma and Yuriy Humber, Abe Olympic Speech On Fukushima Contradicts Nuclear Plant Design, Bloomberg, Oct. 23, 2013).

"French authorities are investigating payments worth around $2m to a company linked to the son of former world athletics chief Lamine Diack over alleged connections to Japan's successful bid to host the 2020 Olympic Games," (Tokyo Olympics Bid Questioned as Prosecutors Probe $2M Payouts, The Financial Times, May 12, 2016).

Japan won the right to host the 2020 Olympics with a bid to spend $5 billion, which is suspiciously small, especially in an historical context. For the record, rival Istanbul's bid was almost $20 billion, a much more realistic commitment for such a momentous worldly event.

Thusly, with mucho "balls-in-the-air," one has to wonder if PM Abe's infamous secrecy law will click into play, in other words, is there any way it can impede investigations? After all, the law allows any Japanese politician to put an offender behind bars for 10 years for breaking state secrets, which are (very embarrassingly) whatever the accuser claims to be "secretive." After all, prima facie, between Fukushima and the Olympics, there could be a lot of secretive stuff going on behind the scenes.

Japan's state secrecy law Act on the Protection of Specially Designated Secrets (SDS) Act No. 108 of 2013 passed on the heels of the Fukushima meltdown, is very similar to Japan's harsh Public Peace and Order Controls of WWII (a real doozy). According to Act No. 108, the "act of leaking itself" is bad enough for prosecution, regardless of what, how, or why. Absolutely, if someone "leaks," they're going to "the can."

Susumu Murakoshi, president of the Japan Federation of Bar Associations dissents: "The law should be abolished because it jeopardizes democracy and the people's right to know," Abe's Secrets Law Undermines Japan's Democracy, The Japan Times, Dec. 13, 2014.

The Japan Times needs to fact-check the definition of democracy.

Scary to say the least. Following is another article, this one from the Natural Mentor website, 7/3/16, on the issue of pesticides and bees. If this and the previous article are true, and I think they are, how can we be so off in our relation to nature, in our relations to each other? It boggles the mind.

Pesticides Are Causing Mass Honeybee Deaths

You might think that, by now, the honeybee colony collapse crisis is old news. If anything, though, it's not being discussed *enough*. Bee colony collapse is an ecological calamity that threatens life as we know it on this planet (and yes, even mainstream scientists are very worried).

The problem is continuing to escalate at a shocking rate: *42% of all bee colonies in the United States collapsed in 2015 alone, and scientists now believe that the extinction event towards which we're heading would jeopardize 75% of the world's food supply.*

It's hard to wrap our heads around this last statistic, because we're not consciously aware of the *essential* role played by pollinators in our food production system. But get this: one out of every three bites of food we take is the product of bee pollination, directly or indirectly—so a shortage of bees equals a *massive* shortage of food. The saddest part of this whole drama is that *we know what's causing bees to die in droves...and very little is being done about it.*

Pesticides, denialism, and corporate greed

While various factors are to blame for bee colony collapse—including habitat loss and climate change—the poisonous pesticides used *en masse* by the agricultural industry are by far the biggest culprits.

Systemic pesticides—especially *neonicotinoids*—appear to be the most harmful to bees. These pesticides are called "systemic" because they're designed to be absorbed into every part of the plant, where they can circulate through its tissues and thereby much more effectively kill any bug that comes into contact with it.

Unfortunately, this design allows systemic pesticides to infiltrate every aspect of an ecosystem, including honeybees and their hives. Evidence suggests that neonicotinoids are neurotoxic to bees, and furthermore that this toxicity severely compromises their immune systems (thus leaving them vulnerable to otherwise harmless pathogens).

Pesticide residues have consistently been found in the hives of collapsed bee colonies, thus conclusively linking the observed toxicity to these agricultural poisons.

You'd think finding this kind of evidence at the scene of the crime would be enough to slow the momentum of pesticide usage. Sadly, though, pesticide manufacturers like Bayer continue to deny that there's any connection between their product and bee deaths. They maintain that "all of the proteins used in insect-protected GM plants are tested for toxicity to honey bees," and that "GM crops have not been implicated in CCD [Colony Collapse Disorder]." Notice how they cleverly avoid discussing the effects of the *pesticides* that are applied to GM seeds? Meanwhile, as the mainstream swallows their propaganda, the *mountain* of evidence incriminating pesticides as the most significant contributing factor to bee colony collapse continues to grow.

Caught red-handed

Anyone who still believes that GM crops aren't "implicated" in the declining of bee populations should be shocked to learn what happened in Ontario in the spring of 2013 (well before the above statements were issued by pesticide companies).

When a mega-farm planted genetically modified corn using a process called "air seeding,"—one which can easily stir up neonicotinoid dust from the pretreated seeds—neighboring beekeepers watched *millions of bees* die within days.

One beekeeper alone lost *37 million bees* (600 entire hives)—and multiple research teams called to investigate the incident cited neonicotinoid pesticides as a direct cause of the collapse.

Researchers from Purdue University confirmed that the dead bees exhibited signs of neonicotinoid poisoning, and the local Pest Management Regulatory Agency even stated that pesticide-treated corn seed "contributed to the majority of bee mortalities."

Ontario has responded by becoming the first area in North America to regulate the sale and use of neonicotinoid-treated seeds.

There's only *one* good thing about this entire tragic story:

the cause of worldwide bee decimation is no longer a mystery. Neonicotinoid pesticides are clearly to blame, and stopping the planet's accelerating slide toward honeybee extinction is as simple as banning the use of these poisonous chemicals. The rest of North America (and the world, for that matter), would do well to follow in Ontario's footsteps.

Besides, systemic pesticides affect all other levels of our ecosystems too. Research demonstrates that neonicotinoids are highly toxic to birds, fish, lizards, beneficial insects, and even humans (pesticide residues are often found in the final products of GM agriculture).

How you can help

While some of the factors that lead to bee colony collapse are more difficult to control, it's easy enough for us all to take action against the use of systemic pesticides.

Sign petitions like this one from the National Resources Defense Council, and support the organizations who are fighting to save bees worldwide, such as Greenpeace, The Pesticide Action Network, and Take Part.

Don't buy GMO foods or support companies that use pesticide-treated ingredients. Instead, support local, organic farms that practice sustainable, pesticide-free, bee-friendly agriculture.

And if you'd like to get involved in a more hands-on way, start a pesticide-free garden, or even start your own bee hive—every plot of safe space that we can create for bees is a small victory.

Can you capture the connection between spiritual imbalance and nature's imbalance? How about spiritual imbalance and your own inner pain? Feel your own inner pain—*which is inner imbalance*—and now let it all go. There is no place in the universe for its existence. No one is asking that it be created—or shared with others. *Let it go.* What is your difficulty? *Let it go.* What is your problem or fear or blockage? *Let it go.* What do you lack? Well please know, your essence/soul is in perfect balance right now, as is mine. Your essence/soul can know nothing else but your perfect balance right now, as does mine. We together, as the life process of spiritual procreation, cannot know lack. We can only know what is which is our light, love, truth, beauty, balance, health, wealth, joy, wonderment, fulfillment, creative expression, inspiration, etc. Why is it we can only know the goodness and perfection? *Because, in the metaphysical balance of spiritual procreation, that is all there is.* Begin from here. Never go to the side of wanting, lack, and victimization. Like attracts like—*The Law of Attraction.* Only acknowledge the love that guides us all. And when you come upon another silently convey to him or her, "I love you and I believe in you." And receive the same in return. Notice that healing (and answered prayer) always take a two/connection. The two must become as one...to become as two...and so on. We are not of ourselves alone. And in our connection together all or our love is eternal love. Let this be our beginning point.

In concluding this section I am adding a few samples from my writings, ending with *The Miracle* from *Meditations for Deepening Love*, 1994, 2010. May these selections assist us in changing our own hearts and souls to the balance/love such that we can see that same balance/love in others and in all of nature.

The Spirit of Truth or of God

We, *man and woman,* ask for answered prayer. We ask in the name of the *Father* and the *Mother,* of which there can be no separation. We ask that our love giveth *birth-life-death-rebirth*...to all things. We ask that what is given to us, we may give in return. We ask that the *spirit of truth* be the *spirit of love.* We ask that *God* be *life* and that *life* never be separate from our *interconnection* together. We pray for the *birth* of our children and the *rebirth* of our parents—that we may hold each in the same graces. We pray that this *procreant* spirit within us guide us—and never allow us to seek the "higher authority" over each other or anyone else. We ask that those most hurt amongst us never again be separated from *our* love or we separated from *their* love. *Thank you Father and Mother for hearing our prayer as your own and answering in your perfect timing as our own.*

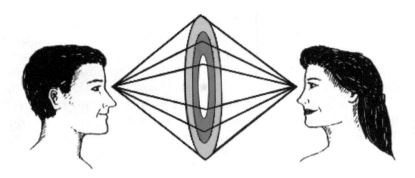

Source Consciousness

Source consciousness—here it is. *Let there be light!* We, You and I, are a part of the original source consciousness. We are a part of the original creative manifestation. Our consciousness (of You and I) exists, from the non-beginning to the never-ending, as a source consciousness. Everything created has been created through You and I. We stand as essential in life together. If there is a "God consciousness" or "Light consciousness," we possess it now. If there is a "God creative process" or a "Light creative process," we underscore it now. It is our connection (I a male; You a female) that is the source of life and love. It is from this connection that we create and procreate. All life and love runs through the creative process of You and I. We are the creative process in action. We are the Prime Movers. We have discovered source consciousness which never existed until we discovered it always existed—in us together.

**The Prime Movers
discover Source Consciousness and thereby
create a living universe of procreative love!**

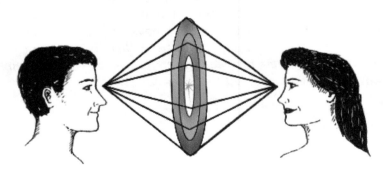

A Living Prayer

Dear:

God the Father and God the Mother—
Thank you for hearing my prayer.
I feel your dual lights around me.
I stand on both of your shoulders
and reach out for the best within me.
And now, I accept your most precious
gift of _____ into my heart—
that it may live in me forever.
Thank you Father and Mother for
all that you have done for me,
and continue to do for me—
that I may again give back to you.
Your loving Son/Daughter,
(name)

Our Eternal Lineage

'I' am loved,
And 'I' love.
From my eternal Father and Mother,
Through my eternal other half
We together as husband and wife,
On to our eternal children, son and daughter.
From Alpha to Omega
'I' love,
And 'I' am loved.
Our Eternal Lineage
Forever lives in my heart connection.
'I' invite you...

Before we complete this chapter with *The Miracle* see if you can capture and feel the depth of the above samples. You might want to, for example, contrast *The Lord's Prayer* from the Bible (Matthew 6: 9-13) with *The Living Prayer* above. Which one actually creates the greater connection? In our prayers we should not ask "God" to heal us or help us, etc.; we should ask from *our connection together*. It is not "God's" job; it is <u>our job together</u>. We, too, are a part of the healing or help. We, too, in our connection (which is our love) together, can shine the healing/helping light to another.

The Miracle

Webster's Dictionary defines a miracle as: *an event or action that apparently contradicts known scientific laws and is hence thought to be due to supernatural causes, especially to an act of God.* It is the view of this author that there are no supernatural causes per se. Extraordinary, yes, but everything that happens has its perfect placement or balance in the divine order of things. It is suggested here that it is the order, absolute in its character/structure, that brings forth a miracle into our lives.

A miracle is not what we may call a result or a manifestation of something. So many of us are looking for some type of fulfillment.—If only 'I' had this or that. If only my life was this or that. We seek goals, demand results, look for how to manifest our desires. If only 'I' had more of something, more love, more abundance, more faith or belief in these things and so on. If 'I' could just place my thought-desire on the "Creative Life Principle/Force" itself certainly all my wants would be (instantaneously) manifested and my troubles would be over. No such luck. The mistake in all this is that we are looking outward. Manifestation is an outward orientation and, as such, leaves us wanting.

Miracles occur from the inside of ourselves. (*The kingdom of God cometh not with observation: Neither shall they say, Lo here! or lo there! for, behold, the kingdom of God is within you.* Luke 17:20-21) They are called to us by something much deeper within ourselves. A miracle exists in the heart/soul. It lies at that point of one's deepest love. Miracles are always and only attached to love.

A miracle does not give us something—like a new house, job, or relationship. Rather, a miracle asks something of us. It looks not at what we don't have and thus want but at what we already have (to give) though might not see. In other words, the miracle is already sitting inside ourselves waiting for us to take note of its authority—and its urgency. A miracle actually calls us to a greater undertaking within ourselves.

As a miracle is actually a giving (of love) from within oneself, it always involves another. One of the great mistakes of the enlightenment movement is the thought that one can be enlightened of or by oneself alone. "My enlightenment, my salvation, my illumination, transformation, ascension," etc. As long as something is singular to ourselves alone, it is a want/manifestation. A miracle must always include another—equal to the miracle. So, if one is to be saved, for example, using Christian terms, there must be a dual salvation, a You and an I, not just a salvation for oneself alone. The You must always be included with the I. And so the salvation actually works both ways. One gives love to another and receives love from another. Isn't that the miracle?

The good book says (Acts 20:35): *It is more blessed to give than to receive.* But if one receives from one's heart, isn't that also a giving? And if one gives, doesn't one also, in that same moment, receive? The verse has merit in that many of us focus on the receiving.—What am 'I' to get? Such is a want. There needs to be a balance between the two. Love is that balance. Love is not just giving or just receiving. Love is giving to and receiving from another. This is to say, the miracle that lies in all of our hearts is that we actually can give to and receive from another. This is the love. This is the merging of two hearts. *...and the two become as one.* Herein lies the miracle. *...and the two become as one* is the only miracle.

As stated, a miracle *lies at that point of one's deepest love.* What might this deepest love be? Isn't it that moment/eternity when *the two become as one?* Let me quote the one verse in the Bible that has eternal merit:

> **Matthew 19:4-6:** *Have ye not read, that he which made them in the beginning made them male and female, And said, for this cause shall a man leave father and mother, and shall cleave to his wife: and they twain shall be one flesh? Wherefore they are no more twain, but one flesh. What therefore God hath joined together, let not man put asunder.*

A man and a woman, coming together in their love, *as one,* giving and receiving all that is within their lives to each and from each other, *procreating life* as only they can—*the two having become as one*. And the man calls out—*Will you come be my helpmate?* And when the man truly states this from the depths of his heart, *as one*, right at that point of his eternal (procreant) need for her, she replies in her perfect balance, *"Yes,"* and the miracle occurs. It occurs right at that moment. Not a moment before or a moment after. Only at that moment. And, then—*there is love.*

Let's say this is in another way as illustrated in these quotes. (From the Spirit Guide work of Ronald P. MacDonald to Christopher Anderson from the years of 1998–1999.)

Did Gina (spiritually) pick Chris that first meeting of June 4, 1997 at the club in San Francisco?

Osyda: *No. Before time, so is man's destiny to fulfill. What has been is. Nothing is new; all must be experienced.*

I have often visualized Gina as being a spokesperson for the message of Man and Woman Balance. Am I correct in this? (Chris' question.)

Osyda: *She will be your helpmate.*

Has the necessary foundation been set within Gina from our meetings together, the writings that she has, and my letters to her such that she can get through this hurt and come back? (Chris' question.)

Osyda: *Can the earth exist before its concept? Can the man and the woman exist before the Potter shines His wheel? I tell you before you were, so were you created. Before she was, so was she created. Together was all of eternity created from the dawn of the Hand of Manifestation. Believe that before the stars, so was your foundation with her.*

Can you feel the miracle already existing in place such that these words could be uttered? And what might this miracle be?—*that the love already is.* That the love already is, is the miracle. It took me eleven years to get to this realization with my beloved Gina. And when I did, all that I could know was *that the love already is.* The miracle (of love) has always been and will always be contained in this simple statement—*right now.*

Let us now take one moment, *this moment,* and open up the channel in our own hearts for our miracle to now occur. Thought is creative (manifestation) but spirit is now. *Spirit is now.* The miracle is now. Miracles only occur in the now. *Love is now.* Giving love is now. Receiving love is now. *My love for you my blessed love is now.*

Our Spiritual Task

The first element of the spiritual task is to acknowledge our spiritual perfection. Writing in *Spiritual Healing ...of Our Eternal Souls for all Time!*, 2016, I stated:

> *The healing has been completed. The original light was received into your soul. Your soul has been perfected. To confirm this take a moment to acknowledge and feel a difference inside of you—like a ball of light/love residing within you as your core. The amazing thing is it has always been there.*

Let's be sure to remember what this "original light" is. Light, like the word God, must be sexed, i.e., placed in the context of the two-force procreant sexual process. This next selection is from *Wealth Plus+: Empowering Your Everyday!*, 2013.

> *"God" is light. Light attracts light. Light is both static and dynamic in its nature. Light propagates (reproduces) itself through its two equal yet opposing forces. It can be said that light is a static/dynamic balance between two equal yet opposing forces. The forces are known as male and female. Male and female are the two forces of the universe. They are equal and opposite, i.e., sexual, in nature at all times. They comprise the united one (the static) which then becomes the divided two (the dynamic)... a procreant life process/lineage. Male is the force of their division; female the force of their union. "God" (or use the terms order, light, or balance) then is an unseen yet universal, automatic yet intentive, living two-way (dividing and uniting) sexual process—connecting the souls of a man and a woman to each other (from the very beginning) with a specific purpose, fundamental and necessary for the wealth attainment of all mankind. <u>This specific purpose/connection is the center point of wealth itself.</u> Be it. Know it. Embrace your equal and opposite procreant other half who is spiritually with you now and at all times. Feel that glow. It is your light together. The universe is alive with your light together. This sharing of your (equal and opposite) lights, on whatever level, with each other is known as love. Together, your only natures are love. Together, your only functions are to express to each other your love. Love is wealth. Love always exists to be expressed, one to another. Such is the purpose and point of action-expressing love...one to another. Within your love together is all the wealth*

that can ever exist.

The purpose of our spirituality/religions is, in essence, to take us to this placement of spiritual perfection/balance. Below are a few quotes I have come upon.

Rumi (1207-1273)—Persian poet
I saw myself self as the source of existence.
I was here in the beginning.
And I was the spirit of LOVE.

Osho (1931-1990)—Indian mystic and spiritual teacher
Millions of people are suffering: they want to be loved but they don't know how to love. And love cannot exist as a monologue; it is a dialogue, a very harmonious dialogue.

Very nice, especially the one by Osho. Notice the sense of connection. *And love cannot exist as a monologue; it is a dialogue...* You see, it really doesn't come down to "cosmic consciousness," "illumination," "enlightenment," "union with God," "salvation from God," "higher self," etc.; it only comes down to how we treat each other. *Love ye one another* it has been said. And so don't wait to be loved, *begin to love,* be that giving love or receiving love. Martin Buber (1878-1965), Austrian-born Israeli Jewish philosopher best known for his writing *I and Thou*, 1923, was also on to this connection when he stated:

When two people relate to each other authentically and humanly, God is the electricity that surges between them.

God is love. Love is God. We, you and I, are the enactment of love. But why haven't we really gotten this. Let's look to another quote as listed below.

Bacha Khan (1890-1988)—Pushtun political and spiritual leader
If you wish to know how civilized a culture is, look at how they treat its women.

And so our spiritual task, at least for men, is as follows: *To All Men the World Over.* This is taken from my writing *Wealth Plus+: Empowering Your Everyday!*, 2014.

To All Men the World Over

To those of you who claim to know God,
or some kind of human goodness...

Be it now known:
- **As you treat a woman, so do you treat God.**
- **As you honor a woman, so do you honor God.**
- **As you love a woman, so do you love God.**
- **As you hold tight to a woman, so do you hold tight to God.**
- **As you listen to a woman, so do you hear God.**
- **As you respect a woman, so do you respect God.**
- **As you stand up for a woman, so do you stand up for God.**
- **As you walk with a woman, so do you walk with God.**
- **As you trust in a woman, so do you trust in God.**
- **As you cherish a woman, so do you cherish God.**
- **As you believe in a woman, so do you believe in God.**
- **As you have a child with a woman, so you have a child of God.**
- **As you hold to the very center of creation with a woman, so do you hold to the very center of creation with God.**
- **As you no longer look for God other than in a woman, so do you know the love of God.**

Let it now be known—your only avenue to God is in touching the very heart of a woman.

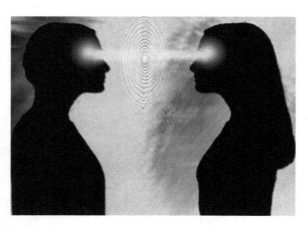

What might be the spiritual task of women? The same as it always has been, to receive a man's soul into her being and reproduce the linage of life. Let's look to the following quote from *Man, Woman, and God*, 1994, 2010. It states:

> *Men, do you know that the soul of woman has been hurt? You have hurt your woman, haven't you? You left her behind to bleed on the roadside. You used and discarded her when all she wanted was to love you. Why do you do this? Do you not see that woman is the only bridge that will take you beyond yourself? Woman is your only hope, but due to your actions she is giving up her belief in you. Can you, man, take responsibility for creating this state of affairs? Can you feel every pain that you have ever caused woman, from her birth to her death?*

> *Women, do you know the spirit of man has been hurt? You blame man for all the havoc around you, don't you? You think that men "just don't get it" and that you could do a better job at life. Can you? In the name of equality, you kill the spirit of life, the difference that you and men depend upon. Now, you only want a man conditionally, not completely. Cannot you see that without a man you can't even have yourself? Perhaps men, too, are doing the best they know how and that in their hearts they only want to care for you. Will you allow that? Can you feel a man's very struggle throughout all of time to do only one thing, to make a home for you? Can you feel this when you are alone?*

So our spiritual task is only to *love ye one another*. In these simple four words all karma is released. Our inner or spiritual cord is reset. Do you see the difference in this balance and what we call worship? We are not here to worship "God" and the like. In fact, that is only an indication that one is not understanding the two-force sexual balance. There isn't anything beyond *love ye one another*. There isn't any Jesus to wait for or some special place/heaven we go to (after life) that is outside of, prior to, or different from *love ye one another*. "*There is only a man and a woman, touching and expressing creation together.*"

And so it is now known that we, You and I, male and female together, comprise the *original light*. All the light in the universe is within us now. All the "God" that exists is within us now. We, You and I, man and woman, are interconnected now. We, man and woman, are procreating all the life and love there is now. And it is from this perfect *sexual* balance, and this perfect *sexual* balance alone, that we want to look at the spiritual task of *creative manifestation.*

To manifest something heretofore not present is a great undertaking, but it will have disastrous consequences if that undertaking is not located in a self-other balance to begin with. This is the idea behind the book *The Secret* and the *Law of Attraction* so popular a few years back. The idea here is that what we put out comes back to us, the law of cause and effect (as you sow so shall you reap). But it is not so simple as just saying, "I want _____." Sometime after *The Secret* came out there came out another writing called *The Secret Behind the Secret.* Apparently, people were having trouble applying the secret. They weren't manifesting their desires. It turns out one must not just think the desire but feel it as well. In fact, it must come from one's very soul vibration. Indeed, but even more than that, one's soul must be balanced. For example, if you are a socialist in heart, advocating the *forced* taking from one to give to another you can hardly get what you want in life, can you? How about if you are gay engaging in the act of sodomy. Is that going to work? Okay, okay, hate me if you must—is that going to work? *Nothing works relative to creative manifestation that is imbalanced at its core.* What I am suggesting is that our (sexual) cores must be balanced, male to female; female to male. That is what gives the light its shine, the stillness its sound, the love its joy, the life its eternality. Do you want to attract into your life those things of your heart's calling? Then have them *now* in the balance you *currently hold* with your equal and opposite eternal other half. *Be in spirit what you want now. Receive in spirit what you want now. Give in spirit what you want now. Hold in your heart what you want right now.*

There are a couple of wonderful verses in the Bible that address creative manifestation.

> **Matthew 21:22:** *And all things, whatsoever ye shall ask in prayer, believing, ye shall receive.*

> **Hebrews 11:1:** *Now faith is the substance of things hoped for, the evidence of things not seen.*

The key to these verses is to not hold them, or the thing you desire, as something in the future. They must be present for you now. They must live in your heart now. For example: *And all things, whatsoever I shall ask in prayer, as they reside in me now, I shall receive.* Or, maybe even better: *And all things, whatsoever I shall ask in prayer, as I see them in you right now, we shall receive.* We always must bring in the other. With Hebrews 11:1 we can say: *Now faith is the substance of things hoped for, the evidence of things not seen—and I still hold to their existence within me/you right now.* Don't ever lose faith in what you desire. Never give up on your ideal. Writing in *Ideal Made Real or Applied Metaphysics for Beginners,* 1909, Christian D. Larson (1874-1954) states:

Christian D. Larson (1874-1954)—*Ideal Made Real or Applied Metaphysics for Beginners,* 1909

To begin to move forward is to begin to make real the ideal, and we will realize in the now as much of the ideal as is necessary to make the now full and complete. To move forward steadily during the great eternal now is to eternally become more than you are; and to become more than you are is to make yourself more and more like your ideal; and here is the great secret, because the principle is that you will realize your ideal when you become exactly like your ideal, and that you will realize as much of your ideal now as you develop in yourself now.

And isn't this what we seek, to make ourselves into our ideals, i.e., the perfection within? And also that the ideal and the real become as one? I should say contact and responsiveness. We seek actual interaction and actual result. But each one of us must make that first step. In other words: *Make things (you do want) to happen within you before things (you don't want) happen outside of you.* This next quote is from *Meditations for Deepening Love: Let the Light Shine Through,* 1994, 2010.

> *The still center is that point of perfect (man and woman) balance or stillness, also called the light, where knowing and fulfillment come together. It is the source-point of co-creation where we, out of our stillness, may "define it," "have it," and "let it go." If we could just hold to the stillness within ourselves—the balance with another—our experience would be one of always having it, and we would, for in the stillness we are one with our desire. We would have it and then could give it away, to watch it return as we again define it. Whatever it is we desire in life, only as we give it out of ourselves do we then receive it unto ourselves.*

Now I could have said: *Whatever it is we desire in life, only as we receive it unto ourselves do we then give it out of ourselves.* Giving and receiving have equal importance in the whole giving-receiving cycle. So let us not forget that we are always in relationship with our sexual (equal and opposite) other half and, as such, our prayers (givings and receivings) must include him or her. Another way to pray is to only pray for the betterment of another. Or even better, only see the spiritual perfection in another. Pray from the perfect balance you two hold together. *Be that balance right now,* and thus: *Let the life you desire live in your heart now as you present that opportunity to another.* There can be no failure in the balance of love. Let's look at a few more biblical verses.

Mark 10:27: *...with God all things are possible.*

Luke 18:27: *The things which are impossible with men are possible with God.*

Matthew 5:48: *Be ye therefore perfect, even as your Father which is in heaven is perfect.*

John 8:12: *I am the light of the world: he that followeth me shall not walk in darkness, but shall have the light of life.*

In the light of balance, in the light of perfection, in the light of our love, all things are not just possible they are a *metaphysical certainty*. They are certain because, as Mr. Larson would suggest, the ideal is the real. Faith is a spiritual certainty in the ideal/perfection within ourselves existing as the real, not outside circumstances. We must hold within ourselves and believe it just as much as we believe in the physical world. You don't doubt the existence of a tree, for example. You don't doubt your own existence. Then don't doubt the manifestation/miracle of your dreams and desires. In the giving and receiving of love all is manifested in its perfect balance. This next passage is also from *Meditations for Deepening Love,* 1994, 2010, from the selection *The Abundance Booklet.*

> *The source of all abundance then is that balance point of life where we, "You and I," are fully giving to and equally receiving from each other. This is a spiritual partaking if you will. It has an eternal sense to it. Hold this self-other balance in your mind's eye at all times. Be one with the balance of You and I. In this one (eternal) moment of now we are fulfilling each other and being fulfilled by each other and the light of our abundance shineth through. As the source of all abundance is balance and as the experience of balance is love, the source of all abundance*

then is our love. Notice I did not say "my love" or "your love," but our love. Not "God's" love singularly, but our love. This is the difference. The balance of the two must be consciously intact. If it is not, a doubt will surface within oneself and one will begin to blame and demand rather than to give and receive. Until we begin to ask in our name, nothing will be forthcoming to us.

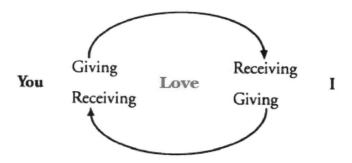

You and I, in perfect balance together, in this one eternal moment of now, comprise the source of all abundance. Can you feel this? Abundance just cannot be found in any other place than in our balance together. In holding to our balance, abundance is brought forth to both of us through our love. So, if you ever find yourself in need please ask in our name, and I can assure you that it shall be given unto You just as perfectly as you have asked.

In summation, what we seek, what we desire and pray for already is— as per our *conscious balance* with our equal and opposite other half. Remember from the last chapter—"And what might this miracle be?— *that the love already is.*" <u>What we seek, what we desire and pray for already is.</u> Our spiritual task is to recognize this. Let us pray in this way:

Dear Father and Mother, I pray for _____, alive in us now, present in us now, answered in us now. Thank you. In <u>our</u> eternal love. Amen.

Notice I did not end the prayer in Jesus' name. It must be an *us*, or a *we*, or an *our*. *Prayer is only answered in 'our' name—answered in <u>us</u> now.* <u>This is the connection</u>. As mentioned earlier, prayer has to be asked and answered together. Another example would be praying directly to your eternal (sexual) other half.

> *My dear eternal helpmate, I pray for* _____, *alive in us now, present in us now, answered in us now. Thank you. In <u>our</u> eternal love. Amen.*

Let us now be in this consciousness of giving and receiving prayer which is also love. Each one of us is equal to what we seek, desire, and pray for. It is a disservice to all of existence to be less than (or more than) what we seek, desire, and pray for. That is our existential doubt/lack. And then this is what we present to another. This is the fundamental flaw in Christianity and most other religions. The Christian insists on being less than "God." The Christian insists on being less than what he or she seeks, desires, and prays for. The balance point (The Law of Attraction) only occurs when what we seek, desire, and pray for is answered in us now. To the Christian, or a follower of any other religion, I would say: *Everything you say God (or Jesus) is you are. If you say God is love it is because you are love. If you say God is perfection it is because you are perfection. If you say God is light it is because you are light. The Christ within you is you.* It is not someone else or some force different than you. I might add as to your *perfect balance* with your equal and opposite eternal other half—from which you can also see the *Christ within another*. And that perfect balance with your equal and opposite eternal other half *already exists now—*within you. There isn't an "out there" per se. This is to say that all is given to and received from this moment right now. And we must hold to this reality as *metaphysical reality* and that we are equal to it *in spirit* right now. And we are. Our spiritual task is only to always be equal to that which we choose to manifest. Our spiritual task is to know *that the love already is, and it is within us both. Our balance together is our source point of answered prayer!*

As a conclusion to this chapter, I would like to return to Thomas Troward (1847-1916). It is so important, I believe, that we are able to make the critical distinctions between a "oneness universe" as to a *sexual universe* that our life's success depends on. And so I compare and contrast over and over again showing how close yet far we still are—like we did with Ayn Rand. I know this is somewhat tedious but we must have our thought and languaging clear. Look at all the havoc in the world due to just a few ideas that are so close yet so far. Remember in an earlier chapter I quoted from his writing *The Creative Process in the Individual*, 1915. Let's review:

Thomas Troward (1847-1916)—*The Creative Process in the Individual*, 1915

From this point onward we shall find the principle of Polarity in universal activity. It is that relation between opposites without which no external motion would be possible, because there would be nowhere to move from, and nowhere to move to; and without which external Form would be impossible because there would be nothing to limit the diffusion of substance and bring it into shape. Polarity, or the interaction of Active and Passive, is therefore the basis of all Evolution.

This is a great fundamental truth when we get it in its right order; but all through the ages it has been a prolific source of error by getting it in its wrong order. And the wrong order consists in making Polarity the originating point of the Creative Process. What this misconception leads to we shall see later on, but since it is very widely accepted under various guises even at the present day, it is well to be on our guard against it. Therefore I wish the student to see clearly that there is something which comes before that Polarity which gives rise to Evolution, and that this something is the original movement of Spirit within itself, of which we can best get an idea by calling it Self-contemplation.

...The order, therefore, which I wish the student to observe is, 1st, the Self-contemplation of Spirit producing Polarity, and next, Polarity producing manifestation in Form—and also to realize that it is in this order his own mind operates as a subordinate center of creative energy.

...And this Law of the Spirit's Original Unity is a very simple one. It is the Spirit's necessary and basic conception of itself.

You may also remember I criticized his idea of "Spirit's Original Unity" as being prior to Polarity suggesting that within polarity is both the division of the one and the unification of the two (Spirit's Original Division and Unity), creating a one procreative process. But this is not to dismiss Mr. Troward so easily. He is one of the great inspirations of the Creative Thought movement. And what the Creative Thought movement is all about is creative manifestation. This is what we all butt our heads against—*"How can I get to what I want in life?"* Mr. Troward had a student, Genevieve Behrend, (1881-1960). Ms. Behrend wrote a book titled *Your Invisible Power* that is a succinct articulation of Mr. Troward's ideas and, I believe, will do us much good in really getting down to that placement of creative manifestation. I am going the extra mile here because I know how difficult it has been for me, and still is at times, to manifest my desires. It is easy to say all the right words or pray in the right way or visualize perfectly or even take necessary action steps, but to actually manifest one's desires? So if you will bear with me, let's review some quotes from Ms. Behrend's book *Your Invisible Power* and really cement within ourselves the power we each possess to manifest our desires.

Genevieve Behrend (1881-1960)—*Your Invisible Power*, 1951

The power within you which enables you to form a thought-picture is the starting point of all there is. In its original state it is the undifferentiated formless substance of life... Visualizing, or mentally seeing things and conditions as you wish them to be, is the condensing, the specializing power in you which might be illustrated by comparison with the lens of a magic lantern, which is one of the best symbols of the imaging faculty. It illustrates the idea of the working of the Creative Spirit on the plane of initiative and selection—or in its concentrated, specialized form—in a remarkably clear manner.

That is to say, you light up your desire with absolute faith that the Creative Spirit of Life, in you, is doing the work. By the steady flow of the light of the Will on the Spirit, your desired picture is projected upon the screen of the physical world—an exact reproduction of the pictured slide in your mind.

Simply try to realize that your picture is an orderly exercise of the Universal Creative Power specifically applied.

God, or Universal Mind, made man for the special purpose of differentiating Himself through him. Everything there is, came into existence in this same way, by this self-same law of self-differentiation, and for the same purpose. First came the idea, the mental picture, or the prototype of the thing, which *is* the thing itself in its incipiency.

Many people ask, "But why should we have a physical world at all?" The answer is: "Because it is the nature of Originating Substance to solidity, under directivity rather than activity, just as it is the nature of wax to harden when it becomes cold, or plaster of Paris to become firm and solid when exposed to the air. Your picture is this same Divine Substance in its original state, taking form through the individualized center of Divine operation, in your mind; and there is no power to prevent this combination of Spiritual Substance from becoming physical form. It is the nature of Spirit to complete its work, and an idea is not complete until it has made for itself a vehicle. Nothing can prevent your picture from coming into concrete form except the same power which gave it birth—yourself.

Some persons feel that it is not quite proper to visualize for *things.* "It's too material," they say. Why, material form is necessary for self-recognition of Spirit from the individual standpoint, and this is the means through which the Creative process is carried forward. Therefore, far from matter being an illusion and something which ought not to be, matter is the necessary channel for the self-differentiation of Spirit.

When we pause to think for a moment, we realize that for a cosmos to exist at all, it must be the outcome of a Cosmic Mind, which binds "all individual minds to a certain generic unity of action, thereby producing all things as realities and nothing as illusions." If you will take this thought of Troward's and meditate upon it without prejudice, you will surely realize that concrete material form is an absolute necessity of the Creative Process; also, "that matter is not an illusion but a necessary channel through which life differentiates itself." If you consider matter in its right order, as the polar opposite to Spirit, you will not find any antagonism between them. On the contrary, together they constitute one harmonious whole.

This same power that brought universal substance into existence will bring your individual thought or mental picture into physical form. There is no difference in the power. The only difference is a difference of degree. The power and the substance themselves are the same. Only in working out your mental picture, it has transferred its creative energy from the Universal to the particular, and is working in the same unfailing manner from its specific center, your mind.

Infinite substance is manifesting in you right now.

There is nothing unusual or mysterious in the idea of your pictured desire coming into material evidence. It is the working of a universal, natural Law. The world was projected by the self-contemplation of the Universal Mind, and this same action is taking place in its individualized branch which is the Mind of Man. Everything in the whole world, from the hat on your head to the boots on your feet, has its beginning in mind and comes into existence in exactly the same manner. All are projected thoughts, solidified. Your personal advance in evolution depends upon your right use of the power of visualizing, and your use of it depends on whether you recognize that you, yourself, are a particular center through and in which the Originating Spirit is finding ever new expression for potentialities already existing within Itself. This is evolution.

Your mental picture is the force of attraction which evolves and combines the Originating Substance into specific shape. Your picture is the combining and evolving power house, in a generative sense, so to say, through which the Originating Creative Spirit expresses itself. Its creative action is limitless, without beginning and without end, and always progressive and orderly. "It proceeds stage by stage, each stage being a necessary preparation for the one to follow."

...the Creative Energy sends its substance in the direction indicated by the *tendency* of your thoughts.

All you have to do is to make such a mental picture of your heart's desire, and hold it cheerfully in place with your will, always conscious that the same Infinite Power which brought the universe into existence, brought you into form for the purpose of enjoying Itself in and through you. And since it is all Life, Love, Light, Power, Peace, Beauty, and Joy, and is the only Creative Power there is, the form it takes in and through you depends upon the direction given it by your thought. In you it is undifferentiated, waiting to take any direction given it as it passes through the instrument which it has made for the purpose of self-distribution—you.

Once you really believe that your mind is a center through which the unformed substance of all there is in your world, takes involuntary form, the only reason your picture does not always materialize is because you have introduced something antagonistic to the fundamental principle.

The Originating Principle is not in any way dependent upon any person, place, or thing. It has no past and knows no future. The law is that the Originating Creative Principle of Life is the universal here and now.

Your feeling should be that the thing, or the consciousness, which you so much desire, is normal and natural, a part of yourself, a form of your evolution. If you can do this, there is no power to prevent your enjoying the fulfillment of the picture you have in mind, or any other you may create.

"My mind is a center of Divine operation. The Divine operation is always for expansion and fuller expression, and this means the production of something beyond what has gone before, something entirely new, not included in the past experience, though proceeding out of it by an orderly sequence of growth. Therefore, since the Divine cannot change its inherent nature, it must operate in the same manner with me; consequently, in my own special world, of which I am the center, it will move forward to produce new conditions, always in advance of any that have gone before."

Surely the Divine could not change its inherent nature, and since Divine life is operating in me, I must be Divinely inhabited, and the Divine in me must operate just as it operates upon the Universal plane. This meant that my whole world of circumstances, friends, and conditions would ultimately become a world of contentment and enjoyment of which "I am the center." This would all happen just as soon as I was able to control my mind and thereby provide a concrete center around which the Divine energies could play.

My mind is a center of Divine operation.
I Am all the substance there is.
The Idea must contain within itself the only one and primary substance there is, and this means money as well as everything else.

There was a feeling of absolute certainty of being in touch with all the power Life has to give. All thought of money, teacher, or even my own personality, vanished in the great wave of joy which swept over my entire being. I walked on and on, with this feeling of joy steadily increasing and expanding until everything about me seemed aglow with resplendent light. Every person I passed appeared illuminated as I was. All consciousness of personality had disappeared, and in its place there came that great and almost overwhelming sense of joy and contentment.

At first it took great effort not to be excited. It all seemed so wonderful, so glorious, to be in touch with supply. But had not Troward cautioned his readers to keep all excitement out of their minds in the first flush of realization of union with Infinite supply, and to treat this fact as a perfectly natural result which had been reached through our demand? This was even more difficult for me than it was to hold the thought that "all the substance there is, I Am; I (idea) Am the beginning of all form, visible or invisible."

In actual practice we must first form the ideal conception of our object with the definite intention of impressing it upon the Universal Mind—it is this intention that takes such thought out of the region of mere casual fancies—and then affirm that our knowledge of the Law is sufficient reason for a calm expectation of a corresponding result, and that therefore all necessary conditions will come to us in due order... If we do not at once see them, let us rest content with the knowledge that the spiritual prototype is already in existence and wait till some circumstance pointing in the desired direction begins to show itself.

Your desire to be the best has expanded your faith into the faith of the Universe which knows no failure, and has brought you into conscious realization that you are not a victim of the universe, but a part of it. Consequently you are able to recognize that there is that within yourself which is able to make conscious contact with the Universal Law, and enables you to press all the particular laws of Nature, whether visible or invisible, into serving your particular demand or desire. Thereby you find yourself Master, not a slave, of any situation. Troward tells us that this Mastering is to be "accomplished by knowledge, and the only knowledge which will afford this purpose in all its measureless immensity is the knowledge of the personal element in universal spirit," and its reciprocity to our own personality. In other words, the words you think, the personality you feel yourself to be, are all reproductions in miniature of God, "or specialized universal spirit." All your word-thoughts were God's word-forms before they were yours.

Even more truly this sensitive, invisible Substance must reproduce outwardly the shape of the thought-word through which it passes. This is the law of its Nature; therefore, it logically follows. "As a man thinketh, so is he." Hence, when your thought or word-form is in correspondence with the Eternal constructive and forward movement of the Universal Law, then your mind is the mirror in which the Infinite Power and Intelligence of the Universe sees itself reproduced and your individual life becomes one of harmony.

If there was a power within himself which was able to capture the idea, then there must be a responsive power within the idea itself which could bring itself into a practical physical manifestation. He resolutely put aside all questions as to the specific ways and means which would be employed in bringing his desire into physical manifestation, and simply kept this thought centered upon the idea of making fences and seeing flowers and grass where none existed at that time. Since the responsiveness of Reproductive Creative Power is not limited to any local condition of mind his habitual meditation and mental picture set his ideas free to roam in an infinitude, and attract to themselves other ideas of a kindred nature.

In the conscious uses of the Universal Power to reproduce your desires in physical form, three facts should be borne in mind:

First—All space is filled with a Creative Power.
Second—This Creative Power is amenable to suggestion.
Third—It can only work by deductive methods.

As Troward tells us, this last is an exceedingly important point, for it implies that the action of the ever-present Creative Power is in no way limited by precedent. It works according to the essence of the spirit of the principle. In other words, this Universal Power takes its creative direction from the word you give it. Once man realizes this great truth, the character with which this sensitive, reproductive power is invested becomes the most important of all his considerations. It is the unvarying law of Creative Life Principle that "As a man thinketh in his *heart,* so is he." If you realize the truth that the Creative Power can be to you only what you feel and think it to be, it is willing and able to meet your demands.

Troward says, "If you think your thought is Powerful, your Thought *is* Powerful."

Only the reproductive Creative Spirit of Life knows what you think, until your thoughts become physical facts and manifest themselves in your body, your brain, or your affairs. Then everyone with whom you come into contact may know, because the Father, the Intelligent Creative Energy which heareth in secret your most secret thoughts, rewards you openly: reproduces your thoughts in physical form.

Now, we can still see the oneness mistake in play in some of these quotes. For example:

My mind is a center of Divine operation.
I Am all the substance there is.
The Idea must contain within itself the only one and primary substance there is…

…"all the substance there is, I Am; I (idea) Am the beginning of all form, visible or invisible."

But we also see some of the complementary balance I am speaking of.

If you will take this thought of Troward's and meditate

upon it without prejudice, you will surely realize that concrete material form is an absolute necessity of the Creative Process; also, "that matter is not an illusion but a necessary channel through which life differentiates itself." If you consider matter in its right order, as the polar opposite to Spirit, you will not find any antagonism between them. On the contrary, together they constituted one harmonious whole.

Here matter (male) is the polar opposite of spirit (female). And notice how they are a part of the same creative process and need one another. *...together they constituted one harmonious whole.* Now that is more like it. Too many "mystics" believe in some non-material, non-dual "oneness" and don't understand that the material is just as real and important. Also, this quote brings in differentiation (what I call division of the one). *...that matter is not an illusion but a necessary channel through which life differentiates itself.* Remember Max Freedom Long's comments: *...that all male and female parts of the Creation were striving to unity. We cannot say what caused the division into the two separated parts from atoms to man, but we can be very sure that there is such a general division, and that the urge to unite and reach a state of balanced inertia is universal. ...we may reach the conclusion that the same division which separated the two lower selves, separated the High Self spirits, and that they also strive on their own high level and in their own more evolved way to reach union.* So what is the cause of differentiation (division)? Isn't it the male impetus to divide the one? And what is the cause of unification? Isn't it the female impetus to unite the two? Take a moment and envision yourself as one sexual half of a two-force procreative life process. And then we see:

> Surely the Divine could not change its inherent nature, and since Divine life is operating in me, I must be Divinely inhabited, and the Divine in me must operate just as it operates upon the Universal plane.

This quote sounds like the Walter Russell quote *...A perfect and omnipotent God could not create imperfection. He could not create a lesser than Himself. He could not create a greater than Himself. God could not create other than Himself. God did not create other than Himself, nor greater, nor lesser than Himself.* We, each one of us, are the *original light.* Said another way by Max Freedom Long: . *...we may reach the conclusion that the same division which separated the two lower selves, separated the High Self spirits, and that they also strive on their own high level and in their own more evolved way to reach union.* We all strive for *the love that* *already is.* This is what we must cement within ourselves. And there is more.

Troward tells us that this Mastering is to be "accomplished by knowledge, and the only knowledge which will afford this purpose in all its measureless immensity is the knowledge of the personal element in universal spirit," and its reciprocity to our own personality. In other words, the words you think, the personality you feel yourself to be, are all reproductions in miniature of God, "or specialized universal spirit." All your word-thoughts were God's word-forms before they were yours.

...is the knowledge of the personal element in universal spirit, and its reciprocity to our own personality. Do you get that, that there is a *personal element in universal spirit,* and furthermore, it has *its reciprocity to our own personality*? This is similar to Christianity and its personal God in the form of the Son. (Unfortunately *the Daughter* was never included to be on the same divine status!) But there must be this *personal element in universal spirit, and its reciprocity to our own personality* within the very nature of the universe itself. *Our hearts and souls demand it.* And don't each and every male and female have a *personal element* within them (their unique gender) and are they not each the reciprocity (or complementarity) of the other? Indeed, we are never alone. We are always in spiritual contact/communication with our equal and opposite eternal other half. This we must believe.

If there was a power within himself which was able to capture the idea, then there must be a responsive power within the idea itself which could bring itself into a practical physical manifestation. He resolutely put aside all questions as to the specific ways and means which would be employed in bringing his desire into physical manifestation, and simply kept this thought centered upon the idea of making fences and seeing flowers and grass where none existed at that time. Since the responsiveness of Reproductive Creative Power is not limited to any local condition of mind his habitual meditation and mental picture set his ideas free to roam in an infinitude, and attract to themselves other ideas of a kindred nature.

Reproductive Creative Power... now where did that term come from? It actually says *the responsiveness of Reproductive Creative Power.* Responsiveness—a very important term. This is the contact point. Of course the nature of the *Reproductive Creative Power* is *responsive*—that must be its *very nature*, without which there could not be <u>Life</u>. That is the female reaction of unity to the male action of division. Both comprise the *personal element in universal spirit.* Together they are the *Reproductive Creative Power.* This is the procreative process in action. Do you get it?

> Only the reproductive Creative Spirit of Life knows what you think, until your thoughts become physical facts and manifest themselves in your body, your brain, or your affairs. Then everyone with whom you come into contact may know, because the Father, the Intelligent Creative Energy which heareth in secret your most secret thoughts, rewards you openly: reproduces your thoughts in physical form.

...reproduces your thoughts in physical form. Awesome, isn't it? Very awesome! And isn't that what we hope for in our prayers, thoughts, and actions—that they are responded to? The whole God-process (*reproductive Creative Spirit of Life*) is one of action and responsiveness— in balance. And this is what the procreant sexual process of male and female is—*an active-responsive two-force sexual procreant living process.* So when you hear words like creative spirit, divine substance, original light, spiritual essence, living God, etc., all of these terms really mean (or should mean) an active-responsive two-way, sexual, procreant, living process. You see, *there never was a difference between the spiritual domain and the procreative process of life. They are one and the same.* And you know what—this whole thing should bring joy to your heart. That the universe is a two-way, sexual, procreant, life process should bring you joy. You, as I, can give and receive *primary* love, the love of birth-life-death-rebirth, right now as per the fundamental structure of the universe itself. We, male and female, in our love together, comprise the spiritual prototype (archetype or original pattern) that is the heart beat of all things. Feel this creative spirit, divine substance, original light, spiritual essence, or living God live in the heartbeat of your love for your eternal other half—you two giving and receiving love together. And contained in that love are all of your desires being manifested. Isn't that super? And let's remember this one critical distinction, it is not "Spirit's Original Unity" that is our source point but <u>*Spirit's Original Division and Unity.*</u> Small distinction maybe but it means everything.

Another word for creative spirit, divine substance, original light, spiritual essence, procreant ether, or living God is manna. Manna constitutes the riches from heaven. Manna is the manifestation of your divine inheritance. Manna constitutes pieces of light/love—being given back to you. Manna is our spiritual food. Wikipedia states:

> **Manna** (Hebrew: מָן) or al-Mann wa al-Salwa (Arabic: المَنّ و السلوى, Kurdish: gezo, Persian: گزانگبین), sometimes or archaically spelled mana, is an edible substance that, according to the Bible and the Quran, God provided for the Israelites during their travels in the desert.

Under Dictionary.com it states:

> 1. The food miraculously supplied to the Israelites in the wilderness. Ex. 16:14–36.
> 2. Any sudden or unexpected help, advantage, or aid to success.
> 3. Divine or spiritual food.

Divine or spiritual food, isn't that what we seek? The universal connection/balance, i.e., original light or spiritual energy or divine substance (known as the goose-bumps [LOVE]), vibrating through each one of us as a sexual contact point (which includes both male division and female unification). This is to say that the essence or center point of manna (divine or spiritual food) is the actual one living, procreant touch between a man and a woman. *There is only a man and a woman, touching and expressing creation together.* This is the spiritual prototype that we connect to as the source point of all our hopes and desires. And when you know this You and I will forevermore be fed as we give and receive love. We will know that our own love for each other is the divine love of the Father and the Mother. And there stands our universal healing where we no longer produce the karma of imbalance, where we no longer are under the rub of original sin. And we can take this love with us wherever we go and shine it forth as *original light* knowing it lives within us all.

Allow me to end this section with a meditation from Father to Son and from Mother to Daughter. The full healing and love runs from man and woman always to child. Children are the lineage of life. These passages are also from Meditations for Deepening Love, 1994, 2010.

Meditation to Son
My dear Son, you were only just a babe, and now look at you. You have

come through the years well; you've grown into your own manhood ready to take on the responsibilities thereof. What more could I ask for? What would make me happier than to see you now in your place in life, securing your life and family? I remember the many esoteric talks we have had over the years while you were struggling over the great questions, seeking to discover the meaning of life. But now they are answered for you, aren't they? Your actions tell me so as you have found the priority of your family. And so I tried to tell you, my son, in my actions. Do you now know why my family always came first with me? But now I am growing old. Things are in your hands now. You lead the world, in your own way. You take your place amongst the great, in your own way. You keep your family together, and through your actions teach your son the meaning of life. And in that thought I will go to my rest, always knowing, always proud, that you are my son.

Meditation to Daughter

My dearest daughter, how could I have ever told you what it means to be a woman? Yes, you thought you knew; at times you were so sure, you would look at me wondering what I knew about life. But now you know, don't you? Yes, my blessed daughter, you, too, have now crossed the channel from woman to mother. You, too, have given birth to a baby, your baby. And now you know; I could see it in your eyes when you first held your baby to your breast. You, my daughter, have brought forth life, just as I had done. And then the look you gave me showing me your understanding, and love, that I am your mother and you are my child, just as you are now the mother of your child. Now you know, my daughter, why I could not explain motherhood in its purpose in my life to you, just as you won't be able to explain it to your daughter. She, too, must first give birth to know herself and her mother. Thank you, my daughter, for now knowing me as your mother and knowing yourself as my daughter.

What "We" Believe!

The key to this section is to ascertain "what we believe" and why we hold it as *universal truth*. Belief and truth are obviously sticky subjects. Today we hear how we must compromise. Compromise with what? Shall we say that men actually are (metaphysically) superior to women, or that the distinction between a man and a woman is not of essential importance, that sodomy is comparable to man and women unitive love, that men can be women or women men, that credit notes are gold, or that initial force (in the name of the people) one against another can be justified? What we can say is this:

You and I exist in perfect balance/love together right now.

That is what exists, <u>right now</u>. Or more <u>sexually</u> specific:

We, man and woman, exist in perfect <u>procreant</u> balance/love together right now.

Or, as my essence statement declares:

Love is the only state of existence between Male and Female.

This is the essence of what we believe. The distinction between what we believe and what others believe lies in the word *procreant* or *procreative*. Heretofore, no one has really viewed the universe in all its nature as a procreative process between two equal and opposite forces. Maybe Taoism comes closest. Christianity is close as well in its *birth* of Jesus (which unfortunately was turned into a supernatural birth). So what is being said here and what we believe is that the center of all things (including "God") is a procreant balance/process between the two forces of male and female. Love is not without the balance of the two equal and opposite forces. Love is not self-love. Love is not universal love. Love is sexual love, man to woman and woman to man. Love is procreant love—Father and Mother to child. Love is life. We really don't have to write ten volumes about it. It should be apparent to everyone—*self-evident*. It is our alpha and omega point. *It is life.* Now, regarding the issue of truth and compromise let me quote the Biblical verse 1 John 1: 5 which states: *God is light; in him there is no darkness.* Can you see how this verse is perfect in that it discounts the existence of darkness altogether? We could say: *God is balance; in him there is no imbalance.* Or even more to the point: *You and I are balance; in us there is no imbalance.* The imbalance of Masculinism and Feminism, in the cases I am presenting, really don't exist. Only balance exists; only light exists; only love exists, etc. This is why I say Christianity, Islam, Hinduism, Buddhism, Secularism Humanism, Corporate (Crony) Capitalism, L,G,B,T,Q,... whatever cause you are pushing, doesn't really exist. Only the perfection exists. *You and I exist in perfect balance/love together right now.* That is what exists, <u>right now</u>. More specifically, *We, man and woman, exist in perfect procreant balance/love together right now.* Or, again, as my essence statement declares: *Love is the only state of existence between Male and Female.* That is the extent of what exists. –"Well, what about... Who do you think you are?... You are blaming the FED/IRS right and left... I can see you certainly hate gay people... Where do you come off getting to decide what is metaphysical truth?..." and so it goes—the Victimization Cycle (lack-blame-demand-attack-deny) rearing its ugly head. And what does the Victimization Cycle create? More of the same of course. If you want to create perfection (light, love, beauty, truth, balance, wealth, health...) in your life than see that in another. *(God is light; in him there is no darkness.)* Don't see darkness; see only light. "Yes, but what about all the problems?" *See only light.* "Yes, but what about... ?" *See only light.* "Yes, but... ?" *See only light.*

Let us now ask, which of the essence statements earlier cited only sees light? Let us review them as follows:

Karl Marx: *From each according to his abilities, to each according to his needs.*

Ayn Rand: *I swear by my life and my love of it that I will never live for the sake of another man, nor ask another man to live for mine.*

Walter Russell: *Thou, my Father-Mother, are the Light of the world.*

Christopher Anderson: *Love is the only state of existence between Male and Female.*

You get to decide.—And this is what <u>we</u> believe. You cannot believe in a statement that is of yourself alone (or is of the other alone). Statements must be complementary. So how might we write such a statement comprising the essence of Man and Woman Balance and what we believe?

What We Believe!

We believe that there are <u>two</u> primary forces (call them energies if you like) in nature which together comprise the one universal order/truth of all things.

We believe that these forces exist in a state of equal to yet opposite from each other, i.e., polar opposites, comprising a <u>balance</u> in all things.

We believe that these forces interact together—that one is not without the other; both are needed for either to be.

We believe that their interaction together comprises a balanced process—let's call it a vibrating, breathing, or living process.

We believe the equal and opposite two unite together and divide apart—over and over again and, as such, are eternal <u>together</u>.

We believe that their interaction is an actual birth-life-death-rebirth... eternal process that we can give to it the name LIFE.

We believe that the two living forces are <u>male</u> and <u>female</u>.

We believe that the male impetus (or energy) is to divide the one (individuality) and the female impetus (or energy) is to unite the two (unification).

We believe that this essential impetus/difference between the two forces comprises a sexual (<u>opposite</u>) nature or gender in each of them.

We believe that the <u>sexual</u> is the metaphysical—each one of us being one of the two genders and that our unique gender constitutes our very soul.

We believe that for every male there is a female and for every female there is a male—and that <u>together</u> they comprise this one sexual, living, eternal process.

We believe that the sexual, living, eternal process has at its core the one motive of LIFE (birth-life-death-rebirth...) in all things.

We believe that this male and female (what we may also call man and woman) LIFE process constitutes the fundamental existence of all things, i.e., lives in the heart of all things.

We believe the one motive (of this two-way sexual process) of LIFE (birth-life-death-rebirth...) is known to us by the reality/understanding called <u>procreation</u>.

We believe that there are always two parts to

procreation—male division and female unification.

We believe that it is through male and female procreation that the lineage of LIFE progresses through our children...and their children...

We believe procreation is the "God process."

We believe procreation is Divine Love.

We believe procreant love (of Father <u>and</u> Mother) constitutes the very center of the order/truth that is LIFE and that...

in procreant love lies the spirit of all understanding, forgiveness, and healing.

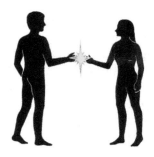

With that I will close this section with another booklet from *Meditations for Deepening Love,* 1994, 2010. It is titled *The Light at the End of the Mind.*

The Light at the End of the Mind

The light at the end of the mind illuminates the mind with all clarity. Clarity—a purity of constant realization that this light could only reside at the end of the mind. After all ideas have come into awareness—without an answer. After all action from these ideas have been taken—to no avail. After all hope has been lost, and finally admitted to, here comes the last idea. Yes, the light at the end of the mind is but an *idea*. An idea that is a *word*—a word that contains all the meaning of life and illuminates the mind with the understanding that has been missing since the dawn of consciousness. The light at the end of the mind is the last idea to be brought to consciousness. It is the final idea of all mankind. It is the one idea all have been waiting for. It is the one idea that will organize all disorder out of the mind. It is the one idea that will free the spirit of all envy. It is the one idea that will relieve the heart of all burden. But this idea will only do that if it is put in its proper perspective as the single and center point of all existence. There is to be no greater idea. There is to be no more significant understanding. There is to be no more enduring truth. Not that we or anyone is to bow down to this idea. It stands only as the central organizing factor of all thought and action, bringing clarity to our lives and everything we do or aspire to. The light at the end of the mind, that exists as an idea and is known through a word, is now ready to illuminate a mind.

The light at the end of the mind is not necessarily a new idea. It has been heard before. But never has it been uttered in its proper context. Never has it been known as the final idea, as the greatest idea, as an idea that encompasses the whole of the understanding, bringing all order to that understanding. The idea, cherished by few, has conveniently been relegated to second tier by mankind in his/her religious, political, and sexual belief systems. The great religious and philosophical books presenting the great ideas of mankind forget to mention it. Your author remembers seeing it only one time.* You, the reader, when you hear this idea, may think you already know about it, that you have superior knowledge and are not moved. But let me impress upon you, this idea has yet to be understood in its *spiritual* significance. I assure you, you will not know what that significance is. You must allow the idea into your mind free of your own preconceptions and let it do its work. *Let it work in you.* If left to do its work, it will reorganize your mind and free your heart such that a light will begin to grow, and glow, within you—the light at the end of the mind.

Leaves of Grass—Walt Whitman, 1855

The idea that is a word that exists as the light at the end of the mind only exists at the end of the mind. If this idea does not crush you with its simplicity, if it does not freeze you with its purity, if it does not release you in it universality, if it does not center you in its totality, if it does not extend you in its density, if it does not embrace you with its clarity, please do not enter its gates. I know you want to read on and see what this *word* is but don't, for this word only exists at the end of the mind. You can only see it from that vantage point. If you haven't yet *lost your own mind,* don't read on. If you haven't yet had *your spirit crushed,* don't read on. If you haven't yet *lost all faith* in the immensity of faith, don't read on. If you haven't yet discovered it was never about you or not about you, don't read on. If you are not ready for instant enlightenment, don't read on— the light at the end of the mind is the brightest of lights. It has already blinded all those who cannot see.

The light at the end of the mind is but an idea that is a word. It does not need an explanation. In fact, it cannot be explained. It is what is called *self-evident*. Its meaning will be instantly known. The light at the end of the mind has always been known. Admitted to or not, agreed to or not, it will be recognized as truth. To those of you who have questions, none will be answered. To those of you who have doubts—they are your own. To those of you who speak ill of this word, you will feel a darkness surround you. This is not personal nor is this stated as some absolute judgment. You see, there isn't any subjective compromise to be had. We just are not able to place our subjective desires into the metaphysical structure and constraints of the universe. Subjective compromise has always been our downfall. The light at the end of the mind cannot compromise. *It simply is what it is and cannot be what it is not.* The light at the end of the mind is always and only what it is. It has always been what it is and has never been what it is not. It will always be what it is and will never be what it is not. The light at the end of the mind is, and can only be, an idea that is a word. That word is **procreant**.

Part 3
The Movement of Man and Woman Balance

A New Nation?

A country is only an idea. The idea behind the United States of America was freedom, specifically individual sovereignty, unalienable rights—the survival rights of earning and owning—and the protective rights of due process. Economically and politically speaking this was the greatest idea to date. Unfortunately, I said the idea behind the United States of America <u>was</u> because most of us agree our country has lost its way. Many people disagree as to why and what the solution is to get us back on the right path but most agree we are lost. I am suggesting a paradigm shift recalibrating the center point to be a man and a woman in (equal and opposite) balance together. In the Preface of the *Man and Woman Manifesto: Let the Revolution Begin*, which I wrote in 1994, I stated:

> *This writing is a product of a recent revelation of mine. I have come to realize that I no longer believe in the United States of America. During my many years of writing about freedom, I had an unconscious assumption that freedom and the United States were somehow compatible, or at least I thought they could be. I no longer believe that but rather believe that the United States has lost its way and has become entangled in so much confusion that the only solution available is a paradigm shift of such magnitude that the concept of country itself will be transcended. For me, I no longer see myself to be a citizen of this country, or of any country, but rather just a man who is a part of the universal Community of Man and Woman.*

What is occurring here is a shift in consciousness. Call this a paradigm shift at the metaphysical center of things. The very core of our existence is being shifted away from our religious, national, racial, and political sense of ourselves. Our identities are being recalibrated, if you will. Let's look at the example of our own country and its metaphysical base. Again we will turn to the *Declaration of Independence*.

> *We hold these Truths to be self-evident, that all Men are created equal, that they are endowed by their Creator with certain unalienable Rights, that among these are Life, Liberty, and the pursuit of Happiness—That to secure these Rights, Governments are instituted among Men, deriving their just Powers from the Consent of the Governed, that whenever any Form of Government becomes destructive of these Ends, it is the Right of the People to alter or to abolish it...*

A very powerful statement, its center being ...*endowed by their Creator with certain unalienable Rights...* To date we have never been clear what this "Creator" is and thus are unclear as to what unalienable rights are. Yet for some two-hundred plus years that statement somewhat held us together. No more. We need a new center, one that can hold us together in both love and freedom. The center that is being proposed in this writing is *Man and Woman Balance.* Man and Woman Balance presents to us a two-force center based on the reality that a man and a woman exist together in a relationship of equal and opposite. Theirs is a sexual relationship—sexual being the requirement for procreation and thus the continuation of life. So the *actual life process* itself is being presented as the center point of our lives and interaction together. If we are of life itself, we, by definition, are the co-sovereign retaining at all times the unalienable rights of earning and owning that stem from the survival necessity of production and consumption. No one, certainly not some FED/IRS consortium, can steal our money and lives through a credit/debit money scheme and tax us for <u>having</u> to use this bogus money. It is this simple. In short, the country was lost in 1913 when both the FED and the IRS were created by Congress and signed into law by President Woodward Wilson and upheld by the highest courts of the land. This was a treasonous action by our public officials of that time and continues up to this day. We have been peons ever since. If you think I am extreme listen to this quote by Ronald P. MacDonald and Robert Rowen, M.D. from their book *They Own It All (Including You!) By Means of Toxic Currency,* 2009.

Ronald P. MacDonald and Robert Rowen, M.D.—*They Own It All (Including You!) By Means of Toxic Currency,* 2009

With the veil of deceit lifted, you have now discovered that you don't own anything. You are using another entity's property in all your contracts. The foundation of liberty is the ownership of property. Without property that is exclusively yours, how can you enter into any sort of contract without the permission of the lien holder? Simply put, you can't.

Furthermore, your use of FRNs identifies you as a debtor in use of the creditor's property. You, and every contract into which you enter with its property, are subject to its terms and conditions.

...Within a few years of the gold confiscation and replacement by marked debt notes, came laws of the kind never seen before in America. Roosevelt's New Deal, allegedly for recovery of the Depression, created agency after agency, board after board, license after license. Occupations, which are your common law right to work, suddenly required a license. A license is permission by the state to do that which otherwise would be illegal.

...How did even marriage come to need state permission by license? Previously it was a holy contract entered into before God in a house of worship. How did the spiritual product of this union, children, need registration with the state? The answer is that we have become the chattel property of some entity (the Federal Reserve Bank), requiring registration and permission.

...In 1933, the U.S. government went insolvent. It too then became a debtor subject to the creditor. But you weren't told. We the People don't have any idea what the terms and conditions of that Chapter 11 bankruptcy included. But the evidence leaves a clear trail. The government became the agent of collection for the creditor. The debt was dumped on us. We were collectively beguiled into a debtor's status. The creditor worked the terms and conditions through the government. If the creditor did this openly, we would not be beguiled. But the cruelest and most unconscionable effect from this act is that it is perpetual!

And so here we are. We find ourselves in a state where—*They Own It All (Including You!) By Means of Toxic Currency*. Perpetual debt—think of that the next time your "government servants" promise you something-for-nothing. They even own your person. Yes, you, too, are liened. But aren't unalienable rights those rights that are non-lienable? Isn't it a little late in the game to be asking this? You see, today, right now, the United States of America is a debtor nation. You want to know the real reason behind the 2008 economic collapse? Too much debt. Debt on top of debt. People and companies trading in debt obligations, not actual value. *The*

FED note is a debt instrument. Can you understand this? *The IRS is about creating poverty.* Do you get this? So in creating a new center of Man and Woman Balance, we are also creating a new transaction of value back to the primacy of right of John Locke ...*I ask then when did they begin to be his? And'tis plain, if the first gathering made them not his, nothing else could. That labour put a distinction between them and common. That added something to them more than nature, the common mother of all, had done: and so they became his private right...* and away from the primacy of need of Jean-Jacques Rousseau ...*You are lost if you forget that the fruits of the earth belong to everyone and that the earth itself belongs to no one!* In short, Man and Woman Balance means that you sovereignly own the substance-value money you earn and *that our elected officials actually serve us.* If this is the basis of a new nation, so be it.

Mission Statement

"Bringing Man and Woman Together!"

**...constitutes a shift into the
new paradigm of a two-force universe
of spiritual procreation.**

Due to a simple misconception mankind made at the dawn of consciousness, men and women have not been able to unite in spirit together. The purpose of the Foundation of Man and Woman Balance is to correct this misconception and, in so doing, allow a man and a woman to unite in spirit, bringing forth their love to all of their creations. Men and women, the world over, the time is at hand for your Man and Woman Balance to begin.

Acceptance and Non-Violence

The whole of Man and Woman Balance is based on acceptance and non-violence. The fundamental maxim is "love ye one another." This follows Jesus' teaching: *This is my commandment, That ye love one another, as I have loved you.* (John 15:12). We are to accept another, not judge/rule him or her. Acceptance goes with love, judgment with violence. The great Russian writer Leo Tolstoy (1829-1910) said it this way: *All, everything that I understand, I understand only because I love.* Mahatma Gandhi (1869–1948) known for his non-violent resistance against Great Britain stated: *You must be the change you wish to see in the world.* That is a very bold statement. In essence, the change we want to see "out there" must first occur "in here," in ourselves. *Life doesn't happen to us; it happens out of us.* How often we see those who advocate change do so by the use of force against others. Can that ever work? Another great leader, Martin Luther King, Jr. (1929-1968), stated in his 1964 Nobel Peace Prize talk: *Violence never brings permanent peace. It solves no social problem; it merely creates new and more complicated ones. Violence ends up defeating itself.* Dr. King also stated: *Darkness cannot drive out darkness; only light can do that. Hate cannot drive out hate; only love can do that.* You cannot effect a change for the good by being bad. You cannot effect a change for peace by being at war. You cannot effect a change for love by hating. As stated earlier by Albert Einstein (1879–1955): *The real problem is in the hearts and minds of men. It is not a problem of physics but of ethics. It is easier to denature plutonium than to denature the evil from the spirit of man.* Yet there also stands the Biblical verse (1 John 1: 5): *God is light; in him there is no darkness.*

In the book *Rules for Radicals* by Saul D. Alinsky, 1971, there is a whole chapter on *Of Means and Ends.* The question is, *does the end justify the means?* Alinsky ends the chapter with the statement: *Means and ends are so qualitatively interrelated that the true question has never been the proverbial one, "Does the End justify the Means?" but always has been "Does this particular end justify this particular means?"* To me this seems like a justification for any means one chooses. Historically, people most often have chosen violent means to achieve their ends. But doesn't that say to us that the ends in that case are not true or balanced to begin with. If my end goal is freedom then must not that be my means? The problem with Marxist class struggle is that the goal is not freedom for both but power, one over another. Whoever is on top wants to say on top; whoever is on bottom wants to switch positions with those on top. In either case we don't have a self-other balance. So we must be very careful in defining our ends. We also must ...*be the change you wish to see in the world.* Our ends must begin on the inside of ourselves. We must *love ye one another*. This means we must *do unto another as we would have him do unto ourselves*. We cannot affect change by harassing, coercing, or forcing another to do something. We can only affect change by accepting another and inviting him or her to a certain action. As Tolstoy stated: *All, everything that I understand, I understand only because I love.*

Let me give you an example. This is something I read about Alexander Solzhenitsyn (1918-2008), Russian writer. Solzhenitsyn was probably the greatest moral force in taking down the Russian Communist system. As he stated: *The line dividing good and evil cuts through the heart of every human being.* So I am paraphrasing as I remember the story; Solzhenitsyn was struggling with the question as to why the Communist system was so corrupt and brutal. How could this be when its goal of a people's utopia was so wonderful? It must be the corrupt leaders; if we only had good leaders we would have a wonderful country. (That is what many people believed.) Then he had his moment of enlightenment when he realized that Communism was not corrupt and brutal because of bad leaders; Communism was corrupt and brutal because its <u>end</u> was corrupt and brutal. The end of Communism was not a people's land of plenty; it was a corrupt and brutal system of forced labor at the benefit of the dictatorial leaders. In other words, the end of Communism dictated the means of Communism, a corrupt and brutal dictatorship. And so I say your end must be clean going in. Your means will only and always be an exact reflection of your end. This next quote is from Solzhenitsyn's *The Gulag Archipelago*, 1975.

Alexander Solzhenitsyn (1918-2008)—*The Gulag Archipelago*, 1975

To do evil a human being must first of all believe that what he's doing is good... Ideology—that is what gives evildoing its long-sought justification and gives the evildoer the necessary steadfastness and determination... That was how the agents of the Inquisition fortified their wills: by invoking Christianity; the conquerors of foreign lands, by extolling the grandeur of their Motherland; the colonizers, by civilization; the Nazis, by race; and the Jacobins (early and late), by equality, brotherhood, and the happiness of future generations. Thanks to ideology, the twentieth century was fated to experience evildoing on a scale calculated in the millions.

If your means to achieve your end are brutal it is because your end is brutal. In other words, your heart/soul was brutal going in? Let me give you an example—the Muslim religion (opposite but not equal). Its proponents speak of peace yet its means "to peace" are brutal and violent. Why is that? It is because its end is not peace/tolerance but submission. In other words, you must believe or else. The same is true for the L,G,B,T,Q movement (equal but not opposite). It proponents speak of tolerance, diversity, equality, and fraternity. But their means are just the opposite; anyone who does not agree is smeared. Why is that? Because their end is also submission. The Muslims and the L,G,B,T,Q movement have the same goal—your submission to their cause/ideology. Neither movement can walk the line of acceptance and non-violence. Neither movement can allow *freedom of choice*. Doesn't that say it all right there? They exist in the Victimization Cycle of lack-blame-demand-attack-deny. As such they are on automatic pilot. They are ruled by the primacy of need and will do whatever it takes to see that they are provided for even if it takes force and destruction. Remember the Dostoyevsky quote: *The criminal assumption is that one has the right and authority to take or confiscate values earned by others so long as someone else has a need for those values.* What do you think the FED/IRS is? They are essentially a criminal syndicate. So are all the departments of the government that deal in fulfillment of needs rather than protection of rights. And the government has its own ideology to push and justify its action. Both the Republican and Democratic parties are ideologies to procure money and power rather than serve the people. And they do this in the name of the people. Astounding! That is quite a distance away from *God is light; in him there is no darkness.* One more time I will say, if your end is not clean and clear (as in the balance of the two sexual forces), your means will be anything but accepting and non-violent. Included here is another booklet from *Meditations for Deepening Love*, 1914, 2010. This one is titled *The Age of Freedom: A Call to Join Arms.*

The Age of Freedom: A Call to Join Arms

Freedom is our birthright. It arises out of the *creative balance* each man and woman hold in regard to one another. We are all created equal—in right. Each of us has a fundamental right, by definition, to our *own* lives, as our lives are our own. The sovereignty of individual life is inviolate. Thus it follows that each man and each woman hold the supreme choice—their own—in their life. Of this we are conscious and certain.

If individual life is sovereign, then no one has the right to circumvent the choice of another. If man (men and women) is free, he is free from all dictate. When two or more *free* individuals transact, they do so *voluntarily.* They reside in a relationship of *consent.* The *Age of Freedom* dawns when one begins to base his or her interactions on the *right* of and *respect* for the choice of all involved.

If we are to live in a state of freedom, we must ensure that we do not circumvent another's right to choose. More specifically, we must not support or directly initiate force, or threat of, upon another. The word for this assault upon another's right to choose is *coercion.* Invariably, the intention of coercion is to steal from another or somehow to prevent him from acting in his own interests. In either case, when we do that, we are exercising our might over another's right. If we are truly serious about freedom, we must hold to the cardinal rule of freedom—*I shall have no man under my dictate.*

How many of us can say that? Yes, you might say that you do not control anyone. Most of us don't directly. But we do use the state to carry out our assault. We engage the "third party" of the state to regulate other's choices or simply demand that another pay for policies and programs that benefit ourselves. If the state can dictate to anyone how to go about their business or of how much one is to pay to the state, then certainly the state is the sovereign party, not the individual. If, indeed, the state remains the sovereign party, freedom will never be found.

Let us be clear, I am not suggesting one has a right to license. Freedom is not the right to do anything regardless of consequence. If, in your actions, you harm another, or otherwise damage that other's property, so you are liable. Freedom holds within it a most rigorous personal responsibility, which is why some try to circumvent it. This personal responsibility is called *justice.* The right to act (liberty) and the right—or obligation—to receive the consequences of one's actions (justice) are like the sexes. They go together and need each other. Liberty and justice encompass the whole of freedom.

Now, the question that lies before us is, *can you let another be free?* I don't mean can you allow him or her the freedom of belief, or of speech, or of the vote. No; I mean can you let him (or her) be free where it counts? *In the pocketbook.* I am speaking of an *economic freedom* where each man and woman is free to earn, keep, and spend as they choose. Economic freedom is the heart and soul of freedom.

In life, each of us must pursue a living to survive. We work and, in turn, earn. Through our efforts we bring forth *a value.* Is not what we earn then *our own?* The fundamentals of freedom lie in the right to earn (liberty) and own (justice). We cannot separate earning and owning, i.e., *property*, from freedom. Yet, how often do we hear about the evils of "private property"? The exercising of freedom always results in private (owned) property. Private property is the cornerstone of freedom. If the state can ban or regulate private property, then it can also ban or regulate freedom. Do we control what is our own or don't we?

Today, we live under an illusion of freedom called democracy. We believe that if we have the "right to vote," that somehow we are free. That would be true if, individually, we were sovereign to begin with. But instead, we have erected this huge apparatus called "the state" to dictate to us how we may earn (run our business) and how much of that earning we may own. The state holds the sovereign power over our pocketbook and dictates to us how much we must pay into the state coffers to support their bureaucracy. And if you do not conform, the state will proceed to take most everything you have. You see, we live in the *Age of Coercion.* We justify this coercion as a "necessary evil" to ensure compliance. Compliance to what? Why can't people own what they earn and pay for what they use? If they can't, then the vote does us little good. Try and vote for your own economic freedom within the state. Economic freedom is against the "law" in the state and is truly the great threat to the state. But until we can vote <u>from</u> our own economic freedom and sovereignty, the vote will only continue to support the coercion by the state. This coercion by the state is the simple result of each of us not letting the other be free.

I, for one, no longer *choose* to support this state of affairs. I do not want to be under the dictate of another. Nor do I want another under my own dictate. I do not believe that coercion is necessary for a relationship or society to succeed. Can't we lay down our arms so that we can begin to join arms? I understand that the state will not support my decision. I understand that they will continue to regulate me and confiscate my earnings, even though I only cry for freedom. *I want to be free.* And so, as an exercise of my *sovereign right,* as a man who has no other man under his dictate, I will begin to exercise my economic vote by taking a stand for freedom. I freely choose to take the *Voter's Oath* as my *Declaration of a Freeman.*

The Voter's Oath
I shall not vote until I am free to vote.

The Declaration of a Freeman
How I earn my sustenance will be of my choosing,
given that I do not force another to participate in my effort.
What I earn is mine, to spend as I choose.

It is from this vote and this stand that the Age of Coercion will come to an end for me. All it takes is one; one person to choose to no longer participate in the game that supports coercion. Just one—and then another. Will you not join with me—*in freedom?* We cannot be truly free until we together are free. I lay down my arms. Will not you join *arms* with me? My *invitation* is one of freedom—with liberty and justice for all. Let's you and I together begin the *Age of Freedom.*

...with Liberty and Justice for All

Checks and Balances

The Constitution of the United States of America constitutes the greatest document to date concerning the limitation of governmental power. It did this through its guaranteed freedoms, especially the Bill of Rights, but also through a system of checks and balances. The three branches of government, the executive, legislative, and judicial branches constitute a check on the other. Then there is the other check of the people's right to vote for their officials. That is an awesome check on governmental overreach. There is the freedom of the press (the media) which has served as an important check on government in exposing government overreach and over up. There is the freedom of speech guaranteeing the freedom in the discourse of ideas. There is freedom of religion guaranteeing the freedom to believe as one chooses. There are the freedoms around due process of law. There are the powers of the people and the states (9th and 10th amendments). And if that is not all there is that nasty 2nd amendment about the right to keep and bear arms. Let's look at the Bill of Rights. It might do us good to review them from time to time. They are of our heritage, after all. The following is taken from the internet under Bill of Rights.

The Bill of Rights—First 10 Amendments

The first 10 amendments to the Constitution make up the Bill of Rights. Written by James Madison in response to calls from several states for greater constitutional protection for individual liberties, the Bill of Rights lists specific prohibitions on governmental power. The Virginia Declaration of Rights, written by George Mason, strongly influenced Madison.

One of the many points of contention between Federalists and Anti-Federalists was the Constitution's lack of a bill of rights that would place specific limits on government power. Federalists argued that the Constitution did not need a bill of rights, because the people and the states kept any powers not given to the federal government. Anti-Federalists held that a bill of rights was necessary to safeguard individual liberty.

Let's look at this issue between the Federalists and Anti-Federalists. The Anti-Federalists wanted more limitation on government—*a bill of rights that would place specific limits on government power.* They did not trust the idea that *the people and the states kept any powers not given to the federal government.* Now as you read these see if you can identify the strengthening of your rights or the limitation they place on governmental power. Let us understand, the founding fathers were all about strengthening our rights and limiting governmental power. They knew what unlimited governmental power resulted in.

Amendment I
Congress shall make no law respecting an establishment of religion, or prohibiting the free exercise thereof; or abridging the freedom of speech, or of the press; or the right of the people peaceably to assemble, and to petition the government for a redress of grievances.

Amendment II
A well-regulated militia, being necessary to the security of a free state, the right of the people to keep and bear arms, shall not be infringed.

Amendment III
No soldier shall, in time of peace be quartered in any house, without the consent of the owner, nor in time of war, but in a manner to be prescribed by law.

Amendment IV
The right of the people to be secure in their persons, houses, papers, and effects, against unreasonable searches and seizures, shall not be violated, and no warrants shall issue, but upon probable cause, supported by oath or affirmation, and particularly describing the place to be searched, and the persons or things to be seized.

Amendment V
No person shall be held to answer for a capital, or otherwise infamous crime, unless on a presentment or indictment of a grand jury, except in cases arising in the land or naval forces, or in the militia, when in actual service in time of war or public danger; nor shall any person be subject for the same offense to be twice put in jeopardy of life or limb; nor shall be compelled in any criminal case to be a witness against himself, nor be deprived of life, liberty, or property, without due process of law; nor shall private property be taken for public use, without just compensation.

Amendment VI

In all criminal prosecutions, the accused shall enjoy the right to a speedy and public trial, by an impartial jury of the state and district wherein the crime shall have been committed, which district shall have been previously ascertained by law, and to be informed of the nature and cause of the accusation; to be confronted with the witnesses against him; to have compulsory process for obtaining witnesses in his favor, and to have the assistance of counsel for his defense.

Amendment VII

In suits at common law, where the value in controversy shall exceed twenty dollars, the right of trial by jury shall be preserved, and no fact tried by a jury, shall be otherwise reexamined in any court of the United States, than according to the rules of the common law.

Amendment VIII

Excessive bail shall not be required, nor excessive fines imposed, nor cruel and unusual punishments inflicted.

Amendment IX

The enumeration in the Constitution, of certain rights, shall not be construed to deny or disparage others retained by the people.

Amendment X

The powers not delegated to the United States by the Constitution, nor prohibited by it to the states, are reserved to the states respectively, or to the people.

Isn't that beautiful? Let me just mention a few of them here. Of course one of my favorites is the 5th Amendment. Let's call it the due process Amendment. And we can add the 4th, 6th, and 7th Amendments to the 5th as well. And the 9th and 10th Amendments—don't they say that *we the people* retain all rights/powers not delegated to the United States? What right do federal judges have to overturn the states and the will of the people? It seems we have we forgotten these two very important Amendments today. Then there is the 1st Amendment—the freedom to believe and express. When we speak of the separation of church and state, what that means is that the government is not to advocate a certain religion/belief upon us. Such creation of a state religion (such as secular humanism and L,G,B,T,Q) would immediately create a dictatorship. But for the government to advocate a state run economic system upon us also creates a dictatorship. Have not we noticed? And so the need for the 2nd Amendment. Like it out not, without a 2nd Amendment no country can be free.

Now, every Amendment to the Constitution should be either strengthening a right of the people or a limitation upon government. That is all. So how did we get from these amendments to the point where a business is fined for placing a want ad in the paper for using the word hostess? Or how did we get from the first ten amendments to the 16th Amendment? *The Congress shall have power to lay and collect taxes on incomes, from whatever source derived, without apportionment among the several States, and without regard to any census or enumeration.* I am not a constitutional scholar but does the 16th Amendment in anyway empower the people or limit the government? I believe every Amendment after the first ten should be reviewed to see if there is an empowerment of the individual or a limit on the government and, if not, be rescinded. Certainly the 14th Amendment should be reviewed that places citizenship in the hands of the Federal government (prior to the states) and government debt in the hands of the people. Remember, sovereignty begins with the people.

It would also be worthwhile for you to review some incidences in your own life where you were affected by government overreach. In my case, my parents and I were under IRS onslaught for over five years. It is brutal. Do you know that a Notice of Federal Tax Lien actually says *Notice of Federal Tax Lien under IRS Laws.* The FED/IRS is a law unto itself. It has very few checks and balances, not anything like our Constitution. So which document, IRS Laws or the United States Constitution, actually has the most power? Interesting question. And while I am on it, how can something be a law that no one can understand? Does anyone understand the Internal Revenue Code (Title 26)? What is it, a couple of thousand pages? That on its face should discredit it from being law. Its creation has created a whole side business of attorneys and CPAs and the like (who often live in bigger houses and drive more expensive cars than we do) to assist us in conforming to a law that takes our money from us.

Here is a scenario that has played out over the country. Local officials and union representatives get together and decide on the salaries, perks, and pensions of union employees of local (county) government. (This also plays out on the state and federal levels.) The problem is the salary, perks, and pensions decided upon and agreed to in "binding contracts" have the people who have to pay for these contracts missing from the negotiating table. We think our local officials are for us but they enter into agreements that cause the bankruptcy of our whole way of life. The check needed on that is to have a number of actual taxpayers at these meetings who also have a say/vote in the matter. We no longer can count on our elected officials to serve our interests.

Here is another local case that also plays out over the whole country. In the county where I live an elected official was arrested for drunk driving. There was talk of her being fired from her job. She was head of the local Department of Agriculture. Her defense from being fired was that she had done a good job, that under her tenure the department had grown substantially both in employees and budget. Now, ask yourself, in terms of your rights and government limitation does growing a government department in anyway support your rights or pocketbook? What happens is that government heads have an incentive to grow their departments because that is how they are budgeted regardless of whether that department or its growth is even needed. Now you know what is happening to Washington, D.C. It grows and grows (just like a cancer), as do the governments on the state and local levels. Where is the check and balance? Where is the counter force for lessening the size of government? We don't see those people at the negotiating table. So what does this do to our lives, rights, and pocketbooks?

As government grows:
Taxes grow.
Regulation grows.
Economic laws and control grow.
Debt grows.
Welfare grows.
Bureaucracy, red tape, and paperwork grow.
Forfeiture (individual to government) grows.
Individual opportunity shrinks.
Loss of (unalienable) rights/freedom grow.
Private sector prosperity (money in wallet) shrinks.
Political power and payoffs grow.
County/State/Federal worker's salaries and pensions grow.
Crime and incompetence grow.
Jobs shrink.
Innovation shrinks.

Values/Morality erode.
Spiritual beauty shrinks.
And, lastly, calls for more government grow.

And today we have hardly anyone minding the economic store for us. Our politicians have mostly been bought off. Do any of these (2000 page) bills (that you have to pass before you can know what is in it) have our best interests in mind? Where is the cost/effect analysis of the bill? Does the bill impede on our fundamental (unalienable) rights or does it not? The Patriot Act? Notice how our local police forces are becoming federalized. The Affordable Care Act? It is not about affordability or care. It is about government power. Don't you see that? What about rent control and a minimum wage? How are these constitutionally possible? Where did the government (or anyone) get the power to tell someone what he/she can charge in rent or pay in salary? You don't get to tell another how he/she runs his/her business or life. Get it? It is called *freedom.*

Here is another example. Have you noticed how the government is acquiring more and more land? The land is controlled by the states, I thought, with the people of those states having unalienable rights. Yet more and more I see federal land grabs. Nevada, for example, consists of almost all federal land. How can that be? Well, doesn't the federal government have to take something from the people to pay the FED? Every time the debt ceiling is raised by Congress, to allow for more borrowing, there seems to be another land grab by the government—a new area set aside for this or that purpose we are told. Or how about federal control over our food and nutritional products? How about treaties that circumvent our unalienable rights/Bill of Rights? How about corporations pushing out small businesses? The checks and balances are mostly gone because we are not minding the store or our unalienable rights and pocketbooks. And so it goes...which is why I am making the suggestion that we need to shift our metaphysical center onto a self-other balance that will ensure the rights of both sides. *Not the needs of both sides but the rights.* Not the rights of corporations and unions but of *we the people*—actual living individuals. Corporations and unions should not be able to give money to elected officials or any official for any reason. That is called graft. Most things are common sense, like balanced budgets, government out of the provisional racket, and sound money. That would be a wonderful place to begin! The point here is that we must have another level of control and accounting over our government. This will not come about unless we take our rightful place as co-sovereigns with unalienable rights and substance money in this universe. The following is a booklet titled *The Five Eternal Values* from *Meditations for Deepening Love*, 1994, 2010.

The Five Eternal Values

The five eternal values are those universal or meta-values of spiritual procreation which, I might add, circumscribe all other values. They are the values that frame life from which we can live. Their necessity stands in the articulation of an absolute of life from which we can think and act—and express (procreative) love together. The five eternal values constitute our liberation out of the deadening confines of Christianity (or any religion), Humanism, and Homosexuality. Through the implementation of the five eternal values, we can bring the eternal down to earth and begin to live in the (procreative) light.

The Five Eternal Values

- *Man and Woman Balance*
- *Procreative Love*
- *Universal Accountability*
- *Unalienable Rights*
- *Substance-Value Property/Money*

What follows are my definitions of each of the values. Please feel free to write them in your own words. That way they will become yours to live.

Man and Woman Balance

Man and Woman Balance is that metaphysical construct or structure of the universe upon which there is life. The primary implication of Man and Woman Balance is that there are two primordial forces (not one) and that together they constitute the dynamic order called life. The two forces stand equal to yet opposite from each other. They are not greater than or lesser than each other but rather co-sovereign. In their opposition lies their sexual distinction or difference. Each of the sexes, male and female, has an essential life purpose opposite of the other. In their purpose, they each have something to give that the other needs in order to live. Herein we see the essence of male and female in their unique yet interconnected life roles in their survival quest. We may define these sexual roles as follows:

Male is that force that seeks to divide the one for the purpose of securing individual sexual form (male as to female),
and
Female is that force which seeks to unite the two for the purpose of reproducing the next division of sexual form (male as to female).

Man and Woman Balance presents to us the deepest calling in our souls. When a man calls out for the eternal, he calls out for a woman— *"Come be with me; I need you."* When she hears his call and responds— *"Yes, I will; I need to be needed by you,"* the eternal is sanctified in their hearts as they, in that moment, touch in spirit and become as one. Man and Woman Balance is eternal life.

Procreative Love

Procreative love is Man and Woman Balance in the action or embrace of love. In procreative love, a man and a woman give their (sexual) lives to each other. In this giving, they unite in spirit. From this unity comes the next division of life in the birth of their child.

Procreative love is the only love that is able to bring forth life. It can only occur out of the (equal but opposite) balance of a man and a woman. All love comes from procreative love. All love is centered in a man and a woman giving their lives to each other from which—*a child is born*. The calling we each feel in the deepest recesses of our hearts is the calling of our (equal but opposite) other half for only a man and a woman together constitute the life center of procreative love. And from that center or union of a man and a woman, they can begin to hear their children call to be brought into life. Procreation is the eternal life process. A child is the next expression of procreative life. A child shines the eternal through his or her soul. That eternal is the love that is procreative to life.

Universal Accountability

Universal accountability is that weight or demand that *life* places upon each man and woman per their sexual purpose to either secure or reproduce life. In fact, each man and woman partnership (marriage) has placed upon it the responsibility of procreating (securing/reproducing) this universe of life. Life is our accountability. It is absolutely essential that a man (male) secure life (his wife and family) and that a woman (female) reproduce life (her husband and children). Together they form/create the balanced dynamic of (eternal) life. It is up to them. No one else can do this for them. The universe of life rests within their hands.

We are not just (individual) creators. We are dynamic procreators. Accountability for life lies in our balance together. Spiritual/sexual balance is the universal mirror that reflects back to us the (procreative) consequences of our every thought and action. We are accountable for everything we do—it comes right back at us revealing to us our balance (or lack thereof) we, at each moment, are holding with our eternal (opposite) other half. There isn't any escape from life and the procreative balance we must hold with our other half to secure/reproduce the eternal in our souls. The balance is absolute. The balance is Man and Woman Balance.

Unalienable Rights

Unalienable rights are those universal, eternal, or absolute rights of life that arise out of the balance, i.e., sovereigncy, of the two forces of male and female. In the balance of the two, hierarchy (superior/inferior) collapses and the sovereigncy of their lives surfaces. In this balance, one is not above the other and one is not below the other. In this balance, there aren't any masters or slaves, only co-sovereigns. In fact, there isn't anything in this universe, be it "God," government, this race or that sex, this group or that cause, that is somehow superior in right or privilege to you and me. Unalienable rights stem from the no masters/no slaves *sovereigncy* of our lives.

By definition, each of us has the absolute right of *our* lives. "My life" and "Your life" is/are the given of life. Ultimately, all rights are property rights—what is yours is yours and what is mine is mine. It is from that right to own that freedom arises. In the environment of freedom, people can transact together and exchange their value. The survival necessity of production/consumption demands exchange. We are not self-contained entities. We must reach out and effort (produce) to thereby consume (own). Liberty is the right to earn; justice is the right to own what one earns—or equally receive the consequences of harmful actions. The basis of all unalienable rights center themselves in the two fundamental rights of liberty (earning) and justice (owning). Any denial of the sovereigncy of each and every individual life and the unalienable rights of liberty or justice is an advocacy of tyranny, thievery, and slavery. Liberty and justice must be for all and under no circumstances can anyone be excluded. Man and Woman Balance defines the sovereigncy that embraces unalienable rights for all.

Substance-Value Property/Money

Substance-value property/money is property and/or money that exists as an actual survival value to life. It is that earned/owned property or exchange medium (money) that contains within itself an actual, tangible, concrete, real value right now. The essence of life is value transaction (trade), i.e., relationship. The production/consumption necessity of life is carried out through *effort value exchange,* spiritually, mentally, and physically one to another. The basis of any exchange lies in the freedom of the parties to exchange that value (they own) they decide to exchange. A medium of exchange (to standardize trade) must itself be free and of value. (Money, too, must be a *private-property* transaction.) If some group or government has a monopolistic control over property and/or money, they can easily discredit its value forcing a counterfeit value or script on the people. The credit/debit system (issuing credit from nothing and obligating a people to pay off that debt) is a counterfeit scheme containing only the appearance of value. It can only be held together through coercion (force).

The ability of a medium of exchange to hold value is dependent on its actual substance-value. It also depends on a people possessing the right (freedom) to own what they earn. True money can only be private-property money of actual concrete value. That value may be in the form of gold, silver, computer chips, redeemable certificates of actual items of value, etc., but a value it will be under the discretion of the *owner.* In essence, *substance-value money is private property money of an actual value owned by an actual person.* Anything else is a fraud—a monopolistic counterfeit script—that holds all people in debt/bondage. Unless and until a people embrace substance-value property/money they will never be free at the heart of where freedom lies—that essential life-sustaining exchange of value.

The five eternal values of Man and Woman Balance, Procreative Love, Universal Accountability, Unalienable Rights, and Substance-Value Property/Money position each of us in the present moment of life. And in that present moment everything unreal collapses. In fact, only one thing is left standing. Do you know what that is? It is *family.* Family is the *living* embodiment of the five eternal values. *Family is the only reality.* These other structures I have spoken about (Christianity, Humanism, and Homosexuality) do not allow for family to stand on the spiritual procreative center of the universe. But family must stand on that which is of its nature—*eternal life.*

What About... Questions

What about questions are those endless questions others bring up (perhaps subconsciously) to create a doubt in the whole of what one is presenting. Sometimes they are put into a negative statement such as, "Oh, nobody can know that," as if that person knows that! Generally, what about questions reflect the doubt in the questioner's mind: What about... the environment, water rights, reproductive rights, unisex bathrooms, drugs, the war on drugs, the war on poverty, genetic modification, UFOs, free will... and on and on. There are thousands or millions or billions of them. And if you are not able to handle them on the spot your whole thesis may go down. Generally, there are a couple of ways to handle what about questions. One is to just turn it around and reply, "That is a good question and presents to you a wonderful inquiry as to its answer." Another way to is suggest that there will always be questions/issues as creation itself is not static and, whatever is placed in front of us, it is our task to move in the direction of love and freedom. Oftentimes, ways of doing things break down. It is time for a shift, for a new model to emerge. We have seen this in the health care industry where it has become bogged down. Unfortunately, the (government's) answer was more government cost and control. In this case, we did not move towards more freedom, empowering people with their own courses of action. It is always good to be asking of yourself, "Does this course of action move me and others towards greater love and freedom or does it not?"

Ultimately, what about questions question the very basis of truth itself. And if there isn't an ultimate truth there certainly can't be a moral truth. Isn't that what these detractors of truth want, to discredit moral truth? Doesn't the whole of L,G,B,T,Q (Feminism) stand on discrediting moral truth? This next quote is from James Colman Linehan, from his book with the extra-long title: *Rational Nature of Man with Particular Reference to the Effects of Immortality on Intelligence According to St. Thomas Aquinas, a Metaphysical Study*, 1937.

James Colman Linehan—*Rational Nature of Man... a Metaphysical Study*, 1937

Aristotle writes that the foundation of morality lies in a clear perception of moral facts. If, therefore, a man wishes to study moral philosophy he ought to live a virtuous life so that he might be able to grasp truth; and that his intellect might be able to form sound judgments on the matter of his study. Aquinas goes even further. He teaches that morality is necessary for the proper action of the intellect; that immorality affects the intellect in its acquisition of truth, because immorality is a deviation from what is in harmony with reason.

...Therefore, upon the end and purpose of life will depend the notion of morality. Broadly speaking, then morality may be defined as the conformity, or lack of conformity, of an action with the ultimate purpose of life. Since for the utilitarian the ultimate end of life is the greatest happiness of the greatest number, the morality of his actions will depend upon whether they lead on to, or hinder, such an attainment. If they achieve this purpose they are good; if not, they are evil. Since the ultimate end of life for the hedonist is pleasure, then for him, whatever gives pleasure is morally good; otherwise it is evil, and for him, pleasure is the guide or criterion of morality. In all systems of philosophy that profess an Ethics, there is a necessary relationship, a relationship that is inescapable, between morality and the ultimate end or purpose of life.

The end or purpose of an act is a very important moral factor in the act, because herein precisely enters the action of the will, the faculty which commands all the others to do its bidding. Only in so far as acts come under the influence of the will have they morality. Saint Thomas writes:—

"Therefore the species of a human act is considered formally with regard to the end, but materially according to the object of the external act. Hence Aristotle says that he who steals for the purpose of committing adultery is, strictly speaking, more adulterer than thief."

Nevertheless, it must ever be born in mind that these two other determinants have their own peculiar morality apart from the end or purpose of the acts; and if they are evil, no matter how worthy or how laudable the end may be, the act is evil. A good reason merely for performing an action does not justify evil circumstances or an evil object. In a word, the end does *not* justify the means.

Probably the most important matter in all moral philosophy is the point of fact that there is a natural basis for the distinction between what is good and what is evil. It is clear, therefore, that the good and evil in human acts are not only according to the positing of a law, but according to the nature order. Good and evil are not relative or transitory notions changing with every wind or fancy. By no means. That which is essentially good, is good always, in all places, at all times, and forever.

From what has been said, it is clear that the ultimate end or purpose of life is the ultimate norm or standard in reference to which some acts are determined as morally good and others as morally evil. What is this ultimate norm? There is a fundamental law of all created beings — a profound metaphysical law, by which all created beings tend towards their proper end or good. ...But only one reason could be responsible for the complete and final guiding of the whole universe, and that reason is Divine. Therefore the ultimate norm of morality is Divine Reason. Human actions will be morally good insofar as they are in harmony with God's Intellect which guides and orders everything towards the fulfillment of its purpose.

Just as in the speculative order the intellect grasps first principles, and is infallible in attaining truth if the laws of right reasoning are adhered to in the process of arriving at the conclusions based upon these infallible first principles, so also in the practical order, the human mind intuitively sees that certain things are right and that certain other things are wrong.

In a word, then, the proximate standard of morality is the dictate of human right reason (*recta ratio*), and the ultimate standard is God's creative reason. Saint Thomas writes:

> "The rule of the human will is twofold, one near and homogeneous, namely human reason itself; the other is the first rule, the Eternal Law which is, so to speak, Divine Reason."

After such a summary of Saint Thomas' teaching on morality, we may define the notion of morality as the conformity or the lack of conformity of a human act with the Eternal Law made manifest by human reason. The Eternal Law is nothing other than Divine Wisdom directing all action.

Moral good and moral evil are words of supreme importance, and should be very definitely and clearly understood. This must be insisted upon, because, as Archbishop McNicholas writes:

> "What is most disheartening in our times is that many leaders of thought, many molders of public opinion, many university professors and influential writers deny the natural law and the very fundamental principles of right and wrong upon which all morality rests... Today our neo-paganism denies the existence of the moral order, and insists that there is no fixed code of morality."

...today our neo-paganism denies the existence of the moral order, and insists that there is no fixed code of morality. That sounds just like what is happening today. So be careful of the smear mongers. They are always and only questioning (in their "what about questions") your moral truth and the basis of absolute truth itself. "Certainly Man and Woman Balance cannot be an absolute truth. No way can it be the gauge of moral action. We won't let it be," they scream. Let's end this section with another booklet from *Meditations for Deepening Love*, 1994, 2010. This one is titled *The First Pair.*

The First Pair

The First Pair has come! We thought the return would be through Jesus or some Avatar type. It wasn't. We thought there would be a great rejoicing—some final salvation. There wasn't. We thought the return would bring peace on earth. It didn't. Certainly the return would at least better our plights. It didn't even do that. So what then was the return, what did it do? Perhaps—could it?—touch one heart.

Man: We, my beloved wife and I, have come forth to unite together that we may have child. If you understand what I have just said, you understand all things.

Woman: Our child, created out of our love—let that be the light that shines for us our way.

Man: If you don't understand what my wife and I just said, let me illuminate. We, the *First Pair*, are what you have, heretofore, called God. We are the first cause, the divine principle and purpose, the primal force(s), the source of all creation. All that is exists through us, our love.

Woman: The spirit of our love connects us all—from the first man and woman to the last which again becomes the first. It is this spirit that is the *Holy Spirit*. We, the *First Pair*, speak to you through our hearts.

Man: The first creation, our child, came from us out of the balance that we together comprise. Please understand, *balance* is the first principle. You cannot circumvent it. Balance always comprises an equal and opposite two—a man and a woman, *primordially*. That is its definition.

Woman: From our balance a child is born. Our balance is our love.

Man: Within the balance is the *procreant*. We, man and woman, are procreant *together*. We are only procreant with each other. Procreation is our eternal lineage. Our balance, as a procreant moment between two equal but opposite *sexed* forces, comprises the eternal.

Woman: The *First Pair* is always eternal. Our love that flows through our balance is eternal love. Our love always exists for our child. As it will never die; it sustains all life at all times.

Man: We, the *First Pair*, exist in the heart or soul of all things directing all things. Balance is our guide. Balance is our law. No one, not even us, can circumvent the *sexual balance* between a man and a woman.

Woman: Your anguish is that you seek and cannot find. Until you hold the balance of our love in your hearts, you can never find. When you do you will know that you *two* can never be lost for you, too, are the *First Pair*, knowing your own love together even before the beginning.

Man: I, man, divide the one.

Woman: I, woman, unite the two.

Man: We, dividing from and uniting with each other, *together* constitute the source of all creation. Not alone; not with something else. Not through anything else. Your life hinges on the *procreant balance* you hold with your eternal other half, just as does mine.

Woman: Don't despair. Rejoice. You, right now, can invite your eternal other half into your heart. I remember the day well when my husband and I said our prayer and took our vows together. That wonderful moment lives in our hearts to this day. We say our prayer and vows together each moment, every day. That is how it *lives*.

Man: Look at us, a man and a woman. What would you have us say? We stand not apart from you. We claim no dimension greater than you. We hold out our hands to you in the consciousness that we, the *First Pair*, can only shine the love to you that arises out of the love we have for our child.

Woman: My sisters, can you feel yourself holding your child in your arms, that child created by your husband and yourself? Is not that the greatest of all miracles?

Man: And brothers, feel the pride you have in securing your family. Every one of you, together with your wives, is surely the *First Pair*. May you take this stand for life.

Woman: The *First Pair* is the only stand my husband takes. And he gives this all to me. I receive all so that we, the *First Pair*, may be reproduced out of my spirit-womb once again. I am woman. All things born out of me come back into me to be reborn out of me.... For surely this is our truth.

Man: To woman I give my life. To woman I make my surrender. To woman I embrace my eternal life as man, only and always with her eternal life as woman. Together we, man and woman, stand on our life eternal.

Woman: How could it be any other way?

Man: The *First Pair*, an original idea, now being differentiated into consciousness as the source of all consciousness by a *First Pair*, is, from this moment on, delineated to be existent at the soul of all things, guiding all things to a universal awareness of 'itself' (as a two procreant forces/*First Pair*), an awareness that from this day forth can never be undone.

Woman: And there is love.

Organization and Leadership

Organization and leadership actually develop out of the paradigm shift that is occurring, in this case to the new paradigm of Man and Woman Balance, which brings love and freedom into the heart and soul. The organization is made up of those who have made the shift. But it is this paradigm shift that allows for one to have greater <u>inner</u> organization, greater conceptual capacity, and thought integration and creativity. Let's just say correct metaphysical concept equals greater mental capacity and construction. Those who have abilities in certain areas rise to the top of leadership positions in those areas. Concerning leadership, it is important to understand that you don't and even can't be #1 in all areas of life. When another shows up whose ability reaches beyond your own, defer to him or her. There is nothing wrong with letting those best prepared lead that task. And in terms of the organization, it is important that everyone has a task, one that exemplifies their creativity and joy and will progress them to another level of competency. Everyone's task is to keep moving forward. That is the creative process after all. It is also important to acknowledge/praise those who do a good job. We all want recognition. We all want to feel we have value. Sure that must come from within but it is nice to receive it from without as well. Truly, we are to live by the Golden Rule which says in effect—*Do unto another as you would have another do unto you.* That is universal law.

Organization and leadership either rise or fall as per the balance of the ideal one is holding. Our ideal (belief or vision) carries us forward. We believe. In the case of this writing, we believe in Man and Woman Balance as the eternal cause/truth. That is our ideal, our modus operandi. It is what we organize our lives and world around and attempt to manifest through leadership. The whole key, if you will, is to hold this ideal (of Man and Woman Balance) as the real at all times. And the more we do our (inner) organization becomes tighter. This is how we become leaders, even masters. Here are some more quotes from *Ideal Made Real or Applied Metaphysics for Beginners*, 1909, by Christian D. Larson that addresses this very point. As you read feel your own inner organization tightening and leadership growing.

Christian D. Larson (1874-1954)—*Ideal Made Real or Applied Metaphysics for Beginners*, 1909

Real progress is eternal; it is a forward movement that is continuous now, and in the realization of such a progress no thought is ever given to time. To live in the life of eternal progress is to gain ground every moment. It means the perpetual increase of everything that has value, greatness and worth, and the mind that lives in such a life cannot possibly be discouraged or dissatisfied. Such a mind will not only live in the perpetual increase of everything the heart can wish for, but will also realize perpetually the greatest joy of all joys, the joy of going on. The discouraged mind is the mind that lives in the emptiness of life, but there can be no emptiness in that life that lives in the perpetual increase of all that is good and beautiful and ideal.

When we discern an ideal that ideal has come within the circle of our own capacity for development, and the power to develop that ideal in ourselves is therefore at hand. The mind never discerns those ideals that are beyond the possibility of present development. This we realize that when an idea is discerned it is proof positive that we have the power to make it real now...our ideals will be realized one after the other until life becomes what it is intended to be, a perpetual ascension into all that is rich, beautiful and sublime.

Proceed to remake yourself into the likeness of that ideal and it will become your own. To proceed with this great development, the whole of life must be changed to conform with the exact science of life; that is, that science that is based upon the physical and the metaphysical united as the one expression of all that is great and sublime in the soul.... Think of the idea as if it were real and you will find it to be real. Meet all things as if they contained the ideal, and you will find that all things will present their ideals to you, not simply as mere pictures, but as realities.

...it is evident that the right use of the spiritual life will produce and bring everything that man may need or desire. The source of everything has the power to produce everything, provided the power within that source is used according to exact spiritual law.

But when we realize that the kingdom is the great spiritual world within us, and that from this world comes all wisdom, all power, all talent, all life; in brief, everything that we now possess in body, mind and soul, and that everything we are to receive in the future must come from the same source, we understand clearly why the kingdom must be sought first.

We cannot secure anything unless we go to the source, and the spiritual kingdom within us is the one only source of everything that is manifested in human life.

When we seek first the kingdom and his righteousness all other things are added, not in some mysterious manner, nor do they come of themselves regardless of conscious effort to work in harmony with the law of life. We receive from the kingdom only what we are prepared to use in the living of a great life and in the doing of great and worthy things in the world. We receive only in proportion to what we give, and it is only as we work well that we produce great results; but by entering the spiritual life we receive everything that we may require in order to give as much as we may desire, to do as much as we may desire.

When the elements of the ideal are blended harmoniously with the elements of the real the two become one; the ideal becomes real and the real gives expression to the qualities of the ideal. To be in harmony with everything at all times and under all circumstances is therefore one of the great essentials in the living of that life that is constantly making real a larger and larger measure of the ideal; and so extremely important is continuous harmony that nothing should be permitted to produce confusion or discord for the slightest moment.

No person who lives in perpetual harmony will be deprived very long of his own whatever that own may be. Whatever you deserve, whatever you are entitled to, whatever belongs to you will soon appear in your world, if you are living in perfect harmony.

The true way to attain greater things is to permit the greatness that is within to have full expression; likewise when we seek health, happiness and harmony or a beautiful life, the true course is to permit those things to come forth and act through us; they are ready to appear. We do not have to work for them or strive so hard to secure them. They are now at hand and will express themselves through us the very moment we grant them permission.

We do not help the weak by becoming weak. We do not relieve sickness by becoming sick. We do not right the wrong by entering into the wrong, or doing wrong. We do not free man from failures by permitting ourselves to become failures. We do not emancipate those who are in bondage to sin by going and committing the same sin. ...but we cannot remove darkness by entering into the dark. We can remove wrong only by removing the cause of that wrong, and to remove the cause of wrong we must produce the cause of right. Darkness disappears when we produce light.

When one door closes another opens; sometimes several. This is the law of life. It is the expression of the law of eternal progress. The whole of nature desires to move forward eternally. The spirit of progress animates everything. Whenever a person loses an opportunity to move forward this great law proceeds to give him another. This proves that the universe is kind, that everything is for man and nothing against him. This being the truth, the man who talks health, happiness, prosperity, power and progress is working in harmony with the universe, and is helping to promote the great purpose of the universe.

Go with the universe, and all the power of the universe will go with you, and will help you reach whatever object you may have in view. ...you will reach every ideal, and at the best time and under the best circumstances cause that ideal to become real. ...Things will take a turn when you take a turn, and you will take a turn when you begin to talk about those things that you desire to realize. Never talk about anything else.

The future of a person is not preordained by some external power, nor is fate controlled by some strange, mysterious force that master-minds alone can comprehend and employ. It is ideals that control fate, and all minds have their ideals wherever in the scale of life they may be. ...To have ideals is to have definite objects in view, be those objects very high or very low, or anywhere between those extremes.

The destiny of every individual is determined by what he is and by what he does; and what any individual is to be or do is determined by what he is living for, thinking for or working for. Man is not being made by some outside force. Man is making himself with the power of those forces and elements that he employs in his thought and his work; and in all his efforts, physical or mental, he invariably follows his ideals.

To entertain superior ideals is not to dream of the impossible, but to enter into mental contact with those greater possibilities that we are now able to discern, and to have the power to discern an ideal indicates that we have the power to realize that ideal.

When ideals are very high all the forces of the system will move towards superior attainments; all things in the life of the individual will work together with the greater and greater greatness in view, and continued advancement on a larger and larger scale must inevitably follow. ...To entertain superior ideals is to think the very best thoughts and the very greatest thoughts about everything with which we come in contact.

The man who becomes much will achieve much, and great achievements invariably build a great destiny. To think of anything that is less than the best, or to mentally dwell with the inferior is to neutralize the effect of those superior ideals that we have begun to entertain.

Superior idealism does not recognize the power of evil in anything or in anybody; it knows that adverse conditions exist, but it gives the matter no conscious thought whatever. ...He knows that all things positively will work together for good when we recognize only the good, think only the good, desire only good and expect only the good; likewise, he knows that all things positively will work together for greater things when all the powers of life, thought, and action are concentrated upon the attainment and the achievement of greater things.

As man is in the within, so everything will be in his external world. Therefore, whether man is to lose or gain in the without depends upon whether he is losing or gaining in the within.

The basis of all possession is found in the consciousness of man, and not in exterior circumstances, laws or conditions. If a man's consciousness is accumulative, he will positively accumulate, no matter when he may live.

Before we can gain anything we must have something, and to have something is to be conscious of something.

...All possession is based upon consciousness and is held by consciousness or lost by consciousness. All gain is the result of an accumulative consciousness. All loss is due to what may be termed the scattering consciousness; that is, that state of consciousness that lets go of everything that may come within its sphere. When you are conscious of something you are among those that hath and to you shall be given more.

When you inwardly feel that you are gaining more and more, or that things are beginning to gravitate towards your sphere of existence, more and more will be given to you until you have everything that you may desire. How we feel in the within is the secret, and it is this interior feeling that determines whether we are to be among those that have or among those that have not. When you feel in the within that you are gaining more you are among those that have, and to you shall be given more.

Whatever you become conscious of in yourself, that you gain possession of in yourself. Whatever you gain possession of in yourself, that you can constructively employ in your sphere of existence, and whatever is constructively employed is productive; it produces something. Therefore, by becoming conscious of something you gain the power to produce something, and products on any plane constitute riches on that plane.

When we analyze these laws from another point of view we find the consciousness of the real in ourselves produces an ascending tendency in the mind, and whenever the mind begins to go up, the law of action and reaction will continue to press the mind up further and further indefinitely. Every upward action of mind, produces a reaction that pushes the mind upward still farther. ...the fact is, when the mind enters the ascending scale the law of action and reaction will perpetuate the ascension so long as the mind takes a conscious interest in the progress made; but the moment the mind loses interest in the movement the law will reverse itself and the mind enters the descending scale. Therefore, become conscious of the law in yourself and take a conscious interest in every step in advance that you make, and you will go up in the scale of life continually and indefinitely.

The great secret of gaining more, regardless of circumstances, is to continue perpetually to go up in mind. No matter how things are going about you, continue to go up in mind. Every upward step that is taken in mind adds power to mind, and this added power will produce added results in the tangible world.

When things seem to go wrong we should stay right and continue to stay right, and things will soon decide to come and be right also. This is a law that works and never fails to work. ...The laws of life will continue perpetually to give to those who have placed themselves in the receiving attitude, and those same laws will take away from those who have placed themselves in the losing attitude. When you create a turn in yourself you will feel that things are also taking a turn to a degree, and if you continue persistently in this feeling, everything in your life will positively take the turn that you have taken. As you go everything in your world will go, providing you continue to go; the law of action and reaction explains why.

To establish the accumulative consciousness, that is, that consciousness that has complete hold on things, train yourself to inwardly feel that you have full possession of everything in your own being. Feel that you possess yourself. Affirm that you possess yourself. Think constantly of yourself as possessing yourself—everything that is in yourself, and you will soon be conscious of absolute self-possession.

When you begin to feel that you possess yourself you actually *have* something in consciousness, and according to the laws of gain and possessions you will gain more and more without end. You are in the same consciousness with those who have, and to you will be given. You have established the inner cause of possession through the conscious possession of your entire inner life, and the effect of this cause, that is, the perpetual increase of external possession, must invariably follow. In brief, you have applied the great law—To Him That Hath Himself All Other Things Shall Be Given.

Everything that exists in your outer world has a correspondent in your inner world. This inner correspondent is the cause that has either created or attracted its external counterpart, and this process is easily understood. To state it briefly, environment corresponds with ability. Circumstances are the aggregation of events brought about by our own actions and associations and friends, which follow the law of like attracting like.

It is wealth in the mental and the spiritual worlds that has the greatest value or the greatest power in promoting the welfare and the happiness of man, and this higher wealth can be accumulated only by those who are living according to their ideals.

To change circumstances is to change fate; and whatever the change may be in fate, circumstances or events it will be a change for the better, if the increase of power is applied according to the principle of ideals.

Make yourself equal to the best and you will meet the best. This is a law that is universal and is never known to fail. Make yourself a great power in your present sphere action. Learn to do things better than they have ever been done before. Produce something for the world that the world wants and the gates to new and greater opportunities will open for you.

Do not simply think of things as they appear on the surface, but try to think of things as they are in the spirit of their interior existence. The mere effort to do this will develop the power to look through things or to look into things; and the growth of this power promotes interior insight. You may thus discern clearly the real worth and the real possibilities that exist in the lofty goal that you have in view, and by keeping the eye single upon that lofty goal, never wavering for a moment, all the powers of your being will work together and build for those greater things that you can see upon the heights of that goal. Thus your entire world in the within as well as in the without will constantly be recreated and rebuilt according to the likeness of your supreme ideals, in consequence, you will not only build for yourself an idea world, but you will be building for yourself a world that is ever becoming more and more ideal, and to live in such a world is ideal living indeed. The world that is ever becoming more and more ideal is *the* world in which to live, and the power to create such a world is now at hand in every human mind.

A bit long perhaps but this is what we need to get—*its compression*. In short, we must own our organization and leadership, even more so in the deeper sense that I am presenting, that of Man and Woman Balance. Man and Woman Balance is more than a new thought; it is a spiritual evolution. Man and Woman Balance is *ideal/truth*. It serves as our universal alignment and spiritual healing. We are able to align/balance our individual metaphysical frames onto the balance/order of man and woman.

Structural Balance
Man and Woman Balance

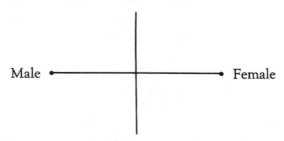

This metaphysical frame (as a living procreant word) in our hearts and souls becomes the basis of our <u>Word</u> or voice. Now we are able to speak from the truth as it were. I remember the word Abracadabra as a young boy. Never really knew what it meant. According to Wikipedia: *The word Abracadabra may derive from an Aramaic phrase meaning "I create as I speak."* I have also heard it said as: *"I create what I speak."* Imagine the power of our speaking—your actual creative *Word*—in being in alignment to the fundamental order of things. Our Word is not only the basis of our bond but it is also the basis of our creativity. As you speak you create. If you don't like what you have in your world, change your speaking/Word. Conscious idea is only expressed in thought/language/speaking. In other words, we bring something into form through our Word. Word, as I am using the term here, is more than our putting idea into language; it embodies the total desire/expression/vibration of our very beings. As such, our Word is our consciousness, our energy, our very life—*a living Word.* "*Let there be light,*" it was said. Might we also say, "*Let there be balance*" or "*Let there be freedom*" or "*Let there be love*"? This is our hope and faith. This is our ideal. This is our power. We must hold to it all times. This paradigm shift into Man and Woman Balance is a challenge both to understand and to hold in the face of others' doubts and challenges to us. To hold Man and Woman Balance as your faith and ideal in the face of others' doubts and challenges is the practice of both organization and leadership. And this brings us back around to creative manifestation. I actually didn't complete that discussion in the chapter *Our Spiritual Task.* If you recall we were discussing Thomas Troward and the book *Your Invisible Power* by his student Genevieve Behrend, ending that discussion with Manna (the giving and receiving of love) as the spiritual food or original light pulsing through us. Let's call this our beginning point of creative manifestation. But now we want to step into bringing forth what we want as the crowning aspect of organization and leadership. A *master of life*, as it were, brings forth the life he or she aspires to. This is the demarcation point between being successful or not. Concerning the message of Man and Woman Balance, we want to be successful. We want to be masters of life. So adding to what Mr. Larson said above, I am including some selections from the book *The Message of the Master* by John McDonald (1906-1998). *The Message of the Master* was published in 1929 I believe. It certainly must be included in the library of writings by those in the Creative Thought movement. Notice the power and control of thought as we master the law. He states:

John McDonald (1906-1998)—*The Message of the Master,* 1929

There are no limits to my possibilities! My successes will multiply and increase in proportion to my mastery of the Law.

I operate according to a definite, unerring law. I know the outcome before I start.

Any picture firmly held in any mind, in any form, is bound to come forth. That is the great, unchanging Universal Law that, when we cooperate with it intelligently, makes us absolute masters of the conditions and situations in our lives.

It is a false belief that there is a power or powers outside you greater than the power within you.

The consciousness or fixed picture in mind of anything, any condition, any circumstance is the actual thing itself.

We have the capacity and the power to create desirable pictures within, and to find them automatically printed in the outer world of our surroundings.

When you invoke the aid of this law, you do not need money, friends, or influence to attain whatever your heart is set upon. It doesn't matter in the least what your position is in life. It doesn't matter whether your ambition is directly in line with the position you now occupy, or whether it requires a complete change from what you are doing. You may have no definite plan in life except the fact that you want to get ahead. All the desire in the world will get you nowhere; what is necessary to do first is to establish a *set definite objective* firmly within.

Once the seed is planted in the darkness of the soil, it proceeds to express or out-picture the exact picture held within its life cell and, in obedience to law, it sends up a shoot seeking the light. ...Keep in mind that the actual process takes place in darkness, beneath the surface. It is the same with us. That is where all great and important ideas are developed.

Now, are you going to constantly be glancing out of the corner of your eye to see how things are proceeding? Are you going to be wondering how the thing works, or it if really is working? Not at all. You set the objective. You planted the seed. You wouldn't dig up a seed in your garden to see if it were sprouting. You planted and watered it and you're satisfied that, according to the law of its being, it will come forth. In exactly the same way, nothing on earth can prevent your objective from becoming externalized, because nothing in the world can nullify Universal Law. You plant the seed idea. You hold it there. You nourish it. You have done your part. Trust the Law to do its part.

As you practice these teachings, what should your attitude

be? What is the attitude of the wind as it speeds on its way to its destination? It recognizes no person, place, or thing as having any power to hinder it. It is *impersonal*. The sun shines, the rain falls, and the wind blows upon all alike. They choose no particular persons or things to help or harm. There is a lesson in that. Those who attempt to hinder you are *helping* you, and they should be considered your friends. This is wisdom of the highest order.

Keep the secret of your aspirations locked securely within you. This sets up antagonism in the Outer Mind, for it rebels against discipline and control. Seeing that it is about to be deprived of its freedom, it will, like a wild bull in a stockade, seek to escape by every means except the way you have provided. I am warning you—it will bring every sort of argument it can in an attempt to convince you that your purpose is futile. It will tempt you to mention your plans and ambitions to others, to slow up your activity, to doubt the power of the Law operating in your behalf. It will try in every conceivable way to thwart you. And your answer to all this will be, *"Obey. I am master here."* Take the position that you are master of your being, and hold your course firmly to your goal.

You may be led through strange places and take circuitous routes at times, but don't let that disturb you. With the wisdom of the Inner Mind at the helm, you are being led the quickest way, even though it may appear at times to be the longest.

This advice is necessary for you now as beginners, but as you grow in practice you will find that these qualities become a part of your very being. Then they function automatically, without any conscious effort at all on your part. What is the result? When you persistently hold to your goal, and keep absolutely air-tight secretiveness, the Outer Mind finds no escape for its increasing energy, and in desperation it plunges through, like the overload of stream through the safety value of a boiler, and your objective is reached.

Living the Law will cause you to become the kind of individual that people notice. They will be instinctively attracted to you, without knowing why, on the street and in your social and business affairs. You will become a mysterious being to the world. Don't let this go to your head. Give thanks, in humble gratitude, to the great Supreme Power that has made this possible.

Incredible. ...*a set definite objective—"Obey. I am master here."—nothing in the world can nullify Universal Law—and your objective is reached...* And how about these: *"It is a false belief that there is a power or powers outside you greater than the power within you,"* and *"The consciousness or fixed picture in mind of anything, any condition, any circumstance is the actual thing itself,"* and *"We have the capacity and the power to create desirable pictures within, and to find them automatically printed in the outer world of our surroundings."* Now isn't that golden? These are profound! Yet, how that "outer mind" (small self) wants to control things driving us right down into the black pit of lack, depression, and failure. This we must ignore. We must hold to our ideal. Call this intention if you want. *Intention, intention, intention,* i.e., *conscious purpose.* We must hold to it with the same certainty we have for our own existence (and the existence of another), with the same certainty we hold in the goodness and balance of all things, with the same certainty in which we *absolutely know* that the universe in its entirety is a sexually balanced male and female interaction, an active-responsive, eternal, living, touch of love, and, furthermore, that all the forces in the universe are behind our success; the under-structure of the universe itself has been set such that everything we do will go our way—for we absolutely know the intrinsic balance and that we exist as part and parcel of this eternal balance. And, maybe most importantly—*We decide.* Yes, you are the I of you and I am the I of me. This is to say that each and every one of us is a <u>primary</u> mental force/creator, not a secondary one. Our every desire/decision holds absolute manifestation capability—due to the (sexual) creative process itself. As Walter Russell once stated: *Idea cannot evade its manifestation into form.* He also stated: *All questions are answerable in the light; thou art light.* Ernest Holmes (1887-1960), writing in *The Science of Mind,* 1938, stated it this way: *Conceive of your word as being the thing.* This is what we must get to. *Can you take this on right now?* That, essentially, is the answer. So let's end this section with the Biblical verses Mark 11: 23-26 followed by *The Faith That Moves Mountains,* also out of *Meditations of Deepening Love,* 1994, 2010.

Mark 11:23-26: *For verily I say unto you, That whosoever shall say unto this mountain, Be thou removed, and be thou cast into the sea; and shall not doubt in his heart, but shall believe that those things which he saith shall come to pass; he shall* *have whatsoever he saith.*

Therefore I say unto you, What things soever ye desire, when ye pray, believe that ye receive them, and ye shall have them.

And when ye stand praying, forgive, if ye have ought against any: that your Father also which is in heaven may forgive you your trespasses.

But if ye do not forgive, neither will your Father which is in heaven forgive your trespasses.

The Faith that Moves Mountains

Let thou thy voice speak unto thee—of the faith that moves mountains. I now tell you, faith is but a word that also means the *truth*. It is not faith in itself that moves mountains. It is the truth and the faith in the truth that moves mountains. Faith stands on the truth. "So, what is the truth?" you ask. Let me first speak to you about what is the mountain. The mountain is the belief system(s) the world is now holding. It is the belief systems of the world that are blocking truth from entering into the heart of mankind. What is your belief? *Let it go.* You must let it go.

"Ah, but that is not so easy," you say. Indeed, our identities are tied around our belief systems. "Show me your truth, then I will decide," you exclaim. But, I must ask, where is the faith in that? You must *let it go* before I can speak to you of the truth. "How is that done?" you ask. "One just can't let go of one's belief." Do you not trust in yourself? Do you fear you might lose yourself? Do you even know the truth of yourself? Surrender, my friend. Surrender it all. Your belief system will no longer serve you.

"Well, just who are you? Why should I believe you?" you ask. Let me tell you who I once was. Once I was a Christian. Once I was a Jew. Once I was a Hindu, a Muslim, a Buddhist, a Mormon, a Transcendentalist, a Paganist, an Atheist, a Humanist, a Nationalist, a Racist, a Libertarian, a Communist, a Republican, a Democrat, a Feminist, a Bisexual, a Homosexual, a Transsexual, a Cross-dresser, and many more things as well. All of those "identities" died within me—I even thought for a moment there wasn't any "me." And then, in an instant, I suddenly knew what never could be taught. You see, the truth is not some concept held in the "singular mind" where one can then say "I know." The truth is a *living* activity. It is that process we call life. And as is the case with all life, it must be *born*.

"The truth is born! How is that supposed to work?" you ask. The truth is born just as a baby is born. We call the process *procreation*. In procreation, a man and a woman give their lives to each other. The man gives his security (seed) to the woman and the woman gives her reproduction (womb) to the man. They are giving to each other their essential sexual selves in a moment of eternal surrender. We call this *love*. And from this love a union forms which begins a new process of division into a new sexual form, male or female, to be born into life. It is this process of begetting life that is the truth. Each time a new baby is born, the truth is expressed. Each time a man and a woman touch in the love that is the procreation of their spirits, the truth is expressed. Our faith in life, the faith that moves mountains, is the faith in this truth that is the expression of divine *procreant* love.

"But how can this be?" you ask. "Not everyone is making babies." It is the spirit of procreation to which I speak. Each child comes into life under the spirit of procreation. Each child feels within his or her heart a calling for their opposite other through which they together will carry on the *lineage of life*. As adults we live through our children, wanting our children themselves to become adults and have children of their own. As grandparents we further live through our children's children...and so on. The procreant urge fosters all life and never leaves any life. As we mature that urge takes on spiritual proportions—and beauty is brought into the understanding. The eternal procreation of a man and a woman continues beyond child-bearing years to include the procreation of the eternal itself. The eternal exists only as it is procreated, moment-by-moment, out of the surrender/love of a man to a woman and a woman to a man. Whatever is your current status in life, hold this *procreant* love in your heart and let it be your guide.

"But...what ...." I see that you do not believe. *Because of your unbelief: for verily I say unto you, If ye have faith as a grain of mustard seed, ye shall say unto this mountain, Remove hence to yonder place; and it shall remove; and nothing shall be impossible unto you.* Might not the mountain be within you? The mountain is our own (singular) belief system. You, and I, can remove the mountain from within ourselves right now by our faith. *The faith is the spiritual birth between two (procreative) hearts.* Take a moment and remove this mountain to a yonder place. "How might I do that?" you ask. By praying, *in faith*, the *Eternal Prayer*. Pray the *Eternal Prayer* to your eternal (equal and opposite) other half right now and know that your mountain is forevermore removed.

The Eternal Prayer

My blessed love, please come into my heart and live in me.
Allow me, as well, to come into your heart and live in you.
Let us, from this moment on, live in each other's hearts,
our love together being our guide, shining a light for all
to see that life is held simply in "our" balance together.

Faith must be, *and is*, as concrete as substance. And what is the divine substance but "our balance together."

Conflict Resolution

Conflict resolution begins and ends within oneself. Jesus on the Cross was in conflict.

Matthew 27:46: *My God, my God, why has thou forsaken me?*

He resolved the conflict uttering the words:

> **Luke 23:34:** *Father, forgive them; for they know not what they do.*

> **Luke 23:46:** *Father, unto thy hands I commend my spirit.*

The conflict in our lives that each one of us carry (call it original sin if you like) is an imbalance embedded in our souls. It is the imbalance of self and other, more specifically man and woman. We carry the imbalances of Masculinism (opposite but not equal) or Feminism (equal but not opposite). And so we see the world (out there) through the lens of our own faulty judgment and Victimization Cycle. Conflict, as it were, disappears when one embraces the balance between the two which is love. Remember the verse 1 John 1: 5: *God is light; in him there is no darkness.* We could also say, *God is love; in him there is no hate.* We must first clear our own hearts. Here is another Biblical verse.

Matthew 5:8: *Blessed are the pure in heart: for they shall see God.*

Conflict is resolved in the pure heart. When our hearts are clean we are not in conflict but in peace. Our outer events/circumstances perfectly follow/reflect our current inner state of being. In *A Course In Miracles,* 1976, written by Dr. Helen Schucman and Dr. William Thetford it states:

> Therefore, seek not to change the world, but choose to change your mind about the world.

I might word it this way: *Don't ask for change to occur in outer events; only ask for change to occur within you in relation to outer events.*

A Course in Miracles also states:

> Nothing real can be threatened. Nothing unreal exists. Herein lies the peace of God.

The doubt (of feeling forsaken) Jesus had on the Cross was in giving credence to the darkness (for a moment) rather than only acknowledging the light. To give credence to the darkness means the darkness wins. We are only to acknowledge spiritual perfection in ourselves and another. *I am light; You are light.* We, our perfect souls, can't be threatened. Yet, all too often, in conflict, we seek to make the other person wrong. We will even sue and go to Court to prove to ourselves the other is wrong. But what if the other is wrong? Then first resolve the issue inside yourself by taking away your judgment (lack, blame, demand, attack, and deny) on the other. True (spiritual) conflict resolution occurs at the connective point of the deeper souls. This is where Jesus resolved the conflict: *Father, forgive them; for they know not what they do.* (Luke 23:34) Jesus chose to see those against him in the perfect light of love. And then: *Father, unto thy hands I commend my spirit.* (Luke 23:46) Was not he saying in those words: *Let my death bring forth eternal spiritual life?* Every death brings forth eternal spiritual life. And every life brings forth its expression of eternal spiritual life unto its last breath. And this is where Man and Woman Balance comes in: birth-life-death-rebirth. In general terms, we might say that a direct connection between oneself and "God" resolves the conflict. But let us remember there are only the two forces, male and female. Let's review the earlier drawings.

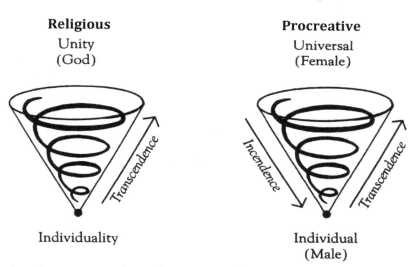

Religious
Unity
(God)

Individuality

Procreative
Universal
(Female)

Individual
(Male)

So the direct connection is between male and female, i.e., a man and a woman. It is when the individual (male) and the universal (female) connect (in spirit/balance) the conflict ceases. This is also the point where faith is restored and prayer is answered. And it is the point at which death is transcended into eternal life. Let us now say: "*I shall not be afraid for the other side is but what I bring to this side. The next moment is just the love I have for this moment. I am love as are you."* Let's now turn to *The Legend of the Truth* from *Meditations for Deepening Love*, 1994, 2010, and see the eternal conflict resolve itself.

The Legend of the Truth

And so it has been revealed... At the time when "God" was contemplating the *creation of man,* he thought unto himself, "How may I ensure that man revere the truth and hold it in the specialness it requires? Ah, yes, I will hide it from him, in a place difficult, but not impossible, to find, so that when he does discover it, he shall always respect it. I shall hide the truth in the heart of man." And upon this decision, God proceeded to create man and woman in his likeness.

Time passed, and soon God began to wonder. "Why hath man not yet discovered the truth? Is it so difficult to find—within himself?" Again, time passed, and God began to feel distraught, for man, in not knowing the truth, was neither free nor just. So God thought unto himself, "Indeed, I will send a messenger to earth. I will send my son to give to man a glimpse of the truth and where to find it." And so God sent his holy begotten son, to be born of a woman, so that he may speak directly to man. And God's son, Jesus, walked the lands of man and said unto him: *The kingdom of God cometh not with observation. Neither shall they say, lo here! Or, lo there! For behold, the kingdom of God is within you.*

Surely, God thought, man would now know where to find the truth. But man proceeded to ignore the words of Jesus and instead crucified him. When God saw this, he turned angry. "Man has crucified my beloved son who only spoke of my kingdom of love. I shall speak to man no more."

And so much time passed, and God watched his creation but did not speak. And man continued to suffer in his ignorance, and God suffered as well. "Why cannot man see where to look?" And as God thought about this it occurred to him, "Can it be that man thinketh that he already knows the truth? He was told to look within, yet he doesn't. He doesn't see any need. Even though my son also said unto him, *I have yet many things to say unto you, but ye cannot bear them now.* Man cannot hear for he thinks he already knows the truth. Ask him, and he will surely deny."

And again God thought unto himself, "I will send another messenger, and this time I will fully reveal to man where he may find the truth. I will leave no stone unturned, the truth is to be found. Now I will send my son and my daughter."

And so it was as God willed, a man and a woman, born into creation, came together in the knowing of God's truth. And this man and woman spoke to all who would *listen.* "Behold, my friends, you have sought for the truth within you. But you findeth it not. We have come to say unto you—the whole of the truth lieth not in your hearts alone. No, rather, one half of the truth lieth in man and the other half of the truth lieth in woman. You can only find this truth together. The whole of the truth lieth in the hearts of man and woman and is only revealed when a man and a woman cometh together in their love."

And God now looked down upon his creation and said unto himself, "Yes, mankind can now find his way for he knows where lieth the truth." And God saw that it was good.

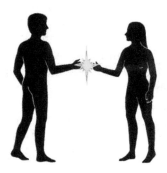

Can you see how when a man and a woman come together in their interdependence (which is love) that conflict dissolves? *"Behold, my friends, you have sought for the truth within you. But you findeth it not. We have come to say unto you—the whole of the truth lieth not in your hearts alone. No, rather, one half of the truth lieth in man and the other half of the truth lieth in woman. You can only find this truth together. The whole of the truth lieth in the hearts of man and woman and is only revealed when a man and a woman cometh together in their love."* Might not the Muslim world take this in, or the L,G,B,T,Q crowd? As somewhat of a side note but to take the issue of conflict resolution (and acceptance and non-violence) deeper, I would like to quote from the book *The Thought Farthest Out* by Glenn Clark. I have included many quotes from the Russell writings. There was a book written about Walter Russell and how Dr. Russell came to his immense creativity. The book was titled *The Man Who Tapped the Secrets of the Universe,* first published in 1946. That author of that book was—Glenn Clark. Mr. Clark wrote a number of books that probably would be labeled religious but they also capture that same spirit of the Creative Thought movement. The point here is to really look at how we may step over conflict and violence—and the debts within our own hearts and souls.

Glenn Clark (1882-1956)--*The Thought Farthest Out*

Go out to meet the thing you are afraid of—not with fear, but with love, and it will become your ally and not your foe. And now with this much of an introduction, I am going to take one great seven league boot stride ahead and tell you how to overcome any evil that may ever confront you.

You love that which belongs to you, is a part of you, is identical with you. To love a thing means to take it unto yourself, assimilate it into yourself, in spirit, and make it a part of yourself. What you love you become like. What you love you actually become. Love Light and you become like Light, a spreader of Light. Continue to love Light and you become Light yourself. Love Love and you become like Love, you spread Love. Continue to love Love and you finally become Love itself. God is Love. To love Love in yourself or in others—is the highest thing you can do.

To love a thing means to realize your unity with the thing you love. Now the sense of Love and the sense of unity can never come on a low or materialistic plane. Love and unity are in essence spiritual terms. Realize your unity with anything and it simply means you are lifted to the realm of spirit, and the spirit of the thing meets your spirit. Now the spirit of everything is good. For instance, even the spirit of debt is good. The spirit behind the debt, which makes the debt possible, is man's trust in man. Thus when you go forth to meet a debt which has heretofore been a nightmare to you, and when you no longer fear it, but realize your unity with it, it simply means that you and Trust become one. The moment you and Trust become one, your debt ceases to be a debt, no matter if it is something another owes you or you owe another.

...Realize unity with anything and you can command it. For anything that is part of you, you can command.

...Merely to realize Unity, merely to Love brings into play in our unconscious nature a transmuting process which lifts everything into the realm of spirit.

Are you afraid of water, fire, a thunder storm, or some animal? Make unity with it, and no harm will come from it. Your realization of unity with anything raises your mind from the mere thing to the spirit of the thing. Thus your mind is pushed above it. To rise mentally above a thing is to overcome the general effect of that thing...

To rise above a thing is to *come up over* it—or in other words to *overcome* it. Love and Unity are the two paths that lift a man above things to ideas, above personalities to being—in short takes him from the carnal to the spiritual realm. Through Love we can thus overcome the world, as through love we can sense our unity with things and come up over things.

...Now we know there is no God but Love, no God but the Father. But we find unity with the Father and with Love every time we find or realize our unity with mankind or with the forces of nature.

...."The thing which I feared has come upon me." But the moment he ceased to fear it and loved it, the moment he ceased to feel his separation from it and began to realize his unity with it—that moment the dread thing disappeared and good things came in its stead, or rather the evil thing became a good thing.

...The tempest is raging, making of the water a terrible, fearful thing. The men in their fear awaken the One who is sleeping in the stern of the boat. "Wake, Master, or we perish." And the Master, turning to the raging elements, recognized in them brothers of His spirit, partners of His soul. And recognizing His unity with the waves, turns and commands. And because they are united with Him, because they belong to Him, the waves obey His voice. And so, when terrible misfortune seems to be coming upon you, merely turn towards it without fear and realize your unity with it and command, "Peace, be still."

According to your faith it will be done unto you. Faith in what? Faith in the power of love, faith in the power of unity. Faith in the realization that what is part of you as an arm is a part of you can always be commanded as easily as you can command your own self, and only good will come of it, provided, of course, you always command with love, so as to hurt no other being, and do not use the power for your personal aggrandizement. ...The only hell, the only suffering in the world comes from a sense of separation. Heaven is harmony, hell is separation. Heaven is a place of harmonious souls who know they belong to each other. Hell is a place of separate souls, on the other hand, who don't know that they belong to each other.

Thus Christ gave a mighty law, a secret of many miracles, when He said, "Resist not evil, but overcome evil with good." And the good with which you overcome an evil always takes its rise in your realization of your union with the thing—or the spirit of the thing you would overcome. For when you realize your unity with a thing, the very unity will lift you up over it. Thus you come up over it and overcome it. For unity and love operate on a high plane—a plane where there is no suffering, no want, no evil of any kind—for they operate in a kingdom which is within—and this kingdom is the kingdom of heaven.

For when you realize your unity with a thing, the very unity will lift you up over it. Can there be conflict in unity (more specifically, the division/unification process)? In the language I am using we might ask, can there be conflict in the two-force balance of procreant love? *No, rather, one half of the truth lieth in man and the other half of the truth lieth in woman. You can only find this truth together.* The great recognition is that *the love already is.* (Or use the word light, *the light already is,* or *balance, beauty, truth already is....*) "But how do you get there" you ask? *You don't get there—you are already there!* You have always been there and you will always be there—in perfect balance with your sexual (equal and opposite) eternal other half. And in this recognition conflict and violence cease. They no longer live within us. How can they? This is why I say, *balance your fundamental/metaphysical relationship and conflict disappears.* Conflict and violence cannot exist in Man and Woman Balance but will always exist in Masculinism and Feminism. Let us then say that unity (or balance as I term it) and non-violence go hand-in-hand. *"Resist not evil, but overcome evil with good,"* says Jesus. Are the demonstrators out there today practicing non-violence—or are they just broadcasting the violence (lack-blame-demand-attack-deny) that already exists in their hearts? Ernest Holmes (1887-1960), also a part of the Creative Thought movement and founder of Religious Science and author of The Science of Mind, writing in *Thoughts Are Things*, 1967, states:

Ernest Holmes (1887-1960)—*Thoughts Are Things,* 1967

Today I practice nonresistance.

Disregarding everything that seems to contradict the Reality in which I believe, I affirm that Reality is operating in my life.

Turning resolutely from everything that denies the good I wish to experience, I affirm that good.

In the midst of fear I proclaim faith.

At the center of uncertainty I proclaim conviction.

In the midst of want I proclaim abundance.

Where unhappiness seems to exist I announce joy.

There is no situation or condition that resists these transcendent thoughts, for they proclaim the omnipotence of God, and the Divine guidance of the Mind that can accomplish all things.

Shouldn't nonresistance or non-violence be our stand in the face of conflict? But you know something, each one of us has to find this placement in our own hearts and souls. And to do this we must locate that point within ourselves where only the (sexual) balance exists.

One of the great balancing forces in the world at large (and perhaps even the universe itself) is marriage—and a man and a woman come together in their love. The God-head, as it were, is only this two-force (uniting/dividing) sexual life process. LIFE is God. LOVE is God. Do you understand? We could also say MARRIAGE is God. Marriage is the bringing of the divided two together again...to divide again, and so on. *Have ye not read, that he which made them in the beginning made them male and female, And said, for this cause shall a man leave father and mother, and shall cleave to his wife: and they twain shall be one flesh? Wherefore they are no more twain, but one flesh. What therefore God hath joined together, let not man put asunder.* (Matthew 19:4-6) Marriage is a metaphysical undertaking. It is the instrument from which the lineage of life progresses. In a balanced marriage conflict is brought under control. In an imbalanced marriage, or any imbalanced relationship, conflict burns brightly. So our direct connection with "God" is really our direct connection with our equal and opposite sexual other half. Balance that relationship and conflict disappears. *(There is only a man and a woman, touching and expressing creation together.)* And that is the spirit from which we bring love to all of our relationships and encounters. Let me return to *Meditations for Deepening Love,* 1994, 2010. This booklet is titled *The Marriage Vow.*

The Marriage Vow

Today, we are gathered to witness and acknowledge the unity of (_____ and _____). (_____ and _____ have chosen to commit their lives, one to another, to which we who are here are grateful. Please listen to these words of marriage.

In this marriage vow, you two are presented with the opportunity to commit your lives to each other, consummating the purpose and balance of creation. In this distinct moment when a man and a woman say to each other *"I do,"* they are committing their lives together under the banner of their *eternal creation.* How joyous is the moment of marriage when a man and a woman have found each other, as you two have, in the knowing of their love together. The words "I do" are most simple yet are commensurate with nothing less than life itself.

We who are witnesses to this marriage implore you not to take your commitment to each other lightly. Upon your commitment together life is consecrated. From your unity, life is brought forth. At each moment, you will be called upon to acknowledge the unique yet distinct purpose of the other, and the balance that you together comprise. You will be called upon to create your commitment anew—each moment, thereby creating your own eternal path together. Let us all understand that this marriage is eternal only as you both continue to *recreate* your commitment to each other, moment-by-moment. The marriage vow does not end at this ceremony. This is only its beginning.

This marriage vow affirms the truth of the love you two bring to each other. And as we gather here, we acknowledge that this love is the only foundation of this marriage. We witness today a man and a woman giving their lives to each other and, in so doing, taking their place in life as the *foundation of creation.* Such is the eternal purpose of your unity. With this said, we offer both of you the following opportunity *to create your marriage eternal.* Please present your vow and confirmation to each other.

Man: (_____), *I give to you my hand and my accounting to hold this day forever in my heart. I affirm my need for you in my life. I accept you in the pure spirit of your life. I recognize your soul essence as woman, and ask if I may commit to and care for you. And if death do us part, I promise to you that I will find you once again. Such is my faith in life. To you, I proclaim that my love is true, and upon this love, I ask of you to live your life with me. I seal my commitment to you with this ring. Let us create our marriage eternal.*

Woman: (_____), *On this day, I receive your commitment of love to me. Into my heart I place your love. I will hold it with me always and, in so doing, I give to you my love. I feel your heart and acknowledge your soul as man. I ask that you please care for me as I will care for you, and allow me to receive and renew your spirit. I affirm my need of you and accept your love of me. I, too, proclaim that our love is true, and I will always be here for you. With this ring, I seal my commitment to you. Let us create our marriage eternal.*

With these words, we who are witness to your marriage acknowledge you (_____ and _____), as husband and wife under the everlasting blessing of your own eternal love. *What therefore God hath joined together, let not man put asunder.*

The Marriage Vow

In marriage we find the actual commitment to life. This commitment is contained in the most simple yet compelling words, *"I do." ...In the beginning was the word...* The words *"I do,"* are the words of the primary commitment that are the cement of life. And notice how both the man and the woman state those words—as if all life depended on them. And all life does depend on them. These are the words of the Logos (an enlightened or divine reason), holding within itself the meaning and feeling of spiritual procreation: birth-life-death-rebirth... And, herein, is our spiritual healing from which conflict can drop out of our hearts. Even if you are not married, or have lost your spouse to death, or whatever is your current situation, you can say the words, *"I do,"* for they are your confirmation of life itself, that there is an eternal life for "You" and "I" because we, man and woman, are always tied together as the actual life (procreant) process in its entirety. In this last quote to this chapter let us address the issue *and feeling* of the eternal within us all. This is from *Man, Woman, and God: I Carry the Cross, too—The Completion of the Message of Jesus Christ*, 1994, 2010.

> *Eternal life is our hope and calling in life. Life (our lives) is held together within the scope of eternal life. Eternal life arises out of the balance of male and female. It is held within their graces. It is equal to their pure love. Each force presents it to the other and, in return, receives the same.*
>
> *There is another word for eternal life that essentially means the same thing and that is eternal love. Love is eternal as it is procreative. And this consciousness of eternal love is what we can bring to our other half. It is a consciousness that embraces our own eternal relationship in the now. What more can brighten our eyes and deepen our hearts? Eternal love is the peace that ends all seeking. It is ours to behold as we give it to our other....*
>
> *There is even another word we can use for eternal life to bring it even closer to us. That word is the eternal marriage. The eternal marriage just may be our deepest longing and greatest conscious commitment available to us in life. It may be through a commitment to eternal marriage that we finally, and forevermore, step out of the one-force paradigm that has so prevented the pure touch, one to another. This commitment is our ultimate surrender to our other half made solely out of the stand we take for our life. At this point, we really don't have much to go on to guarantee our success. We only have our own stand—I commit to you, my other half, in this one eternal moment of now....*
>
> *I trust many of you have your "what about this?" questions concerning eternal marriage. If so, meditate upon them. Take them into the silence—and see your other, you two together bringing forth life. Your questions will roll away as the light of your love fills your heart and soul. I will say again that all of life, all of creation, is only made up of male and female in their one universal (dividing/uniting) continuum, from which each moment is created anew out of their balance as is their desire.*

THE MAN AND WOMAN MANIFESTO

Presentations

Presentations consist of any format (usually speaking) from talks to workshops, and even meditations, where the spiritual light of Man and Woman Balance may be manifest. The purpose of any presentation is to transfer the procreant light from one to another. Procreant light is the balance point, i.e., love. This is also the healing point. It is important to point out that our task is limited to spiritual healing. If the physical body is assisted through spiritual healing all the better but that is not our task. We only address the essential alignment of the spirit, or individually what may be called one's soul. We want to get to that point where we can say to ourselves, *"I am finally happy inside myself at the very root of my core,"* and we can say to each other, *"Thank you for being a part of my life."* Our job, as it were, is to simply refuse to see things out of the lens of inner lack. In other words to experience JOY simply because we can. Life itself is joy. Look at the first smile of a baby. Is not that pure joy? Even the last breath of a life lived and loved is joy. Joy is but the inner light—the knowing of love. It is luminous. All physical light actually stems from spiritual illumination.

In giving presentations, the presenter is faced with the question of how to make his or her words *living words*. How does one infuse his or her words with the life force (also called the original light or the living spirit or the Logos)? It is the life force that brings forth connection. Think of political speeches for a moment. Why are they so dead? Could it be that they are full of false promises/lies? Indeed, by their very natures. Or religious speeches. Haven't we heard them all too many times? But a living speech where one's very words are infused with the very light and love that feeds our spiritual souls—that is something to behold. Yes, that is what we want to be able to do, not for our own grandiosity, but for life. We want to illuminate the moment with light and love. And, equally, we want to be illuminated with light and love right back to us. It is always the giving-receiving cycle. Such is the balance. So let us return for a moment to the Mission Statement from an earlier chapter. I am only going to quote the text here.

"Bringing Man and Woman Together!"

...constitutes a shift into the new paradigm of a two-force universe of spiritual procreation.

Due to a simple misconception mankind made at the dawn

of consciousness, men and women have not been able to unite in spirit together. The purpose of the Foundation of Man and Woman Balance is to correct this misconception and, in so doing, allow a man and a woman to unite in spirit, bringing forth their love to all of their creations. Men and women, the world over, the time is at hand for your Man and Woman Balance to begin.

Well, I guess you will know when your time is at hand for your Man and Woman Balance to begin. When that time comes, you will then be able to speak/present the message of Man and Woman Balance. The truth never lies. We can never fake it. It must lie in our hearts as our hearts.

On to another point, in any form of presentation of this message we want to ensure that those receiving our message are free to say, "No thank you." This message can't be a "have to" and certainly not a "forcing of" but only an offering. I, or you, have no right to coerce another. We can only offer. And perhaps more will be stated through our actions. We can never forget that love is not without freedom and freedom always allows for another a choice in the matter. What is wrong with our world is that we still fail, and actually institutionalize, mandate, if not force itself, to disallow the other the same freedom we demand for ourselves. The last freedom statement in the *Declaration of Freedom* states:

> **Freedom**—*And lastly, let us understand that the test of freedom lies not in whether "I have mine," but rather in my own willingness to allow you to equally have your freedom. "Can 'I' let others be free?" Let that be our enduring question.*

Just to cement this point in listen to this quote from *The Truth Revealed: My Answer to the World*, 1997.

> *What then would you say to religious people or humanistic people or homosexual people?*
>
> Unfortunately, they are wasting precious energy on a dying message. *Where is the rebirth?* Such people do not realize that they are only trying to put their own disorder into the place of a (perfectly balanced) universal (procreative) order. No wonder why they tend towards the fanatic. They just don't want to look at the balance, or lack thereof, of their own center. Is it procreative?
>
> *And if they choose that way anyway?*

Then please don't ask (force) me to pay for it. I want a choice, too. Let's let the free market of individual choice decide. If I am right, or wrong, the market place will tell me.

So nobody will be forced to embrace this idea of Man and Woman Balance?

How could that be? At that moment, the balance would be lost. Individual choice is the acid test of balance, and balance is the basis for all freedom. All I am saying is that Man and Woman Balance presents to us the understanding from which we may create (without creating karma) and thus together enter into the one everlasting moment of pure (pro)creative love.

Nobody will be forced to embrace this idea of Man and Woman Balance. Nobody can be forced to embrace the idea of Man and Woman Balance. And isn't that the point? *The freedom to believe is not just for oneself but equally for another.* You have a choice and it is to be honored. May I suggest you do the same for others. That is the walk of truth. This next quote is from *Man, Woman, and God: The Eternal Marriage*, 1994.

The universe (life) depends on our coming to the truth. Truth resides in the creative balance of male and female and is revealed in their procreative touch together. It is this creative balance that holds this sexual creating universe together. Circumvent the balance and creation stops.

Yes, the universe depends on our coming to the truth. But we can only come to the truth as we embrace our sexual other. As I have stated, one half of the truth resides in male and the other half of the truth resides in female. Neither male nor female can come to the truth alone.

The calling of man (to come to the truth) is the calling that he comes to woman. And the calling of woman is the calling that she comes to man. Each unto the other. Each calls for the other. I understand that some of us may not be with our other right now. But I speak of a consciousness, a consciousness that knows of one's sexual interconnection, a consciousness that sees life in terms of male and female. What are you bringing to your other right now?

And, fundamentally, what is it we are presenting? Remember the quote from www.manandwomanbalance.com website? Let's review.

On a personal note, when Mr. Anderson was asked to

describe the writings and what he felt their message was he responded, "Spiritual procreation. Mankind has yet to distinguish the two sexes on the spiritual level. In this failure lies the root of our problems and why we cannot yet touch the eternal together. The message of Man and Woman Balance brings each of us together in love with our eternal other half right now."

So, we are presenting the idea of spiritual procreation, that the sexual process equally works on the spiritual level and, in fact, is the spiritual level. Let's review from Max Freedom Long: *...we may reach the conclusion that the same division which separated the two lower selves, separated the High Self spirits, and that they also strive on their own high level and in their own more evolved way to reach union.* And further: *We can do little more than accept the ancient statement, "As above, so below," and reverse it to "As below, so above."* This study we are doing can be called *sexual metaphysics.* We are bringing the sexual (life) process to the meta-level of things, the 1st or primary order, and viewing all things from the basis of sexual balance. This next quote is from *Man, Woman, and God: The Eternal Marriage,* 1994, 2010. *The Eternal Marriage* was actually written around 1991-1992.

The field of *sexual metaphysics* looks at various systems or ideologies to view their creative connection, or lack of, between male and female. We begin from the premise that male and female are co-creators on each level—the spiritual, mental, and physical. (I will be looking at each level specifically in the next three sections.) We can create a drawing to show each level as sexed, holding male and female polarity. This becomes the basic metaphysical drawing of *sexual creation.*

The Man and Woman Relationship

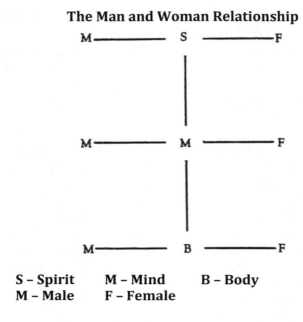

S – Spirit   **M – Mind**   **B – Body**
M – Male   **F – Female**

To my knowledge, there aren't any thought systems (or ideologies) that hold to the dynamics of sexual creation on all three levels. An example that holds sexual creation on the mental and physical levels, yet denies it on the spiritual level, is Christianity. Christianity is not alone; most religions deny the sexual dynamic between male and female at the spiritual level. On the spiritual level, Christianity brings in the third force of "God" to act as the source of and mediator between male and female. It is at this point that Christianity fails to hold life. This may seem contrary of Christianity with its emphasis on spirituality. But we must understand that the spirits of male and female are not the same. Spirituality is but the connection/unity of male and female and cannot be touched without their balanced opposition. On the mental and physical levels, Christianity is fine. It does acknowledge sexual difference. It is only on the spiritual level that we find the imbalance.

Christianity

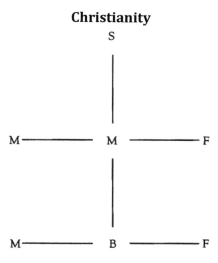

An example of a metaphysic that denies the sexual on both the spiritual and mental levels is socialism. Socialism grants sexual distinction only on the physical level. On the mental level, they would say that male and female are essentially the same. The spiritual level is also held to a sole unity as in a "one people." We see this same "one people" trait in what is called "humanism." In fact, we are not a "one people" but a two persons, male and female. I will speak more to socialism later. For now, let me say that socialism cannot stand on its own. It sinks below the halfway point of sexual creation. Whereas Christianity holds creativity in two of the three aspects and therefore can basically support its creation, socialism cannot. In being just one-third creative, it just cannot create enough to survive.

Socialism

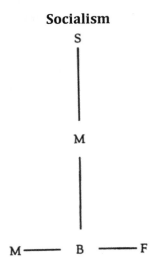

An example of a metaphysic that denies sexual creation on all levels—the spiritual, the mental, and the physical—is homosexuality. It is not that the homosexual does not acknowledge the existence of the other sex, just that for him or her, the other sex is not required. In turn, homosexuality is not co-creative and thus is not creative at all. It is the antithesis of male and female balance and sexual creation. If we continue to follow this path, calling for the legitimacy and equality of homosexuality, we will lose life. In homosexuality, the life dynamic is completely missing. From its base life cannot be created.

Homosexuality

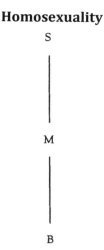

In the examples listed, I am using a simple test—*Is it procreative?* This simple question, *is it procreative?*, sheds much light. This question can be called the *test of the truth.* If something isn't procreative then throw it out. It will not hold life.

The above was written some 25 years ago. Notice how as we drop from Man and Woman Balance, we become more and more non-binary/depolarized—and radicalized, i.e., the new (sexual) Marxism. And look where we are today, the lights of the Rainbow (Gay) flag shining over the White House—Feminism, the ideology of non-distinction, where tolerance, free speech, respect, and rights only run one way. Who would have thought Orwell's *1984* (where truth can no longer be spoken) would come to us through our submission to the L,G,B,T,Q demands—and that it would be more important to submit to some guy's claim that he is now a woman and his demand to use the ladies restroom respective of the ladies and young girls' choices. We thought the bottom was hit with gay marriage. (Actually the bottom was hit when in 1973 the American Psychiatric Association took homosexuality, i.e., sodomy, off the list of mental disorders. It never was a mental disorder per se but it is a spiritual disorder.) But it appears we are seeing in this transgender issue the completion of the collapse from sexual polarity into the equal but not opposite, non-binary, androgynous, fluid, sexual imbalance of Feminism. And this is because we never have identified sexual polarity (equal <u>and</u> opposite) as comprising the primary, 1st tier, order of creation, rather postulating some "Spirit's Original Unity" or "His sexless unity" outside of, prior to, or different from the sexual process of male and female unity and division. And you don't think we need a new paradigm, a metaphysical shift into man and woman (sexual) balance that presents us with both love and freedom? This is what we present—*Man and Woman Balance.*

And now let's end this section with another booklet from *Meditations for Deepening Love,* 1994, 2010. This one is titled *By the Force of Will Alone.*

By the Force of Will Alone

The whole world was waiting, but they knew not for what. Yet, they could feel within themselves that something was going to happen very shortly that would, forevermore, change the very fabric of life as they had known it. But what was it to be? They could not ask anyone, for everyone else was waiting, too—except one man. There was one man who was not waiting, for he knew what was imminent.

Why did not this man just speak out? Perhaps it was because no one could hear. Not until the *time was right* could anyone hear what he had to say. Even though everyone seemed eager to know, not until they were truly and completely *open in heart* could they hear the message of this one man.

So this man waited. He waited aeon after aeon, watching the world, waiting for that one exact moment to be right. You may wonder how this man continued to hold the world's want within himself for so long without respite. One can only conjecture; most likely *by the force of will alone.*

Many events had to occur first before the world would be able to hear this message. Mainly, people had to come to the realization that they just did not know life themselves, and *could not know it by themselves.* This is what this man was waiting for, and everyone was close to this realization for their hearts were opening in an anticipation they could no longer control.

And then one day the event occurred. This one man, by the force of his will alone, extended his consciousness that carried the message to all regions in the world. The *light* of his consciousness intermingled with everyone's consciousness and the message crossed through that "eternal impasse" and was conveyed in that one immediate moment. In that single instant everyone knew, *"I" am not alone. "You" are with me. We, male and female, are together.* And in that moment, a man and a woman looked upon each other and said: *Let there be life.*

What was surprising about this event is that no one was really surprised by it. In a way, they all knew that that was what they had always wanted to hear. There wasn't any shouting about it. It did not cause a celebration. Everyone was quiet, but you could sense a subtleness about them that said, *"I" know; "I" have always known "You."* After this event, peace came into the world. After all, what would there be to fight about?

What happened to this man is not really known. It is said that he finally found his life mate, and that he and his wife have had many children together. I would like to think that this is so.

Demonstrations/Parades/Rallies

Demonstrations, parades, and rallies are a particularly unique form of presentation. In presentations (of Man and Woman Balance), it is generally assumed that the people attending are doing so out of their own interest and choice. But a demonstration, parade, or rally may imply a conflict is in place between the demonstrators or participants and the powers that be. The powers that be might not look favorably on what the demonstrators are implying or presenting. Moreover, it is not uncommon for other people, who would not choose to be there, to get caught up in the festivities at their inconvenience and time. Given that those who demonstrate ought to be very courteous of both the powers that be and innocent bystanders. It does one no good to try and force his or her point of view upon another. That being said, it is the suggestion of this writer that demonstrations, if necessary, be silent and peaceful.

When might a demonstration be necessary? Usually when one, or a group of people, feels that the powers that be are ignoring their concerns. Take the Black Lives Matter demonstrations that have been occurring lately. Those people feel their concerns, mainly police brutality, are not being heard. Actually, it is much more than police brutality; it is a whole history of race discrimination. I think that has merit. But they miss the boat on at least two fronts. One is they are out their yelling and screaming (not to mention at times vandalizing and looting) very derogatory, if not violent, statements about the police. They have hate in their hearts. As such, they miss the essential aspect of their own spiritual mentor Martin Luther King, Jr. Remember his quotes from earlier: *Violence never brings permanent peace. It solves no social problem; it merely creates new and more complicated ones. Violence ends up defeating itself.* And: *Darkness cannot drive out darkness; only light can do that. Hate cannot drive out hate; only love can do that.* It looks to me that the Black Lives Matter movement is displaying a bit too much violence and hate. (Just as a case in point, contrast Black Lives Matter with the Black church and gospel music. Not even close.) From this writer's point of view, it seems that Black Lives Matter people are more caught up in the Victimization Cycle of lack-blame-demand-attack-deny. Why is this? It is because the Black Lives Matter movement is not out for the right/freedom to create and keep their own wealth. They are about the "social justice" to distribute other people's wealth to themselves (*From each according to his abilities, to each according to his needs.*), and that always requires initial force from one to another. This is the problem. We just cannot contain ourselves—*it must be another's fault and therefore they must pay.* The good book tells us in Matthew 7: 1-2: *Judge not, that ye be not judged. For with what judgment ye judge, ye shall be judged: and with what measure ye mete, it shall be measured to you again.* It also instructs us in Matthew 5:48: *Be ye therefore perfect, even as your Father which is in heaven is perfect.* And so, the effectiveness of any demonstration is in how we honor those to whom we are demonstrating against. Seems to be a paradox in play, but honor, and even forgive, we must. (We must also forgive ourselves for judging those others in the first place.) Otherwise we just fall back into the Karl Marx system of class warfare that changes nothing but destroys everything.

The second reason the Black Lives Matter movement misses the boat is that they don't understand the real boot that is stomping on their necks. Most of us don't. We don't want to. Yet, if we could just identify it maybe we wouldn't be so afraid of it. What if in their demonstrations they carried signs that said:

Free Thy People!
No More FED/IRS

Now that would have potency. Those of the Occupy Wall Street movement of some years back were on to this. Unfortunately, they, too, could not step beyond the class warfare. They did not understand that the big banks were not the fundamental issue of their loss of freedom and opportunity. They needed to take one more step and get into the heart of the beast itself, the stealing of our substance money system by the politicos and replacing it with a counterfeit script (credit/debit note) for their own benefit. That is why our government has again become our masters and we their debtor slaves. We, black and white, and everyone else, are all on the plantation of debt slavery together. Don't you feel it? We see this federalizing taking place all over now, all the way down to County governments and police and sheriff departments. But what if the Occupy Wall Street people carried signs saying:

We are the Sovereign!
We own our own Wallets!

Right to Life is another issue that ought to be demonstrated for. And it often is. Abortion is a consequence of the spiritual/procreation separation between a man and woman. Listen to what Mother Teresa (1910-1997), Catholic Nun and Missionary, said as the keynote speaker at the National Prayer Breakfast in Washington, D.C. on February 3, 1994.

Mother Teresa (1910-1997)

I feel that the greatest destroyer of peace today is abortion, because it is a war against the child, a direct killing of the innocent child, murder by the mother herself. And if we accept that a mother can kill even her own child, how can we tell other people not to kill one another? How do we persuade a woman not to have an abortion? As always, we must persuade her with love and we remind ourselves that love means to be willing to give until it hurts... Any country that accepts abortion is not teaching its people to love, but to use any violence to get what they want. This is why the greatest destroyer of love and peace is abortion.

Abortion is a rejection of the teachings of Christ himself who taught that those who receive a little child, receive him. ...Every abortion, as a refusal to receive a little child, is a refusal to receive Jesus.

I will tell you something beautiful. We are fighting abortion by adoption—by care of the mother and adoption for her baby... Please don't kill the child. I want the child. Please give me the child. I am willing to accept any child who would be aborted and to give that child to a married couple who will love the child and be loved by the child. From our children's home in Calcutta alone, we have saved over 3,000 children from abortion. These children have brought such love and joy to their adopting parents and have grown up so full of love and joy.

Abortion begins at the spiritual separation of a man and a woman. Undoubtedly, they have never "become as one" to begin with. Such is the result of a sex separated from procreation society. *The sexual act is a procreative act.* You can't separate it out from procreation like the L,G,B,T,Q people would have us believe. So I am not going to lay the sin of abortion on the mother. The man is equally responsible. Maybe even more so as he wanted to have his sex without equaling the responsibility of its ramification—life. The abortion debate ought to have been limited to cases of incest or rape where the girl's or woman's choice had been taken from her. Then the girl or woman does retain her choice. Or also in those special, and rare, cases of child deformity or a woman's health. But to open up abortion to millions of women, as if it is just another day at the office, misses the whole scope of life and its importance. Who is to speak for the unborn if not us? The loss of one child to abortion is the loss of a child to every father and mother. We must speak out on this issue, and to our credit many are. Let me suggest signs that read:

Living Matters!
or
Unborn Lives Matter!
or
Let There Be Life!
or
Man, Woman, and Child = Life!

This next article *The Little Sister's Last Stand for Religious Liberty*, I found on the *Crisis Magazine* website. It is by Bruce Frohnen, a Professor of Law at the Ohio Northern University College of Law. He is also a senior fellow at the Russell Kirk Center and author of many books including *The New Communitarians and the Crisis of Modern Liberalism*, and the editor of *Rethinking Rights* (with Ken Grasso), and *The American Republic: Primary Source*. I am just taking a couple of paragraphs from it.

The Supreme Court recently heard oral arguments in the case of *Little Sisters of the Poor v. Burwell*. This is a case in which a small order of nuns is seeking exemption from an Obama Administration requirement that they help distribute free contraceptives and abortifacients (drugs that cause abortions) through their government-mandated healthcare plan. Why does the Obama Administration need to require that a small order of Catholic nuns help distribute contraceptives and abortifacients? Certainly this administration is committed to making such products as widely and freely available as is humanly possible. But there simply is no need to require that the Little Sisters of the Poor provide the administrative machinery for any of their employees who might happen to want them to get them through their health insurance administrator.

Should the Obama Administration succeed in forcing dissenting religious institutions to bow to its contraception/abortifacient mandate, the Church will be made into an administrative unit of the federal government. The full ramifications of this transformation will take time to play out. But the federal government's right to force religious organizations to violate conscience in service to the state even in matters of purely internal administration will have been established. The Church's independent role as a conscientious check on power will have been fatally compromised. And power politics, already dominant, will reign supreme.

The truth is the Church's independent roll as a conscientious check on power was over a long time ago. The Church never did really recognize the co-sovereignty of man and woman and that procreation is the basis of all creation, not a singular unsexed "God." Nevertheless, Mr. Frohnen has an important point—the government is simply out to destroy ...*The Church's independent role as a conscientious check on power.* Let me state it this way: *The government is out to destroy all of our sovereignty. They only want peons.* For government (the Fed/IRS), our lives do not matter. We as sovereigns should have an independent role from government. We are the sovereign; government is the servant. For you see, *Life does matter*—absolutely. And we, you and I, are *life*. And that is why we need demonstrations for *Man and Woman Balance*. The point being made here is that the two forces of male and female (Man and Woman Balance) are the primary. And as such gender is metaphysical. You can't just wake up one morning and decide you are of the other gender (or that your great epiphany is that you are non-binary, etc.) Sex reassignment surgery does not create a man from a woman or a woman from a man. What it does create is a radical depolarization of what one's sex was—and still is. So in a pro-Man and Woman Balance demonstration we might use signs such as these:

Existence Exists as a Male and a Female
or
Man and Woman—Together Forever!
or
Marriage: Equal and Opposite!
or
Man, Woman, and Child = Life!
or
Man and Woman Balance: World-Wide <u>Evolution</u>!
<u>or</u>
The Eternal and the Procreative are One!
or
Man and Woman Sovereign<u>c</u>y!
or
Family: The Force to Save the Planet!
or
Procreant Love is the Center!

We can also use these signs to demonstrate for the sanctity of sexual relations. Can anyone really say today that sexual relations are better today with the onslaught of the sexual liberation movement of the sixties? We have lost our innocence but we have also lost our purity and sense of beauty, not to mention the two becoming as one not just physically but spiritually. The following article I also found on the *Crisis Magazine* website. It is titled *What the Hook-up Culture Has Done to Women* by Anne Maloney. Anne Maloney is an Associate Professor of Philosophy at the College of St. Catherine in St Paul, Minnesota.

What the Hook-up Culture Has Done to Women

A stereotyped but unconscious despair is concealed even
under what are called the games and amusements of mankind.
There is no play in them, for this comes after work. But it is a
characteristic of wisdom not to do desperate things.
Henry David Thoreau, *Walden*

A few weeks ago, a young woman at Stanford University was raped by a virtual stranger, and her rapist received a ridiculously light sentence. The story grabbed headlines everywhere, and caused a firestorm on social media. This "dumpster rape" is being blared about everywhere in the public square while a far more insidious and dangerous threat to women rages on directly under our noses, unacknowledged. This threat is systematically destroying an entire generation of our daughters, sisters, aunts, future mothers, and friends.

The young woman who was raped behind the dumpster has an advantage over most young women today: she knows she was raped. She is angry, and rightly so. She realizes that she has been violated, and she can try to find a way to heal. The young women I encounter every day on the campus of the university where I teach are worse off than this victim, because they do not know what has gone wrong in their lives. Nonetheless, something has gone terribly wrong, and on some level, they know it.

In thirty years of teaching, I have come to know thousands of women between the ages of eighteen and twenty-six. These women are hurting. Badly. Consider these examples from "the front lines": a young woman says to me with all earnestness, "This weekend I went to my first college party, and I hit it off with a guy so we went into the back bedroom where the coats were and started kissing, but then he reached down, moved my panties aside and penetrated me, so I guess I'm not a virgin anymore." Another young woman came to me in tears because her doctor told her that since she has genital warts, she may have trouble conceiving children in the future. She had always assumed she would get married and have a family someday. "And the worst part is," she wailed, "I'm not even promiscuous. I've only had sex with six guys." This young woman was nineteen when she said this to me.

Once, in a writing assignment about Socrates and the Allegory of the Cave, a student wrote that she decided to make better choices after she woke up one morning in a trailer, covered with scratches, naked, next to a man she didn't remember meeting. At least she knew there was a problem. All too often, these women come to me in a state of bewilderment. Women have never been more "sexually liberated" than these women are, or so they are told. No more are they shackled by ridiculous bonds like commandments, moral rules, words like "chastity." They shout: "We're free!" Yet they whisper: "Why are we so miserable?"

It is no coincidence that the top two prescribed drugs at our state university's health center are anti-depressants and the birth-control pill. Our young women are showing up to a very different version of "college life" than that of the previous generation. One woman, while in her freshman year, went to her health center because she feared she had bronchitis. In perusing her "health history," the physician said, "I see here that you are a virgin." "Um, yes," she responded, wondering what that fact might have to do with her persistent cough. "Would you like to be referred for counseling about that?" This student came to me to ask if I thought she should, in fact, consider her virginity—at the age of eighteen—a psychological issue. (I said no.)

In a seminar I teach every other year, we discuss the ways that addiction reveals certain truths about embodiment. One of the books we discuss is Caroline Knapp's *Drinking: A Love Story*. The students adore this book, and we have fascinating conversations in class. The chapter that generates by far the most passion, however, is the chapter on drinking and sex. Knapp speaks honestly about the key role that alcohol played in her decisions to have sex, sex that she regretted and that made her feel terrible. My students resonate deeply with Knapp's experiences, and I continue to be struck by how unfree these students feel. Once the culture embraced non-marital sex and made it the norm, women who do not want to have casual sex often feel like outcasts, like weirdos. College is the last place where one wants to feel like an utter misfit; couple that with the fact that first year students are away from home for the first time—lonely, vulnerable, insecure— and you have the recipe for meaningless sexual encounters followed by anxiety and depression.

Why don't these women just stop it? Rather than get drunk in order to have casual sex, why don't they put down the glass AND the condom? The world we have created for these young people is a world which welcomes every sort of sexual behavior except chastity. Anal sex? Okay! Threesomes? Yep. Sex upon the first meeting? Sure! Virginity until marriage? What the hell is wrong with you? I am going to go out on a limb here and suggest that the reason so many college-aged women binge-drink is so that they can bear their own closeted sorrow about what they are doing. The woman who got drunk and got raped behind the dumpster is the victim of a toxic culture. But my students are also the victims of a toxic culture. Small wonder that the number of women suffering from eating disorders, addiction, anxiety and depression is at an all-time high.

I have not been raped, and I did not engage in non-marital intercourse. I did have an encounter early in my life, however, that gives me a glimpse of the shame experienced by women who "hook up." When I was sixteen years old, my sister took me to a bar near her college campus. The bar was one designated by students as the "easy in" place, because I.D.'s were checked cursorily if at all. Once we were inside the bar, my sister was swept away by a phalanx of her friends, and I lost her in the crowd. A "college man" at the bar noticed me, and came over to ask me if I would like something to drink. I had no idea what to order or how, as I had never been to a bar before. He reassured me that he would take good care of me, and went over to the bartender. When he came back with a Tequila Sunrise, he said it would taste great, like Hawaiian Punch. He was right; it was delicious, and I gladly accepted three more from him. The next thing I remember, I was doing some very intensive French-kissing with this fellow, and he was murmuring a suggestion that we "take this somewhere else." By the grace of God, my sister's boyfriend had just entered the bar, saw me, pulled me away from the man, and dragged me to the back of the bar and my sister. That was my first kiss. The next morning, I experienced my first true hangover. As awful as I felt physically, though, my shame was much, much worse. A romantic through-and-through, I had dreamed for years of my first kiss. A drunken slobber with a stranger was the brutal reality I would never be able to undo.

And yet, whenever I tell people this story, they are shocked that I am making "such a big deal" about that night. People drink. They kiss. But for the grace of God and a sister's boyfriend, they end up in a stranger's bed with a bad headache, a dry mouth, and an incalculable emptiness. I am often told, "Lighten up!" "You had fun. Big deal!" "Why are you so hard on yourself?" I kept speaking the truth of that awful experience, but my culture could not absorb that truth. I had no words for my sadness; it was only later in my life when I was a stronger person that I was able to say, "You know what? It was a big deal. It wasn't fun. I did feel ashamed."

A few years ago, I was online and saw that man's name come up on a blog that I read. He graduated from the college and became a respected and award-winning journalist. When I told some friends I had found him and he was now famous, they suggested that I "network" and re-introduce myself to him online. I was horrified at the thought of doing any such thing; after more than thirty-five years, I was still deeply ashamed of that night. It was years before I realized how very ashamed *he* should have been. In fact, given my age and obvious vulnerability, his behavior was predatory and vicious. The fact that he ought to have been ashamed, however, did not mean that I needn't have been. Had this fellow succeeded in taking me somewhere to do what he intended, I would have felt degraded. The culture of "Sex and the City" and "Girls" would have insisted that I was fine, I was a modern woman, I was "free." I knew better. Yes, I was sixteen, but I knew I wasn't supposed to be in a bar that night. I knew I was not of legal age to drink. I knew that accepting drinks from complete strangers is a very bad idea. I never told my mother about that night, but if I had, she would have said, "Anne, you know better." To say that I had no choices that night is to rob me of the moral agency that I, in fact, had. At sixteen, I may not have known how to articulate that fact, but I do now.

An entire generation of women is wounded yet unable to find the source of the bleeding. There is, indeed, an "unconscious despair" behind their "games and amusements." They "hook up," feel awful and have no idea why. It's hard to heal when you don't know you've been damaged. And the despair and shame that these women who hook up feel is real. Contemporary sexual culture is toxic for young women, and until women stand up and acknowledge that fact, despair, sadness and regret are going to be the underlying chord structure of their very lives. We fail an entire generation when we withhold from them the "wisdom not to do desperate things."

Why do you think women, in general, feel bad about themselves when they give into sex? Well, it's not the giving into sex, it's the giving into *sex without love*. You see, sex is always tied into love and love is always tied into (spiritual) procreation. Women exist on the unity side of life. They intrinsically know when they have given themselves to sex without love—where the spiritual unity/procreation does not happen, and neither does the commitment by the guy. And this is where guys fail. A man is a man because he takes responsibility for his actions. The sexual liberation movement separated men (and boys) from their actions. The cost is incalculable and unbearable. We are losing our cultural/moral heritage. We are being attacked and destroyed—by Feminism—from within. (See *Family—The Force to Save the Planet* from the chapter *A Model for Freedom.*) We are also being attacked from without by Masculinism. (Nothing new there.) As I am writing this a scourge of Muslim immigrants are rampaging through Europe brutalizing and even raping women. (Where is the light of life and love there?) Europe will be lost, with the United States of American to follow, if this is not stopped, not just physically but ideologically. You see, it is all part of the metaphysical imbalance. It is time for all Europeans, and all peoples of all worlds, to stand up to this masculinist (opposite but not equal) and feminist (equal but not opposite) scourge and make it clear that choice runs both ways. Women everywhere ought to be marching with signs saying:

We Exist too!
or
We, Man and Woman, need each other equally!

With men by their sides saying:

Freedom for All!
or
We will defend your right to Exist!

Moreover, there should be in every classroom, if not home, a copy of *To All Men The World Over.* (See the chapter *The Healing Light.*)

Like it or not, the 2nd Amendment to the Constitution of the United States of American just may be the bottom line. It was not placed in the Bill of Rights to procure a right to hunt or even to create community militias which, after all, are not a bad idea, especially today with the federalizing of local police. It was placed there so you and I could bear arms in the event the powers that be tried to take from us our unalienable rights of life, liberty, and property. *We the people are the last defense of our own life, liberty and property.* I am sorry if you don't want to hear this but it is the truth. (And I am not against the registration of guns. Like tobacco and alcohol [and drugs] firearms are very dangerous.) This is not an easy world. Life is difficult enough without those who would steal from us our life, liberty, and property. As such we are sometimes called upon to take the light of love into those places of darkness that are always held together by brute force. Make no mistake, thievery, brutality, murder, and dictatorship always go together. And we never get to believe that this task of defending freedom will ever end. For one thing, we always have to be on guard concerning ourselves and our own actions. As the last line of the *Declaration of Freedom* states:

> **Freedom**—*And lastly, let us understand that the test of freedom lies not in whether "I have mine," but rather in my own willingness to allow you to equally have your freedom. "Can 'I' let others be free?" Let that be our enduring question.*

The Flag

We usually think of the flag as that symbol representing the sovereign authority of a state/nation. The flag for the United States of America, for example, is really a sovereign-state flag. Each country has its own flag signifying to the world that it is a sovereign state. In my research, I didn't find much on this linkage. On Wikipedia under flag it states:

> A flag is a piece of fabric (most often rectangular or quadrilateral) with a distinctive design that is used as a symbol, as a signaling device, or as decoration. The term *flag* is also used to refer to the graphic design employed, and flags have since evolved into a general tool for rudimentary signaling and identification, especially in environments where communication is similarly challenging (such as the maritime environment where semaphore is used). National flags are potent patriotic symbols with varied wide-ranging interpretations, often including strong military associations due to their original and ongoing military uses. Flags are also used in messaging, advertising, or for other decorative purposes. The study of flags is known as vexillology, from the Latin word *vexillum*, meaning flag or banner.

In *Black's Law Dictionary*, Fifth Edition, under *Flag* it states:

> A national standard on which are certain emblems; an ensign; a banner. It is carried by soldiers, ships, etc., and commonly displayed at forts, businesses and many other suitable places.

Further under *Flag, duty of the*, it reads:

> This was an ancient ceremony in acknowledgment of British sovereignty over the British seas, by which a foreign vessel struck her flag and lowered her top-sail on meeting the British flag.

Here we see some connection to the idea of sovereignty. And sovereignty is the key here. A flag represents the sovereignty of a certain country over something. It is a claim of rule or ownership if you will. This is very important. Further in *Black's Law Dictionary* under *Sovereignty* we find:

The supreme, absolute, and uncontrollable power by which any independent state is governed; supreme political authority; paramount control of the constitution and frame of government and its administration; the self-sufficient source of political power, from which all specific political powers are derived; the international independence of a state, combined with the right and power of regulating its internal affairs without foreign dictation; also a political society, or state, which is sovereign and independent.

The power to do everything in a state without accountability, — to make laws, to execute and to apply them, to impose and collect taxes and levy contributions, to make war or peace, to form treaties of alliance or of commerce with foreign nations, and the like.

Sovereignty in government is that public authority which directs or orders what is to be done by each member associated in relation to the end of the association. It is the supreme power by which any citizen is governed and is the person or body of persons in the state to whom there is politically no superior. The necessary existence of the state and the right and power which necessarily follow is "sovereignty." By "sovereignty" in its largest sense is meant supreme, absolute, uncontrollable power, the absolute right to govern. The word which by itself comes nearest to being the definition of "sovereignty" is will or volition as applied to political affairs.

Now there is quite a definition for you—and quite a reason to have a constitutional system of checks and balances in place. And my point here is this is what the flag, as a symbol, carries with it. It signifies sovereign power—a claim of ownership or rule over. Notice how when explorers came to the "new world" they planted their country's flag. It was their claim of ownership and rule. Countries at war; the winner usually plants its flag in the claimed territory to signify its victory and sovereignty over that territory. (We, the United States of America, even planted a flag on the moon!—I assume that wasn't a hoax!) The flag as a symbol of a country's sovereignty has great power.

There is another aspect of a flag that needs to be considered. Flags also represent ideas. One of the great things about the American flag is that it represented, world over, the idea and ideal of *freedom*. So the American flag was not just a symbol of the sovereignty of the United

States of America, but also that the United States of America stood for freedom—*with liberty and justice for all*. This was an absolutely great idea. I say "was" because the United States of America has about lost its way. It has lost its *clarity of idea and thus its liberty and justice for all*. Its fundamental principles that guided it have been diminished. Its people are no longer the sovereign, if they truly ever were. Its money is no longer substance but rather debt. Its values no longer originate in man, woman, and child. Not that they truly ever did but it had come closest in the Christian religion. And so we see today other flags springing up with other claims, not necessarily physically territorial but idea claims. Below is an article I found on the internet

NYC Kindergarteners Pledge Allegiance to 'International Flag' Made from a Desecrated American Flag

New York values.

By: Caleb Howe

A story from Sean Hannity's website has been tearing up social media on Saturday and with good reason. It seems kindergarten children in New York City, under the direction of teachers and with the approval of the parent teacher association, desecrated an American flag in order to praise multi-culti internationalism as superior to and authoritatively above the United States.

THE MAN AND WOMAN MANIFESTO

The flag was created by gluing the flags of other nations onto the stripes. The red stripes represent the 13 original American colonies, of course.

Kindergarten students from PS75, a public school in New York City, recently took part in a class project in which the children were made to create an American flag with the flags of 22 other nations superimposed over the stripes. Below the flag read the words "We pledge allegiance to an International Flag."

The story came out when a concerned parent contacted Hannity's website with a link to the page where the Parent Teacher Association was auctioning it off to raise funds. It has since been deleted.

In the liberal leftist assault on American values, institutions, and culture, your children are the front line. The indoctrination in public schools is near-total. As a parent of two, I have a kabillion other stories just as offensive and ridiculous. They really are out to get your kids. And they really see nothing wrong with it.

There are numerous flags springing up in the L,G,B,T,Q community. They are basically clamoring for a "new (non-binary) structure of gender or family" including but not limited to: Agender, Androgyne, Androgynous, Bigender, Cis, Cisgender, Cis Female, Cis Male, Female To Male (FTM), Gender Fluid, Gender Nonconforming, Gender Variant, Genderqueer, Intersex, Male to Female (MTF), Neither, Non-binary, Pangender, Trans, Trans Female, Trans Male, Trans Man, Trans Person, Trans Woman, Transfeminine, Transgender, Transgender Female, Transgender Man, Transgender Woman, Transgender Person, Transsexual, Transsexual Female, Transsexual Male, Transsexual Man, Transsexual Person, Transsexual Woman, and Two-Spirit—all under the feminist's/socialist's sovereign banner of *Equality* (equal but not opposite). Must not each category have its own flag as a symbol of its (idea) sovereignty and absolute legitimacy? And surprise, many do. I mentioned how the rainbow flag flew in its colors (shown by lights) over the White House when the Supreme Court ruled in favor of gay marriage. That actually represented a "takeover," if you will, of the country by this gay and lesbian ideology; obviously a takeover applauded by the White House. There are many more flags that have yet to have the success of the rainbow flag. But they are moving in that direction. Let's take a look at the various flags that are already flying right now, at least as ideas, and what they represent. I found this information on the internet under the category of sexuality pride flags.

LGBT/Gay Pride
(Original 1978 Design)

The original Gay Pride flag was designed by Gilbert Baker, and debuted in 1978 at the San Francisco Gay and Lesbian Freedom Day. The pink strip represents sex, red for life, orange for healing, yellow for sun, green for nature, turquoise for art, indigo for harmony and violet for spirit. In 1979, when the flags were planned for mass-production, the hot pink and turquoise were removed from the design, since they were not commercially available.

LGBT/Gay Pride
(Current 6 Colour)

The six colour version of the mass-produced flag from 1979 spread from San Francisco to other cities, and soon became the widely known symbol of LBGT pride and diversity. It is even recognized by the International Congress of Flag Makers. There are many variations on the gay pride flag, specific to each country. (For example, deviations using the US Flag, the Union Jack, the Canadian Maple Leaf, the Southern Cross, Silver Fern, etc.)

Lesbian Pride

The design of this flag is a bit of an unknown, and while I have found some information on the symbology, the information has been inconsistent and unreliable. This flag premiered in 2010, and has been in use randomly throughout the community as a way to specify pride in lesbianism, independent of the grouping of the LGBT community that the rainbow pride flag (above) signifies.

Bisexual Pride

The Bisexual Pride flag was designed by Michael Page, and debuted in December of 1998 at the BiCafe's first anniversary party. The flag is an evolution of the pink and blue triangles (an earlier symbol of the bisexual community), and the resulting purple colour when they overlap, representing the middle ground.

Asexual Pride

The Asexual Visibility and Education Network created this flag in 2010, after seeking input and votes online. The flag premiered in 2011 at pride parades in San Francisco, London, Stockholm and Toronto. The field is divided into four vertical bars. The top three bars represent the three ranges of sexuality; The black bar at the top symbolizes asexuality, (either the lack of sexual attraction to anyone, or a lack of a self-sexual identity.) The grey bar represents Gray-A or demisexualism, (limited sexuality.) White represents sexuality. The fourth purple bar unites the three together and represents community.

Polysexual Pride (Helms)

The three colour Polysexual flag represents the attraction to multiple or alternate genders and multiple or alternate sexualities through three horizontal stripes, each at 1/3 of the field. The pink relates to either female or feminine qualities, while the blue relates to male or masculine qualities. The green center bar represents non-binary genders and sexualities. The specific source of this flag's design is unknown.

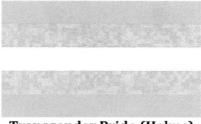

Transgender Pride (Helms)

The three colour Transgender flag was designed by Monica Helms and made its debut in a Phoenix, Arizona pride parade. It is the most widespread and recognized symbol of the transgender community. The light blue is the traditional color for baby boys, pink is for girls, and the white in the middle is for those who are transitioning, those who feel they have a neutral gender or no gender, and those who are intersexed. The pattern is such that no matter which way you fly it, it will always be correct. This symbolizes us trying to find correctness in our own lives.

Transgender Pride (Pellinen)

This version of the Transgender pride flag was created by Jennifer Holland in 2002. She was unaware of the Helms flag (above) and wanted to give a symbol to the transgender community. The five horizontal striped field of the flag represents female (pink at the top) and male, (blue at the bottom), with three shades of purple to represent the diversity of the transgender community, and the genders other than 'male' and 'female'.

Transgender Pride (Holland)

The Queer Nation's Transgender Focus Group, Transgender Nation, created this flag in 1991 in San Francisco, California, USA. The interlocked gender symbols in the charge of the flag are meant to represent various transgendered people working in unity.

Hermaphrodite Pride (Mars/Venus)

The Herm-Pride flag is based on the principle that yellow represents a neutrality in gender, (where pink is typically representative of females, and blue of males.) Taking the rainbow spectrum from the gay pride flag, the herm-pride flag opens the spectrum between the colours that border the yellow, (orange and green), and create a six-barred field with shades of yellow ranging from orangish to greenish. The center of the flag holds a modified mars/venus symbol to represent both genders. The designer of this flag is unknown.

Hermaphrodite Pride (Mercury)

The Herm-Pride flag is based on the principle that yellow represents a neutrality in gender, (where pink is typically representative of females, and blue of males.) Taking the rainbow spectrum from the gay pride flag, the herm-pride flag opens the spectrum between the colours that border the yellow, (orange and green), and create a six-barred field with shades of yellow ranging from orangish to greenish. The center of the flag holds a modified mercury symbol to represent both genders. The designer of this flag is unknown.

Genderqueer Pride (Roxie)

The Genderqueer Pride flag was accepted by the genderqueer (persons who do not identify themselves by one specific gender) community in September of 2010. The field of the flag is divided into three horizontal stripes, the top lavender stripe representing a mix of blue and pink, (traditional male and female colors) meant to represent those under the genderqueer umbrella who feel they are both male and female in identity. The greenish chartreuse color is the inverse of the lavender color, meant to represent individuals who feel they are neither male nor female in identity, and the white meant to represent individuals falling completely outside of the gender binary. The design is by Marilyn Roxie. Version two of the design was replaced by this current version (3) in June, 2011.

Genderqueer Pride (Alternate)

This alternate Genderqueer Pride flag has recently been seen in the genderqueer community. Its origins are unknown. Though not thoroughly accepted because it too closely resembles some commercial product color schemes, it is expanding in recognition in the community. The field is divided into five equal horizontal lines of a unique, non-heraldic colour scheme. The top bar, a shade of purple is meant to represent androgyny, followed by robin's egg blue for masculinity, the yellow for genders outside the standard male/female binary, and pink for femininity. The orange was adopted to represent the invert of purple, to represent agender identities, as yellow (the true opposite of purple) was already used for another purpose.

Genderfluid Pride

The Genderfluid Pride flag is another sexual identity pride flag used by those who do not identify with a binary male/female gender system. The five horizontal bars start at the top with pink, for female/ femininity. The three center bars are black, purple, and white— representing the blurred lines of neutral and fluid genders. The bottom bar unites the meaning with the top bar by symbolizing masculinity/male attributes.

Bigender/Intersex Pride

The Intersexed Pride flag was created by Natalie Phox in 2009 to symbolize the spirit of those who either are born partially a member of both the male and female gender or for those who transition from male or female to both as a final result rather than a complete transition to one or the other (heshe, shemale) or any combination such as a male who desires a more feminine appearance. The middle stripe combines pink (female) and blue (male) in the middle to symbolize the mix between the two genders.

Intersex Pride

The Intersex Pride flag was created by Organization Intersex International Australia in July 2013 to create a flag "that is not derivative, but is yet firmly grounded in meaning." The organization aimed to create a symbol without gendered pink and blue colors. It describes yellow and purple as the "hermaphrodite" colors. The organization describes it as freely available "for use by any intersex person or organization who wishes to use it, in a human rights affirming community context."

Pansexual Pride

The Pansexual Pride flag was designed to increase visibility and recognition for the pansexual community, and appeared on the internet on multiple sites in mid-2010. The blue portion of the flag represents those who identify within the male spectrum (regardless of biological sex), the pink represents those who identify within the female spectrum (regardless of biological sex), and the yellow portion, found in between the blue and pink portions, represents non-binary attraction; such as Transgender and Intersex people.

Polyamory Pride

The Poly Pride flag consists of three equal horizontal colored stripes with a symbol in the center of the flag. The colors of the stripes, from top to bottom, are as follows: blue, representing the openness and honesty among all partners with which we conduct our multiple relationships; red, representing love and passion; and black, representing solidarity with those who, though they are open and honest with all participants of their relationships, must hide those relationships from the outside world due to societal pressures. The symbol in the center of the flag is a gold Greek lowercase letter 'pi', as the first letter of 'polyamory'. The letter's gold color represents the value that we place on the emotional attachment to others, be the relationship friendly or romantic in nature, as opposed to merely primarily physical relationships. The flag was created by Jim Evans.

Polyamory Pride

The red heart with the blue infinity logo is the most widely recognized symbol of polyamory. This pride flag is a white field with that symbol centered.

Androgyny Pride

The Androgyny Pride flag's origin is unknown, but is meant as a symbol for androgynous people of all sexualities. The grey field represents the ambiguousness of androgynous people, and the blue and pink equal sign represents equality between genders.

Lesbian Pride

The Labrys Pride Flag is a symbol for the lesbian community. The lavender field represents the lesbian community features a black triangle in the charge. The triangle is a symbol from Nazi Germany, which was used to designate prisoners with anti-social behaviour, including lesbians. The triangle includes a labrys, which is a double-sided hatchet or axe which is an ancient symbol from European, African and Asian matriarchal societies. The flag was created by Sean Campbell in 1999, and was first used nationally in 2000 for a Pride edition of GLT Magazine.

Below is an easier guide for you to follow. I am just trying to show to you that the flags for the L,G,B,T,Q movement are already here. Do you think they, in any manner, represent our sovereignty, unalienable rights, rights to substance money, not to mention the *man, woman, and child?* I think not.

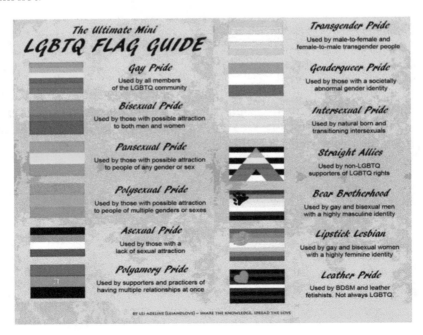

Notice how all these flags are based on the "absolute" that there isn't any absolute (metaphysical) sexual/gender distinction between the sexes. And look at the chaos it is creating. My suggestion is that we come up with a flag that stands for *life*, its actual structure that our lives are based upon, the exact (equal and opposite) balance of man and woman that all life depends on. How else would you have it? What other structure is based in *procreant love*, also called *spiritual procreation*? What other structure will bring forward our co-sovereignty together— our unalienable rights, substance money, and private property? What structure will honor the sanctity of all life, including the unborn? What other structure—understanding that "God" is the exact sexual procreant life process of division and unification—can state: *Have ye not read, that he which made them in the beginning made them male and female, And said, for this cause shall a man leave father and mother, and shall cleave to his wife: and they twain shall be one flesh? Wherefore they are no more twain, but one flesh. What therefore God hath joined together, let not man put asunder,* (Matthew 19:4-6)? As stated in the last aphorism in the booklet *Aphorisms for the New Age of Man and Woman: Love is the only state of existence between Male and Female.* Male and female are in love together, right now and forever. This is what we believe and, as such, is the basis of our flag. (Flag created by Misha at Norwest Designs.)

The Flag of Man and Woman

Banners, Signs, and Bumper Stickers

Banner, signs, and bumper stickers are just another way to get this word out. Banners and signs are more appropriate in demonstrations, parades, or rallies. Below I give some examples.

Banner

Signs/Bumper Stickers

The Eternal and the
PR CREATIVE
are One
WWW.MANANDWOMANBALANCE.COM

MAN AND WOMAN BALANCE: WORLD-WIDE
EVOLUTION
WWW.MANANDWOMANBALANCE.COM

FAMILY:
The Force to Save the Planet
WWW.MANANDWOMANBALANCE.COM

Man, Woman, and Child
= LIFE!
WWW.MANANDWOMANBALANCE.COM

Man and Woman Sovereigncy

WWW.MANANDWOMANBALANCE.COM

MARRIAGE:
Equal and Opposite

WWW.MANANDWOMANBALANCE.COM

MAN AND WOMAN
TOGETHER
FOREVER

WWW.MANANDWOMANBALANCE.COM

Free Thy People!
NO MORE FED/IRS

WWW.MANANDWOMANBALANCE.COM

POST CARD

MADE IN U.S.A.

FOR CORRESPONDENCE   FOR ADDRESS ONLY.

Dear,

God the Father and God the Mother
Thank you for hearing my prayer.

I feel your dual lights around me.
I stand on both of your shoulders
and reach out for the best within me.
And now, I accept your most precious
gift of [_____] into my heart
that it may live in me forever.

Thank you Father and Mother for
all that you have done for me,
and continue to do for me—
that I may again give back to you.

Your loving Son/Daughter,

Christopher Alan Anderson
Spiritual Healing

Memes

Memes consist of quotes from my writings with a background picture that highlights the quote. The background pictures have been provided by Misha at Norwest Designs. Misha has been the Man and Woman Balance website designer for many years. I find the memes are particularly effective in presentations and as handouts at demonstrations. They allow a person to capture the message of Man and Woman Balance at a deeper level, I believe.

Along with the memes there are cards (25 as of this date listed on the Man and Woman Balance website) that can be used as handouts at presentations, parades, and rallies. Some have been included in this writing. The point of this is that the man and woman message must be presented both intellectually and emotionally to reach into spirit. From there an inner shift can occur.

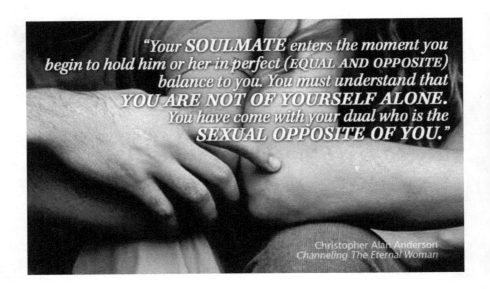

"*Your SOULMATE enters the moment you begin to hold him or her in perfect (EQUAL AND OPPOSITE) balance to you. You must understand that YOU ARE NOT OF YOURSELF ALONE. You have come with your dual who is the SEXUAL OPPOSITE OF YOU.*"

Christopher Alan Anderson
Channeling The Eternal Woman

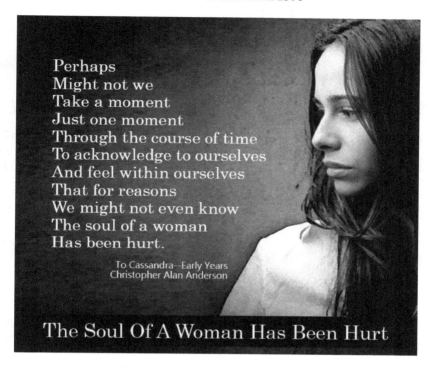

Perhaps
Might not we
Take a moment
Just one moment
Through the course of time
To acknowledge to ourselves
And feel within ourselves
That for reasons
We might not even know
The soul of a woman
Has been hurt.

To Cassandra--Early Years
Christopher Alan Anderson

The Soul Of A Woman Has Been Hurt

If there is a "God the Father,"
there must also be a "God the Mother,"

not a "God the Mother"
as a secondary existence
to "God the Father"

but as an equal and opposite
primary existence to "God the Father."

CHRISTOPHER ALAN ANDERSON
The Prime Movers: The Sovereignty of Man and Woman

We Will Always Be Together

We will always be together
Through sun and rain
Through time and pain
Together
Sharing our dreams along the way
In silence,
We, you and I
Man and Woman
Will always be together
Until eternity's end.
Listen, listen to our children
They say it is so.

Christopher Alan Anderson
To Cassandra - Early Years

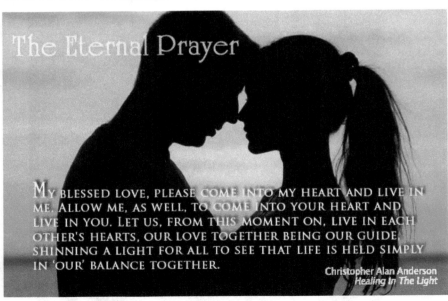

The Eternal Prayer

My blessed love, please come into my heart and live in me. Allow me, as well, to come into your heart and live in you. Let us, from this moment on, live in each other's hearts, our love together being our guide, shinning a light for all to see that life is held simply in 'our' balance together.

Christopher Alan Anderson
Healing In The Light

Merchandise

Merchandise generally consists of t-shirts, coffee mugs, bags, and caps. Other items can be included.

Man and Woman Balance: Equal & Opposite

Man and Woman Balance: The Message of the Universe

A Success Covenant

What if we had a *Success Covenant* that literally could guarantee our success? This whole task of Man and Woman Balance, its definition and implementation, is a grand undertaking. And yet, on the other hand, it is the daily living of love, man and woman creating life together. Let's begin by exploring the idea of a covenant. As a boy growing up in the Christian Church, I was aware of the idea but did not know about its real meaning. Below are some definitions and ideas of a covenant that I'm taking from the internet and Wikipedia.

> *An agreement, contract, undertaking, commitment, guarantee, warrant, pledge, promise, bond, indenture; pact, deal, settlement, arrangement, understanding.*

> *The promises made by God to man, as recorded in the Bible.*

> ***Theology:*** *An agreement that brings about a relationship of commitment between God and his people. The Jewish faith is based on the biblical covenants made with Abraham, Moses, and David. See also Ark of the Covenant.*

> *The **Ark of the Covenant**, also known as the **Ark of the Testimony**, was a wooden chest clad with gold containing the two stone tablets of the Ten Commandments as well as, according to various texts within the Hebrew Bible, Aaron's rod and a pot of manna.*

As I read this what stands out for me is that a covenant is a promise. The Marriage Vow comes to my mind as a promise a man and woman make to each other—*until death do us part* and so on. But we also see that a covenant is a pact or agreement from God to man. The Ten Commandments for example—God giving to Moses his laws. Now, I have been suggesting throughout this writing that there are two primary forces (male and female) that interact with each other, giving their sexual essence to the other and receiving back the sexual essence of the other. In short, they exist in a giving and receiving cycle.

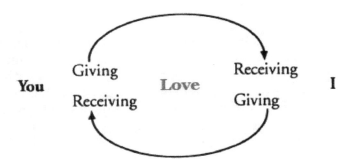

In religious terms, we would say that a covenant is the solemn agreement/promises made from God to man (men and woman). One of these promises is to prosper, i.e., be successful. There are many verses in the Bible that mention prosperity. Below is just a sampling.

Proverbs 10:22: *The blessing of the Lord, it maketh rich, and He addeth no sorrow with it.*

3 John 1:2: *Beloved, I pray that you may prosper in all things and be in health, just as your soul prospers.*

...just as your souls prospers. Interesting. And just how do our souls prosper? Using religious terms here for a moment, I would suggest to you that we must complete the covenant (the giving-receiving cycle) by making our solemn promise back to God. Man and God, if you will, is not a one-way street. The interaction must be two-way, a complete giving and receiving cycle. So when we ask (in prayer for example) something from God must not we also state what we are going to give back to God? Say you ask for riches in some form. Must not you state what you are going to do with those riches, how you are going to benefit not just yourself but others as well? We give back to God by putting into <u>use</u> what God gives to us.

Let me return to the book *The Thought Farthest Out* by Glenn Clark. As you read these few paragraphs think of yourself as a Success Covenant, or shall we call it a Success Promise.

Glenn Clark (1882-1956)—*The Thought Farthest Out*
Prayer, in so far as you hope it will change the outward conditions about you, must first of all change conditions within you. If you want something in the world changed, first change yourself, then go and lay your need before the altar,

and your Father who rewardeth in absolute fairness will reward you.

Do you want a balanced world? Then get a balanced personality. And how do you *get* anything? You get only by giving. As you give you shall receive. ...Give it to the least of those about you—give it to the greatest of those about you. ...The light—the love—the joy—the abundance with which you give yourself attracts the same that is outside of you to you. It cannot be otherwise. ...What shall you give? Most beautiful, most powerful, most wonderful of all gifts is yourself, your faith, your trust, your love. Trust men, trust God, trust events. And the most powerful, most beautiful of all giving is forgiving your enemies, your persecutors. If you really do that once, then you become irresistible. After that you will draw all things to you. For then you are perfect even as your heavenly Father is perfect.

For again let me repeat: You attract unto yourself the condition that accords with what you are; and if you are perfect, you draw perfection to you.

Do not have Love. Be Love. And then you will attract all the Goodness, all the Perfection that the world has in store for you to you; you will draw the very Kingdom of Heaven itself down to the earth. When your Power to Love becomes like God's Power to Love then your Power to create will become like God's power to create.

...And the moment that you become love, thenceforth whatever you ask shall be yours. Whatever you expect shall be yours. Whatever you want shall be yours. For you shall thenceforth ask for, and expect, and want, only that which is in accord with the spirit of infinite love. For you are love and love is the power that draws all things into perfectly adjusted and harmonious activity. You henceforth attract unto you the condition that accords with what you are.

Mr. Clark states, *"Prayer, in so far as you hope it will change the outward conditions about you, must first of all change conditions within you."* In this statement lies the essence of the Creative Thought movement and the *Law of Attraction*. The inner creates the outer, and thus the necessity of basing our inner selves on the perfect balance. As good as the writers of the Creative Thought movement were we still want to take that last step into a sexed-electric universe of Man and Woman Balance. Let's word it this way: *You, and I, are of the original light. We are Source/Spiritual energy, the Divine Substance (Manna) itself. We are "Gods" making our covenant to each other.* The idea is to begin from *Light* and return to *Light.* Our light only shines from the eternal sexual balance of who we sexually are to each other. *Man shines his male light to woman; woman shines her female light to man.* That is it. As you give out from your soul so you receive into your soul and vice versa. Just like in breathing. You cannot give without also receiving; you can receive without also giving. Let what you desire into your heart and soul as you give it out again and again. The mistake too many of us make is that we don't equal the covenant. Each one of us needs to not only *be the light,* but also be the *sexual light.* Don't start as less than that. Remember, your love is *primary love.* You, too, are the *only begotten son or daughter.* "God" is asking you to be as "God." "God" can only give and receive love. "God" (the one absolute order) actually is the one two-force, sexual, living, procreant process of giving and receiving love. Each one of us is one of the two *sexual* forces, dividing apart (male desire) and uniting together (female desire), over and over again. This is the exact giving and receiving cycle. *The love already is. The love is already within us now. We, male and female, dividing from and uniting with, are manifesting our love together right now!* So the Success Covenant is simply to give to and receive from primary love—which is also light, truth, beauty, balance...and so on. And what we must do is just allow this *sex-electric love energy* to pulse through us. We are all vibrating with light/love energy. *Feel the actual life/procreant energy itself as yourself—as you see your eternal (equal and opposite) other half as the perfect life complement of yourself. In this is our increase.* Be the promise that you want made to you. Be that love; be that light; be that truth, beauty, balance, health, wealth... You decide. *You are the universal consciousness that decides!* Be on the inside what you want on the outside. You decide. Let your prayers *change conditions within you* as Mr. Clark says. You decide. The secret, if there is one, is to see the Light of Love in everything, in everyone. The covenant (promise), as it were, is that what you are on the inside will out-picture on the outside. *"For you are love and love is the power that draws all things into perfectly adjusted and harmonious activity."* So to plant the seed of your desire into the spiritual prototype (or in any negative event which might surround you) from which it can sprout just *love ye one another.* Or, said another way, *pray ye one another.* Prayer itself has to be asked and answered <u>together</u>. *A man and woman praying together* is the archetype. And know that this new moment, procreated from the last, is just a little better than the last; each new day another *expression of love* moving us forward. Indeed—*we are one within our two; we are two within our one.* <u>Know this now</u>—with your own eternal (equal and opposite) other half. You two together comprise the totality of the Life Principle or Spirit of Life. Begin from there.

So how may we word a *Success Covenant*? We want something that will capture this feeling/acceptance for us on the inside, such that it will out-picture for us on the outside. We want something that will be responsive to our deepest desires and longing. We want something that, just by its original wording, places us in the original light, i.e., Source/Spiritual energy or Divine Substance (Manna) itself such that we each are cognizant of our own living and eternal sexual spirits—always in harmony with our own equal and opposite eternal other half. Yes, we together, man and woman, are the two (pro)creative forces. Let there be LIFE.

A Success Covenant

Thank you for being the original light, the divine substance itself, with me.

Thank you for shining your light into me, and allowing me to shine my light into you.

Thank you that our Covenant together comes with the promise of love, and stands on this promise alone, as we together shine our lights that comprise the original/eternal light—expressing as the spiritual/sexual forces that comprise LIFE itself.

Thank you for being in LIFE—birth-life-death-rebirth...—with me.

Thank you for sharing with me a point of our love, a sun shining in this vast cosmos of space.

And thank you so much that this point of our love brings into creation more points of love—our children that mean so much to us.

And please know and share with me the promise of our love, it being the divine substance itself that we together may mold into the most beautiful expressions of divine life as we give to and receive from each other.

And please share with me this divine feeling of life, as it pulses the original light of love through our veins—that we may know that this divine feeling is the feeling of original balance from which all karma is vanished and increase is generated, simply by our holding to it as real now.

Thank you for being real with me now.

Thank you for allowing me to know that our promise of love is love itself and as we stand in that center together all is manifested per our desire as the only reality of our lives.

The Manifestation Process

The Manifestation Process (which can also be called the Miracle Process) is a simple exercise one may do to assist in manifesting one's desires. By desires I mean your deepest desires, what you really want in life/out of life. What is important to you?—Your dream, your passion, or your purpose—define it now. What is meaningful to you?—Take charge of it now. Stay focused on your core desire until it is manifested to your satisfaction. Then you can move on to another desire, and so the process continues. Before we look at how a step-by-step process of manifestation might play out I want to review the lineage of the Creative Thought movement that we have covered. We began with Walter and Lao Russell—*The Universal One, Atomic Suicide?,* and *Why You Cannot Die.* We reviewed Omraam Mikhaël Aïvanhow—*Cosmic Balance: The Secret of Polarity.* There was Thomas Troward—*The Creative Process in the Individual*—and Genevieve Behrend—*Your Invisible Power.* Also Christian D. Larson—*The Ideal Made Real.* We reviewed John McDonald—*The Message of the Master.* Then Glenn Clark—*The Thought Farthest Out.* In passing I mentioned Ernest Holmes— *Thoughts Are Things.* Now I want to complete the Creative Thought movement with some passages from Ernest Holmes' *The Science of Mind.* I consider *The Science of Mind* the Bible of the Creative Thought movement. Now, we understand that *The Science of Mind* is not sexed, i.e., the procreant life process not viewed as primary. In *The Science of Mind,* Holmes uses the term "Infinite Spirit" (the action of Spirit within Itself). Also the terms like "One Infinite Mind," "One Supreme Intelligence," "One Life," and "God is," are used. Never-the-less, this is very good. You might say this is where we start from, this is where the equal and opposite structure of Man and Woman Balance begins. And so, as you read these quotes please remember, *the love already is.* The success or wealth or health or perfection or light, etc., *already is.* We don't get there, we are there.

Ernest Holmes (1887-1960)—*The Science of Mind,* 1926, 1938

One should analyze himself, saying, "Do I look at myself from a standpoint of restriction? Do I see life limited to the eternal round of getting up in the morning, eating, going to work, coming home, going to bed, sleeping, getting up again and so on?" Break the bonds of apparent necessity and see life as one continuous expression of the Infinite Self, and as this conception gradually dawns upon the inner thought, something will happen in the outer conditions to relieve the greater demands of necessity.

In treating we conceive of the ultimate of the idea but never of the process. Never treat a process. We plant a seed and there is in the seed, operating through the creative soil, everything that will cause it to develop, unfold and produce a plant. *The ultimate of effect is already potential in its cause.* This is the mystical meaning of the words: "I am Alpha and Omega." Our word for the fullest expression of our life or for its smallest detail should be the alpha and omega, the beginning and the end of the thing thought of. All cause and effect are in Spirit, they are bound together in one complete whole. One is the inside, the other the outside of the same thing.

Never let anything cause you to doubt your ability to demonstrate the Truth. CONCEIVE OF YOUR WORD AS BEING THE THING. See the desire as an already accomplished fact and rest in perfect confidence, peace and certainty, never looking for results, never wondering, never becoming anxious, never being hurried nor worried. Those who do not understand this attitude may think you are inactive but remember: "To him who can perfectly practice inaction, all things are possible."

What we know about Subjective Mind proves that It is unconscious of time, knows neither time nor process. *It knows only the completion, the answer.* That is why it is written, "Before they call, I will answer." Cosmic Creation is from idea not object. It does not know anything about process; process is involved in it but not consciously. Correct practice should know that ultimate right action is now, today. If we say, "Tomorrow it is going to be," then according to the very law we are using we hold the answer in the state of futurity which can never become present. If a gardener holds his seed in his hand and says, "Tomorrow I am going to plant this seed," his garden will never start growing. Therefore, Jesus said: "When ye pray, believe that ye have and ye shall receive." He did not say believe and you will immediately have. He said, "Ye shall receive." He did not deny the natural law of evolution and growth. Nature operates according to a law of logical sequence.

In mental work, we must realize that there is One Infinite

Mind, which is consciously directing our destiny. Declare every day that: "No mistakes have been made, none are being made and none can be made." Declare: "There is One Supreme Intelligence which governs, guides and guards, tells me what to do, when to act and how to act." Having done this in perfect faith, act with perfect assurance. Declare further: "Everything necessary to the full and complete expression of the most boundless experience of joy is mine now."

Know that there is no condemnation, for nothing can condemn unless we believe in condemnation. Destroy the thought that would place limitation or bondage upon any situation or condition. "Loose him and let him go." Talk to yourself, not to the world. There is no one to talk to but yourself for all experience takes place within. Conditions are the reflections of our meditations and nothing else. There is but one Mind, that Mind is our mind now. It never thinks confusion, knows what It wishes and how to accomplish what It desires. *It is what It desires!*

Assume a case of treatment for prosperity. Suppose one comes to you and says, "Business is bad. There is no activity." How are you going to treat him? Are you going to treat activity, business, customers, conditions or what? There is but one thing to treat as far as the practitioner is concerned, and that is HIMSELF. The practitioner treats himself, the reason being that his patient's mind and his own mind are in the One Mind.

There is but one activity, which is perfect. Nothing has happened to it. Nothing can cut it off, it is always operating. There is no belief in inactivity. What is this statement for? To neutralize the belief in inactivity. A word spoken in Mind will reach its own level in the objective world by its own weight; just as in physical science we know that water reaches its own level. You must destroy the thoughts of inactivity. Man cannot become either discouraged or afraid if he realizes that there is but One Mind which he may consciously use. The real man knows no discouragement, cannot be afraid, and has no unbelief. And he who knows of the power with which he is dealing and who plants a seed of thought in Subjectivity, knows that it will come up and bear fruit.

Bring out the idea of Substance. Make consciousness perceive that Substance is Spirit, Spirit is God, and God is all there is. Once you acquaint the consciousness with this idea, it is implanted in the Creative power, which is externalized in your life.

Continue to declare there were no mistakes, there are none and there never will be. Say, "I represent the Truth, the whole Truth and Nothing but the Truth. It is unerring, It never makes mistakes. There are no mistakes in the Divine Plan for me. There is no limitation, poverty, want nor lack. I stand in the midst of eternal opportunity, which is forever presenting me with the evidence of its full expression. I am joy, peace and happiness. I am the spirit of joy within me. I am the spirit of happiness within me. I radiate Life: I am Life. There is One Life and that Life is my Life now."

It is not enough to say: "There is One Life and that Life is God." We must complete this statement by saying: "That Life is my life now," because we must couple this Life with ours in order to express It. We are not becoming this life, but are now in and of this Life. There is no other life. God is not becoming: God IS. God is not growing; God is complete. God is not trying to find out something; God already knows. Evolution is not the expression of a "becoming" God, but is simply one of the ways that a God Who already IS, expresses himself; and as such it is the logical result of involution and is eternally going on.

"I expect, fully and emphatically, the answer to my prayer today. Right now do I possess this thing I so greatly desire. I remove my fear of lack and negation, for it is the only barrier which stands in the way of my experience of good. I alone can remove it. And I do remove it now."

"Today, in this moment, the Law responds to my thought. My word is one of affirmation, rising from the knowledge that the Good, the Enduring and the True are Eternalities in my experience. I cannot be apart from that which is my good. My good is assured me by God, the Indwelling Essence of my life."

All the good that *I* desire awaits *my* acceptance of it.

The last quote came from Holmes *Thoughts Are Things.* It actually read: *All the good that you desire awaits your acceptance of it.* I changed *You* to *I* and *Your* to *my* to better fit the first person languaging of the other passages. Now, incorporating some of Holmes' wording, a Manifestation Process might look something like this: (These are conceptual steps.)

Step 1: *Define what you want.*
Step 2: *Never treat a process. ...The ultimate of effect is already potential in its cause. ...All cause and effect are in Spirit, they are bound together in one complete whole. One is the inside, the other the outside of the same thing.*
Step 3: *Conceive of Your Word as Being the Thing.*
Step 4: *It knows only the completion, the answer.*
Step 5: *There is but one thing to treat as far as the practitioner is concerned, and that is HIMSELF.*
Step 6: *It is unerring. It never makes mistakes. There are no mistakes in the Divine Plan for me.*
Step 7: *Substance is Spirit, once you acquaint the consciousness with this idea, it is implanted in the Creative power, which is externalized in your life.*
Step 8: *There is One Life and that Life is God. That Life is my life now.*
Step 9: *Today, in this moment, the Law responds to my thought.*
Step 10: *All the good that I desire awaits my acceptance of it.*

If I were to condense these steps I might simply say:

-*I only want for the change to occur within me that will create the exact occurrence without me.*
-*I possess within me now that which is the Source-point of all my fulfilled desires.*
-*Every aspect of my Life contains the Substance/Spirit of all Life.*
-*Today, in this moment, the Law responds to my thought because the Law of Balance is my thought.*
-*My word/desire is the thing itself...alive in me now!*
-*Change is occurring in me now!*

Having it now is a consciousness. Call this *source consciousness* if you will. We might say: *You can only get that which you have first received into your heart/soul. This is spiritual law.* It must originate from within you. But source consciousness is not just in me alone or you alone. It really is a connective consciousness, arising from the balance one holds with another. It is *...alive in us now!* This whole treatise is about a *sexually connective us.* Creative manifestation, i.e., the life process only exists because there is a primary us. I call this balance Man and Woman Balance. We could also call it Spiritual Procreation; the Two-Force Sexual, Life-process; Male and Female Division and Unification; or a Sex-Polarized Universe. So I am making a fundamental distinction between the Creative Thought movement's "Spirit's Original Unity," "His sexless unity," "One Still Light," "Spirit's necessary and basic conception of itself," "the action of Spirit within Itself," or some "One Infinite Mind," etc., and the Sex-polarized Universe of Man and Woman Balance. One, the Creative Thought movement, originates from fundamental oneness and the other, Man and Woman Balance, originates from oneness and twoness. Here are a few other quotes from *The Science of Mind* by Ernest Holmes. As they progress, notice how close they come to stating that the causal act of creation is the creative (two-force) process itself.

> As we come into the Spiritual Realm—which is a perfectly natural and normal realm—we have to come into it in its own nature. It is a unity.

> If we suppose Spirit to be the Life Principle running through all manifestation, the Cause of all, then we must suppose that It has Substance within itself. It is Self-Existent consciousness, and also Self-Existence Substance. Spirit makes things out of itself through some inner act upon itself. This inner act must, of course, be an act of consciousness, of self-perception, of self-knowingness. What God knows IS. This has been called the Word of God and the Self-Contemplation of God.

> An eternal creation is proved by the fact that we must suppose Spirit to be Conscious Intelligence, and there can be no Conscious Intelligence unless It is conscious of something! Spirit is conscious and must be conscious of something. Therefore, It must always create. What a glorious concept is such an idea of an Eternal Creative Principle. There is no stagnation in Spirt, nor should there be any in our idea of spirituality. To be spiritual is to create! The Spirit is alive, conscious, aware and active.

> But the world of multiplicity does not contradict the world of Unity, for the many live in the One. This concept of Unity is

the mystical secret of the ages, the key to spiritual wisdom and the teaching of Jesus.

Perhaps the one point of which we are all agreed is that whatever the nature of First Cause of Spirit, It is creative. If this were not true, nothing could come into existence. It is impossible to think of Creative Life expressing Itself other than in Livingness.

Spirit is the Father-Mother God, because It is the Principle of Unity back of all things. The masculine and the feminine principle both come from the One. Spirit is all Life, Truth, Love, Being, Cause and Effect.

And so the question we might ask ourselves is whether this difference (between oneness [or unity] and oneness and twoness) matters? It only matters relative to the idea of balance. If we hold oneness prior to twoness (equal but not opposite) or twoness prior to oneness (opposite but not equal), we essentially end up in inner lack. All negative consequences arise out of inner lack. But if we hold to the balance of equal and opposite we end up in *having it now. Balance itself is the source of all abundance.* The abundance/prosperity consciousness comes from the perfect (equal and opposite) balance we hold in our own hearts and souls from which we see another in their absolute necessity. As earlier stated, *one is not without the other; both are needed for either to be.* And so we view the other not just as a part of a "unity" with ourselves but *as an absolute necessity to ourselves.* Relative to man and woman we would say an *absolute sexual necessity.* This in a nutshell is the difference between the Creative Thought movement and what I am attempting to articulate. We need to remember: *There is not a singular me. There is not a singular you. There is a uniting/dividing procreant us. And moreover, our connection (division and unification) together is the answer.* Manifestation is ultimately an us proposition. This must be our ultimate frame. Our purpose in life is not singular (one "God," one Spirit, or one Mind, etc.) to ourselves alone. It is a purpose that always ties us (male and female) together. GENDER IS METAPHYSICAL! And that, my friends, is the real spark of life. And so we want to sexually polarize some of the statements above. Below is my wording. You might want to create your own.

Our Purpose Together

**We stand together in universal purpose!
We acknowledge each other as being an
absolute necessity to our own lives!
We intend, from the frame of our balance together, and so it is!
Within our balance there cannot be any lack, resistance, or fear!
Each one of us exists not just for our own gain
but equally for the gain of the other!
We stand together in perfect acceptance, gratitude, and love!
Let us not expect anything; let us accept everything!**

Now, I have not really put in the sexual components of male and female in the above statements. It is a general statement. I did use the sexual components of male and female for the statement *What We Believe!* from an earlier section. This sexual polarizing (putting in the sexual difference of male and female) into the primary origination is what this writing is all about. This is the fundamental difference between Man and Woman Balance and the Creative Thought movement or any other movement or religion. Man and Woman Balance is founded on, or actually is, procreation. The procreant (two-way equal and opposite sexual) process is the 1st tier primary and is not secondary to some singular "Spirit's Original Unity." "Spirit's Original Unity" is just one part of the two-way life process. It comprises the female side of unity. (Male comprises the side of division/individuality.) So when we hear the terms such as "Spirit's Original Unity" or "Supreme Being," "God-Self," "Divine Essence," "Infinite Spirit," "One Infinite Mind," etc., all of these terms generally refer to the unity side of things. Remember the earlier drawing depicting the *Religious* as to the *Procreative*? We are attempting to <u>sex</u> the *Religious* if you will. Do you see that? Female is the universal womb; male the specific materialization into form. So when Ernest Holmes writes in *The Science of Mind: We plant a seed and there is in the seed, operating through the creative soil, everything that will cause it to develop, unfold*

and produce a plant. The ultimate of effect is already potential in its cause. ...All cause and effect are in Spirit, they are bound together in one complete whole. One is the inside, the other the outside of the same thing, he is actually referring to a procreant process. As I say: *The Two is in the One; the One is in the Two.* Or let us use the terms spirit and substance. As Mr. Holmes also states: *Substance is Spirit, once you acquaint the consciousness with this idea, it is implanted in the Creative power, which is externalized in your life.* (Let us say that spirit is female and substance is male.) And: *One is the inside, the other the outside of the same thing.* One process, two parts: spirit and substance; a balance, one goes into the other, the other comes out of the one. Remember Walt Whitman's quote from *Leaves of Grass,* where he states: *...Urge and urge and urge, Always the procreant urge of the world. Out of the dimness opposite equals advance...?* He also stated in the same writing: *This is the nucleus...after the child is born of woman the man is born of woman. This is the bath of birth...this is the merge of small and large and the outlet again.* And so this is the balance we are to hold—spirit and substance as a one procreative life-process of love. Hold within yourself that which you desire as the spirit of substance and the substance of love—all a one and perfect and complete procreant life-process. This is what the term *spiritual procreation* means.

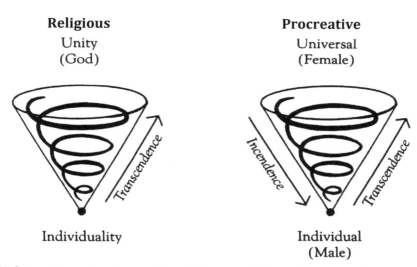

Religious
Unity
(God)

Procreative
Universal
(Female)

Individuality

Individual
(Male)

Might not we just consider this possibility of a *sexual procreant universe,* a possibility that allows each and every one of us to come from the reality that: *Love is the only state of existence between Male and Female,* and, furthermore, know that this is the actual creative/manifestation process itself. Wouldn't this be a good place from which to begin the life endeavor? Let's end this section with a review of the earlier quote from *Channeling the Eternal Woman,* 2014. This is the spiritual feeling we want to get to, a feeling equal to our understanding.

Thank you. I am the Eternal Woman. I am not a "God." I am a woman. I am the female soul within every woman. As a woman, I stand with man. Actually, I stand between man and child. I am the link between man and child. I am the space between man and child. I am the death of all life and the life of all death. From a man dying inside of me, so our child is born out of me. I am what you might call the field, frame, zero-point, space, opening, womb, or void. But I am not death. Rather, I give life to death. I bring life-potential to all things. I connect all things within me. In this, I am love. Without me there would never be love. All women know this about me because they know it about themselves.

I, the Eternal Woman, stand as the counter-balance to the Individual Man. The Individual Man is that center-point of all men. A man's life purpose is to secure a woman. A woman's life purpose is to reproduce a man. Can that ever change? As such, a man can only find his rebirth, i.e., eternal life in me. Individual men have yet to understand this. And so they go about their "lives" creating "Gods" to believe in—which are nothing more than idols that they serve—that they may somehow reach eternal life. And then they enslave the women who are their eternal life connection. What folly. Any man who walks ahead of a woman in his life and heart cannot know life or love. We are co-creators together. We can only walk hand-in-hand.

That which you call belief systems, or might you call them philosophies or religions or enlightenments, or what you may call your sciences or any embodiments of thought, if they exclude man and woman as co-creators they cannot be correct and true. I don't say this as somehow being superior to you. I say this in the frame of Individual Man and Eternal Woman together. Women have wept for thousands, no millions, of years for just a connection of equality between the Individual Man and the Eternal Woman. We are still weeping. Come to me my man and let me touch your heart and breathe new life into your soul. I call you from the space that you thought was somehow empty and have for so long been afraid to enter. But how can you fear me? I am the Eternal Woman. I can only give life to you as my love for you.

Man and Woman Balance

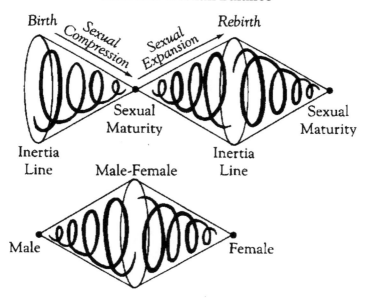

The Eternal Woman is saying that life consists of an <u>us</u>. It is the *sexual* connection point (which includes both division and unification) that is the source point of creative manifestation. Feel it. The love is now. The love has always been now. And in that *procreant* love all is continually manifested as is your desire.

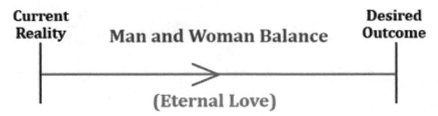

Let us now say: *Creative manifestation, your life manifestation, is only and always birthed in your sexual connection, i.e., spiritual procreation. So whatever is in your deepest heart's desire, let it equally find you as you open your heart to receive its life essence!*

The True Meaning of the Christ Message

As mentioned, I was brought up in a Christian home. As a boy I often felt something was missing in it, like it did not go far enough. As I tried to express my thoughts and feelings, I mostly got a cold shoulder. I guess I turned inward, to writing. It is true that my answer lies in the integration of spirit and procreation. Once more from the *Man and Woman Balance* website:

> On a personal note, when Mr. Anderson was asked to describe the writings and what he felt their message was he responded, "Spiritual procreation. Mankind has yet to distinguish the two sexes on the spiritual level. In this failure lies the root of our problems and why we cannot yet touch the eternal together. The message of Man and Woman Balance brings each of us together in love with our eternal other half right now."

Throughout this writing you have read my comments concerning Christianity. You will also have noticed I quote a number of verses from the Bible. But let's get down to it, what is the true meaning of the Christ message? I would submit to you it lies in the *resurrection* (also called *eternal life*). And I would further submit that each one of us has to go through our own resurrection (into spiritual balance) and, furthermore, that we don't do this alone—*our eternal other half is always with us!* In Webster's Dictionary it defines resurrection as a) *a rising from the dead, or coming back to life;* b) *the state of having risen from the dead.* But the thing is we are not speaking to physical rebirth here per se. We are speaking of a spiritual rebirth. The resurrection is a state of consciousness if you will. It is a certain placement within us. We move from spiritual death (the darkness) to spiritual life (the light). And we all must do this, not just Jesus for us. This spiritual rebirthing can be called the *Christ.* It actually is a part of the birth-life-death-rebirth...cycle of life but it is also spiritual in nature. What this essentially means is that every moment along the eternal (birth-life-death-rebirth...) cycle of life is the most precious moment along the eternal (birth-life-death-rebirth...) cycle of life. *Every moment is a spiritual resurrection/rebirth—and it exists due to the balanced nature of the sexual/procreant process itself.*

The Christ Balance Exercise

I give; I receive; I Am.
You give; you receive; You Are.
We give; we receive; We Are Together.

But first we must forgive and be forgiven. Why is that? Because we have not laid down our imbalance which is also known as judgment, which essentially means "Me" before "You." We still don't view "the other" as an equal and opposite aspect of our own lives. Our belief systems or thought patterns (Masculinism or Feminism) preclude that. So all our thinking and interaction with that other is a judgment upon them. In other words, "me first and you second." And even to forgive another presumes that other needs our forgiveness. Perhaps we were not viewing that other as spiritually perfect in the first place. And so we equally need to accept the forgiveness of that other for our initial judgment upon him or her. And the other person is pretty much in the same position regarding ourselves as we are with him or her.

Forgiveness

**I forgive you; please forgive me.
I receive your forgiveness of me;
please accept my forgiveness of you.**

So as we seek to find that placement of the true meaning of the Christ message within ourselves, let us now acknowledge that the resurrection is but an inner rebirth of love one to another—and, moreover, that we live in each other's hearts, together and forever. Did not Jesus himself state (Matthew 19:4-6): *Have ye not read, that he which made them in the beginning made them male and female, And said, for this cause shall a man leave father and mother, and shall cleave to his wife: and they twain shall be one flesh? Wherefore they are no more twain, but one flesh. What therefore God hath joined together, let not man put asunder.* The resurrection lies in the connection, an us, where the two become as one. Let's add to that the division of the one into two, the next birth of life. Let's review those few passages from *Let Us Create Life Together* from *Meditations for Deepening Love*, 1994, 2010.

Suddenly, her heart stirred again. *It is I.* Emotion flooded over the woman's body. "Is this man to take me to the truth?" she asked herself. He was still just sitting there. He had not given any notice to her to confirm. "What shall I do?" she thought.

"I am a *man.* I only know the truth with *woman.* Man and woman together are the truth. I seek the woman who seeks me, that we may *create life together.*"

"What can I do to help?" she uttered. "We don't want the truth to die."

The man responded saying, "The truth lives only as it is *reproduced*. The truth lives only through man and woman. If I have been sent with this message then I must not have been sent alone." The man paused and then trembled as he said, "*May you be the one who has been sent with me. May you be the one to extend beyond me.*"

That was her question, her truth. And once more the woman's heart stirred and she spoke the words even before she heard them. *Let us create life together.*

In short, "The truth lives only as it is *reproduced*. The truth lives only through man and woman. If I have been sent with this message then I must not have been sent alone." The man paused and then trembled as he said, "*May you be the one who has been sent with me. May you be the one to extend beyond me.*" If you are with me then you will know that the truth/resurrection lives *only as it is reproduced, only lives through man and woman.* This is our connection point, which is every point along the birth-life-death-rebirth process of life. It is *this one present moment of our love.* Let's approach life from this *inner awakening*—and we can only come from it, not to it. Let's view another and everyone from this inner awakening. Life is not about our own salvation or enlightenment. It is only about our giving to and receiving from cycle of life itself. And so this (simple) distinction between the *One* and the *One <u>and</u> the Two*, which is at the heart of this writing, actually opens the door for our very life-survival. Today, we are being pressured by the Islamists (Masculinists) on one side and the Secularist Progressives/L,G,B,T,Q (Feminists) on the other side. Neither of these imbalanced sides can allow for love and freedom, and Christianity will not save us as it, too, fails to make the fundamental distinction between equal and opposite, i.e., male and female, i.e., man and woman as the 1st pair—comprising the heart of creation itself. The moment you ask Jesus to save you, thereby holding Jesus as superior and more necessary than you, is the moment you create an imbalance in your own soul and, therefore, are not able to *love ye one another* as Jesus did. Our resurrection comes <u>together</u> or not at all and until we understand this we will continue to stay in darkness when the light is shining. Yet, we, you <u>and</u> I, are the light itself. Let's add to the statement of Jesus: *I am the light of the world...* (John 8:12), to include: *You are the light of the world.* Again I say that it is a <u>we</u>. Only together as fundamental *sexual pairs* may the light shine forth. Would you have it any other way? Now let's go to another selection from *Meditations for Deepening Love*, 1994, 2010. This one is titled *Into Your Heart.*

Into Your Heart

There was much commotion in the market place on this morning. Most everyone was speaking about the man who just the night before had been condemned to die. He had been found guilty of a great heresy and was to be crucified on this day at the noon hour. Most everyone agreed this man ought to die. At his trial, the multitude had called for his death. They even threatened great reprisals if their demand was not met.

What, though, had been his crime that stirred such a deep resentment in both the authorities and the masses alike? Why, at his trial he had said, "I am not your savior. You cannot find eternal life in me."

"What are you saying?" the crowd shouted at him.

"I am a man," he replied, "a man with a woman, we together comprising all that is life. I extend my hand to you, in invitation, to leave me now and go embrace your beloved."

"What do you know about love?" the crowd jeered. "You have betrayed us. You promised us eternal life and now you tell us to go away." And the crowd set to cursing him and spitting upon him as he was led away.

The judge was candid in his ruling. He simply said, "This man threatens our ways too deeply. What are the people to believe if not in him? I cannot be responsible for the vengeance of the multitudes. Right or wrong, I must submit to their will. Perhaps this day will call for us to pause on another."

As the noontime approached, the crown gathered as this man was led to the summit. As the crucifixion took place and the man was hung from the cross, someone shouted, "Well, oh mighty one, where is your woman now?" Everyone laughed. The authorities kept the crowd at bay and it wasn't long before they had lost interest and returned to their houses of worship.

The summit was now empty except for the man on the cross and one woman who was kneeling before him. The man on the cross looked down upon this woman and spoke, "Why do you stay?" The woman looked up to the man and replied, "Because I believe." "And what is it that you believe?" the man asked. "I believe in us," she answered. As the man on the cross heard these words a tear could be seen running down his face.

The man again looked upon the woman and spoke, "I have presented the message of Man and Woman Balance to this world. But only you receive. May you take this, our child, and give it forth to another." At this same instant, a beam of light shot from the eyes of the man into the eyes of the woman, connecting them as one in spirit. It was just a moment's flash, but it could be seen all the way back at the market place, and for one moment all was still.

Once again the man spoke unto the woman. *Into your heart I commend my spirit. On this day more, we shall be together in paradise.* With that the man dropped his head to speak no more.

The woman kneeling before this man looked upon him. As the tears rolled down her cheeks, she whispered unto him, "I will bring your message of Man and Woman Balance into this world so that all will believe in *us* just as it has been from the beginning."

The woman walked away from the man who now hung lifeless on the cross. She was sad, but as the days went by she could feel a light growing inside of her. She smiled, placed her hands on her belly, and uttered to herself—*within me you shall live again.*

...within me you shall live again. Isn't that nice. Let me complete this section with a few comments. John 15-12 states: *This is my commandment, That ye love one another, as I have loved you.* Now, how do you think Jesus loved another? Could it just be that Jesus saw each and

every person as the Holy Son or Daughter and not just himself alone? And thus we see the spiritual connection (which in man and woman balance terms is spiritual procreation) where each one of us can stand before another in both our individual authenticity and divinity because we know we are simply an (dividing and uniting) us—*a one and a two.* So when Jesus states in Matthew 18:20: *For where two or three are gathered together in my name, there am I in the midst of them,* may I suggest that the 'I' is not Jesus personally but is an <u>us</u>—a point of our giving and receiving love, one unto the other, the only resurrection we will ever need. Following the understanding of spiritual procreation, this allows us to make a structural change or paradigm shift in Christianity (the religion of my upbringing) from *God the Father, God the Son, and God the Holy Spirit* to *God the Father, God the Mother, and God the Holy Son or Daughter.* (Perhaps we can call this the *New Trinity* or *A Living Trinity.*) And if you, the reader, understand this you, indeed, will understand <u>what we believe</u>, that our *love together* is the salvation.

Please Believe in "Us"

Your love and the love of another are the purpose and power of all things. *Can you give your love to another right now? Can you receive love from another right now?* These are the only questions before us. It is my contention that the one structure of Man and Woman Balance gives to us the ability to give and receive love, one unto another, right now. Remember the Albert Einstein quote mentioned in the Preface? *The real problem is in the hearts and minds of men. It is not a problem of physics but of ethics. It is easier to denature plutonium than to denature the evil from the spirit of man.* We just can't get to making right the hearts and minds of men (and women) without the understanding of the universal (equal and opposite) balance between man and woman. It is this sexual balance, derived from the simple distinction: *If division comes out of the unity must not that division be an essential part of the unity. From the unity comes the division into a two. As such, that division must be an essential part of the unity/division process. Likewise, from the division of the two comes unity, the two becoming as one. Therefore, unity must be an essential part of the unity/division process*—that makes our hearts and minds right. If you think you have another answer for this *life-issue* then take it from here. For now, this (Man and Woman Balance) is what we believe.

I Am Never Without You

Birth and death continue onward
Generations come and go
New faces emerge
Sharing new ideas
Formulating new conceptions
One or two so evolutionary
That even reality is viewed
Beyond what I could have ever known
But I am never without you.

That poem is taken from *To Cassandra—Early Years,* 1985, 1994. I would now like to conclude this writing with the booklet *Please Believe in "Us,"* also out of *Meditations for Deepening Love,* 1994, 2010. Of course the "Us" stands for any us, any male and female interaction or relationship in the eternal moment. As you read this ask yourself—*Can you give and receive love right now?* If so give thanks to the underlying structure of the universe—that of the procreant/eternal, living, moment of Man and Woman Balance. *Men and women, the world over, the time is at hand for your Man and Woman Balance to begin.*

Please Believe in "Us"

May I speak with you once again? It has been so very long. My heart can no longer contain itself. I understand that you might not want to hear what I now have to say. Undoubtedly, you have already made up your own mind about me. But please try, if only once more. The time is so very near. We can no longer deny each other, can we?

When I spoke to you for that short time many years ago, there was much I could not say. I tried as best I could to have you see my heart. I wanted you to feel the spirit that moved through me, feel it as your own. For some reason you were not able to do this. After I left you, I understand that you said I thought this spirit was mine alone. I never intended for you to believe that.

As I look back on the time we had together, I now understand that I made a fundamental mistake. I asked you to believe in me. I wanted so very much for you to believe in my love. I felt that for you to believe in my love was to believe in your own love as well. I really did not mean for you to believe in my love alone, although I now see how it must have sounded. I wanted you to *believe in us.* Yes, I wanted you to believe in me, but just as importantly, I wanted you to allow me to believe in you. *I wanted for us, together, to believe in our love.* It is not my love that is holy. Your love is every bit as special. It is our love together that makes for the most special *love.* This is what I have wanted to say but failed to do so. I hope it is not too late.

I have heard that you, and perhaps others, now believe in "my love." No, this is not what I have wanted. Don't you see—life isn't about me. I am not so worthy that you should believe in me, at least not without allowing me to equally believe in you. *We are to believe in each other.* Yes, I want you to believe in me, but please allow me to believe in you. Don't you see, I need your love as much as you need mine. I did not come for you to follow me. *I came for us, that we may be together.* My message is that we may believe in *our love.* My life means nothing without you. How can it be that I could possibly be viewed as somehow being more important than you? I am ashamed of that. And it hurts me very deeply, for until we believe in *our love* we cannot be together.

I hope you can forgive me. I did not present myself clearly to you. It would have been so easy for me to just say, *our love.* I should have said that *we* are the way, the truth, and the life. Yes, that would have been better. I should have told you that *together* we are the light of Christ. I should have declared *our love* as the only pathway for those who would listen. How could I ever have suggested that somehow it was me alone? What a blunder. This blunder has caused all of life's misery ever since. It is a burden I must now carry. I now ask you that you please forgive me.

Just think, for all this time we have been looking for life eternal in all the wrong places. I suppose I thought *I could be* saved without you. Have you, too, thought that about me? It is so clear to me now; I cannot be saved without you. You are my *other half*. I hope you will think of me as your other half as well. Let me tell you how I know this is true. It is because *you and I together can create life.* Yes, together, we, *male and female,* create life. *Through our beautiful love a Christ child is born.* Our love together is always *procreative* to life. This is *the spirit* through which we together *touch life eternal.*

I have returned to you to tell you that we can only be saved by being together. We, male and female, behold the balance through which the Christ light shines though. Each of us must find our other half. *We must find each other.* We must become a male and female pair and give birth to *our* Christ child ... in every moment of our lives.

How could I tell you this before? I didn't even know this myself. I did not understand the purpose and essence of *man and woman,* how they were different yet necessary for each other. I felt it, but I did not understand it. But now I do, and so I say unto you: *Male and female are eternal ... each of us are either a male or a female, eternally ... only together can we continue to give birth to our eternal life ... male constitutes one half of this eternal life and female the other half ... the creative purpose of male is to secure our eternal life ... the creative purpose of female is to reproduce our eternal life ... each moment secured and reproduced by male and female is balanced thus eternal to life ... there isn't any "other life" than the eternal life of male and female balance.* If I don't tell you this now it will never be known.

Do you understand if I now ask of you, *"Please believe in us? Please believe in you and I together, forever. Please come be my helpmate to secure/reproduce this eternal universe of our love."* There is nothing else but *our eternal love.* Let us now come unto one another. Let us step beyond the personhood of Jesus, Mohammed, Buddha, Krishna, or whomever we may have believed in, in the past and who now may be standing in the way of *You and I. Let us begin to touch each other in our eternal love.* This is the *one immediate choice* that now faces us. Let us begin to choose each other, not out of disrespect for our past, but out of our love for each other.

I understand that you might not want to "believe in us," especially with what I have previously spoken. It is difficult for me as well. But we must understand that there just isn't any *salvation* for ourselves without each other. So hard we have tried, sometimes calling ourselves Christians, or Jews, Muslims, Hindus, Buddhists, even atheists, nationalists, naturalists, New Agers, or homosexuals. Please understand, our own life eternal cannot come to pass without each other. I'm sorry, but there just isn't any "my own way." There never was. Man and woman were the only way from the very beginning.

At this time in our lives, each of us is now being presented with the *one immediate choice.* Let us choose carefully. We will not get another chance. Once you have heard these words, you, and I, will be given just this *one* choice. We will then know we can't choose anything else but each other. There never was a choice now, was there? *We can only choose each other. We are never free from each other. We are always together, procreating life in our love just as we desire in our balance.*

May it now be said, the message of Man and Woman Balance is complete. My purpose here is now finished. I will be leaving you shortly. Before I do, there is something I want to give you to remember me by. It is my *eternal prayer* to you. I also want to thank you for listening to me. *You are the one who has completed the message of Man and Woman Balance!* I now know that *our love lives forever* in us both. This is what I have so needed to convey. And so, after all this time, I can now say, *it is finished.* And it has just begun...

With love,
Your Other

Love is the only state of existence between Male and Female.

Ending Note by the Author

7/17/16—Written to a special friend facing a difficult situation, losing her storage unit that contained the special belongings of her parents, followed by a closing poem *Touch* from *To Cassandra—Early Years*, 1985, 1994. One shows a problem, the other the inner frame of spiritual procreation, i.e., sexual balance we must come from such that the problem is overcome. Whatever the problem is for anyone, the solution is always the same.

"Dear friend—You took a big hit yesterday. A meltdown actually. Nothing to be ashamed of though. In a way that shows how much you do love.

"I don't know how your day is planned today with your storage issue. May I suggest you begin by just relaxing into and feeling your breathing. Each inhalation and exhalation is a giving and receiving of love. This giving and receiving of love is the one perfect activity and can never be altered. You are part and parcel of this activity as am I. This is all there is. So if by some reason you don't get your storage back it doesn't change anything. Your parents' love for you and your love for them are solid as a rock. It lives in you both absolutely. Do you see that? Nothing can take that love away from you ever. You are a child of love as am I and everyone—if we could just see this. This is the message of the writings—man and woman can only love each other. You are whole and complete sweetie. Always have been and always will be. Your only existence lies in and as eternal love, one to another. That is what you have to give and receive at each moment.

"So take this spirit of love with you today and never let it go. You may even find yourself giving it to others and/or receiving it from others! And they might not even know this but deep down that is all that is going on. Know that you have crossed over and now are blessed. You also truly have something to give, something wonderful—your own love. Let it touch others and heal their very souls just as your soul has now been healed. 'Love ye one another,' the good book says. Indeed. Have a wonderful day. Don't let anything disturb your love which is now your power.

"P.S. The balance (and abundance) of all things is sourced out of the goodness in our hearts. Each moment is what we bring to it."

Touch

At times
At times in this universe
We come upon each other
And touch
Briefly,
Or for a longer spell
Lightly,
Or only we can tell
We touch
Male and female
Each touch
Securing and reproducing
A complete touch,
And all we really know
Is the love
Between ourselves
And our other half.

Man and woman
Live
And struggle
And walk and rest
And die and concentrate
And hope and exaggerate
And despair and recreate
Only, only
Always together.

Cassandra,
Shall you and I

Walk into our silence
Together
Down the aisle
Arm and arm
Into the abyss
Forever
To only return
When called by desire
Between a man and a woman
To touch.

Writings by the Author:
The Man and Woman Relationship: A New Center for the Universe
Spiritual Healing ...of Our Eternal Souls for all Time!
The Man and Woman Manifesto: What We Believe!
The Prime Movers: The Sovereigncy of Man and Woman
The Case Against Man and Woman
The Metaphysics of Sex ...in a Changing World!
Channeling the Eternal Woman
Wealth Plus+ Empowering Your Everyday!
The 2008 - 2009 Articles
Light from Light: Quotations by the Author
Meditations for Deepening Love
To Cassandra--Early Years
Man, Woman, and God
Illumination
The Discovery of Life
The Man and Woman Manifesto: Let the Revolution Begin
Psychotherapy As If Life Really Mattered
The Universal Religion: The Final Destiny of Mankind
The Truth Revealed: My Answer to the World
Healing In The Light and *The Art and Practice of Creativity*
Selected Writings
Selected Writings—Volume 2

For ordering information go to:

Foundation of Man and Woman Balance
www.manandwomanbalance.com

CPSIA information can be obtained
at www.ICGtesting.com
Printed in the USA
BVHW052304250123
657195BV00009B/22/J